# I Remember Distinctly

## *A Family Album of the American People 1918–1941*

*Assembled by*

AGNES ROGERS

*Assembler of* THE AMERICAN PROCESSION *and* METROPOLIS

*With Running Comment by*

FREDERICK LEWIS ALLEN

*Author of* ONLY YESTERDAY *and* SINCE YESTERDAY

HARPER & BROTHERS PUBLISHERS

*NEW YORK AND LONDON*

I REMEMBER DISTINCTLY



---

# GENERAL PLAN

*This book is a panorama of American life during the years of peace from 1918 to 1941, ranging from politics and business to fashions, sports, famous crimes, entertainments, and popular fads. It generally follows (with a good many excursions) a chronological scheme:*

# I. POSTWAR

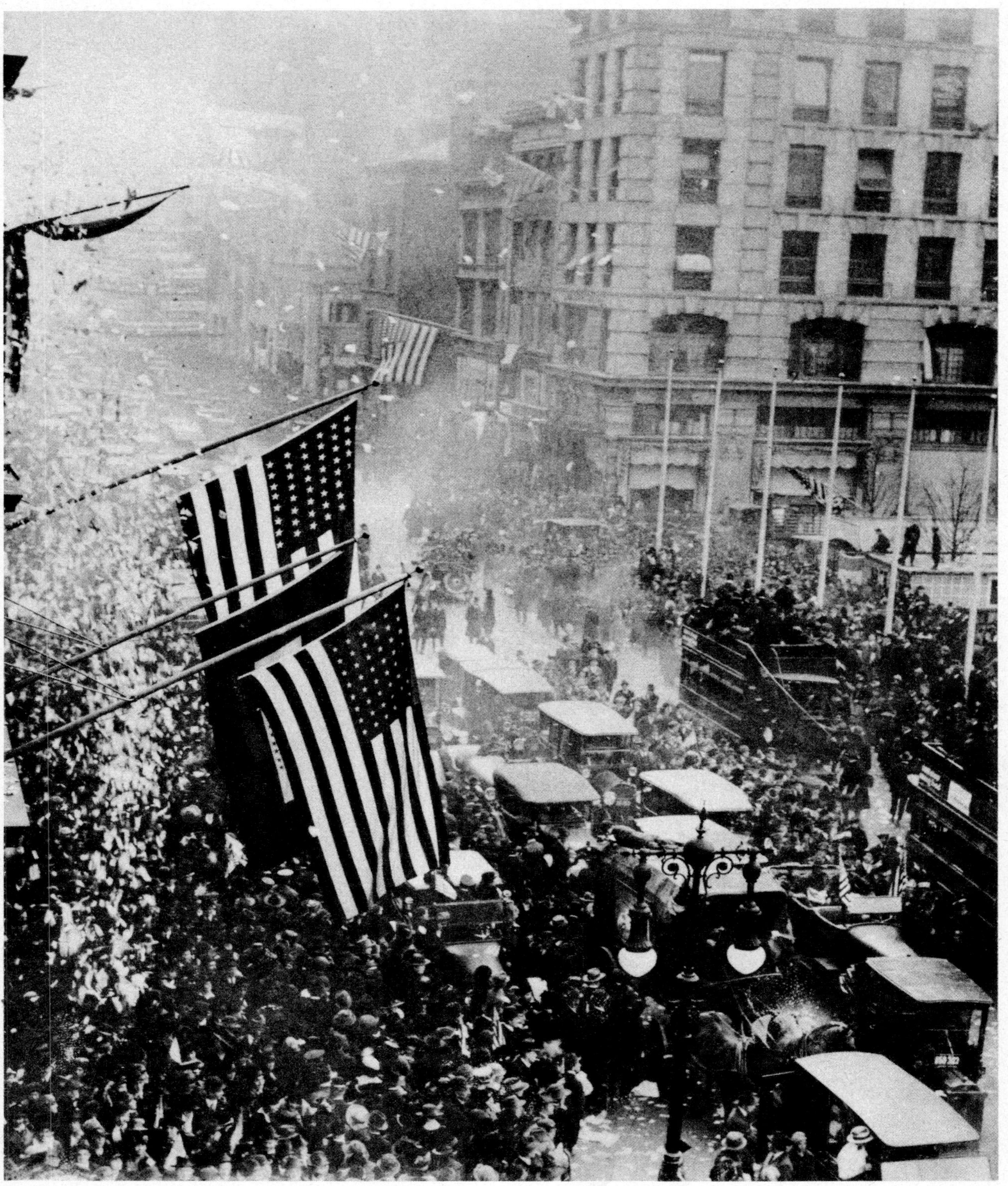

*The war is over!* Crowds in Fifth Avenue, New York, celebrate the signing of the Armistice with Germany on November 11, 1918. The picture above looks southward from a point opposite the Public Library at 42nd Street. Note the horse-drawn vehicles and the absence of automatic traffic lights. In those days traffic on this famous avenue was controlled from high metal traffic towers in mid-street, several blocks apart.

A little before three o'clock on the morning of November 11, 1918, the State Department in Washington gave out the official word that the war—World War I, as we now call it—was over, and that within a few hours the guns in Europe were to cease firing. Great care was taken to assure the public that the news was authentic, for four days earlier a false report of the end of hostilities had caused wild and prolonged celebrations all over the United States. (History came close to repeating itself in this respect twenty-seven years later: remember the false report of German surrender in May 1945, and the premature celebrations of Japanese surrender in August 1945?) All day long there was wild rejoicing. When President Wilson had received the wonderful news in the White House before dawn that morning, he had written out in pencil a message to the American people which reads, perhaps, a little ironically today:

*My Fellow Countrymen: The armistice was signed this morning. Everything for which America fought has been accomplished. It will now be our fortunate duty to assist by example, by sober, friendly counsel, and by material aid in the establishment of just democracy throughout the world.*

Thus began—with hopeful phrases, and with cheering and shouting and blowing of horns, and with dancing in the streets (as caught by the camera in the picture below)—the Period Between the Wars, which was to last twenty-three years and twenty-six days.

The war was over, but there were still over two million American soldiers in Europe, and the terms of peace had yet to be settled. Woodrow Wilson determined to take a leading part in their settlement. He would himself head the American delegation to the Peace Conference, going to Paris with a commission which included only one Republican (a diplomat named Henry White) and no senators. And he would use all his vast influence to get a League of Nations organized and incorporate its covenant in the Peace Treaty itself. (Things were arranged differently in 1945, President Roosevelt having a long memory.)

The task which Wilson set himself was imposing, but he was at the summit of his international prestige and almost anything seemed possible for him. Had he not, as the man most trusted by Allies and Germans alike, been the chief negotiator in the interchanges that had led to the Armistice? Did not his phrases as the spokesman of triumphant democracy ring throughout the world? It was with a confident smile that he stood on the bridge of the *George Washington* on December 4—only three weeks after the Armistice—as the ship left New York to take him to Europe on his peace-making errand, and waved his formal silk hat while whistles blew and guns boomed in salute.

*It was a time when ...*

The Model T Ford was the most plentiful car on the road

"Doug and Mary," and Charlie, were the reigning stars (here shown with D. W. Griffith)

Women's afternoon dresses were elaborate

Paul Whiteman's band played for many a *thé dansant*

Babe Ruth (right) was a pitcher for the Boston Red Sox

Douglas MacArthur (left) was about to be chosen as the head of West Point

*It was a time before . . .*
red fingernails
and women smoking
cellophane,
*Reader's Digest,*
and the new *Life*
zippers
cocktail parties
radio
broadcasting
drum
majorettes
tourist cabins
crossword
puzzles

*People looked different then.* In those days of 1918 and 1919, when the war was just over and the nation was gradually settling back to the uneasy ways of peace, there were striking contrasts with today. We have suggested some of them on the preceding page, but there were many others. For instance, there were no talking pictures; the movies—overwhelmingly popular—were silent, with the actors inaudible and their remarks conveyed to the audience in titles flashed on the screen in brief interruptions of the action. Not only were there no cocktail parties, but a bar was a place frequented by men only, and if it was not connected with a hotel or a club but operated independently, it was called a saloon. Few women smoked. And as for the appearance of women, it was extraordinarily different. There were no short skirts then, or flesh-colored stockings; short hair was associated in the public mind with Bohemianism and radicalism; and make-up (unless well concealed) was associated with actresses and "fast" women. The picture shown above, from *Vogue* for May 1, 1919, illustrates well the sort of silhouette that fashionable women hoped to present. The skirt comes to within six inches of the ground, the shoulders are sloping, the figure flat (and slouching), and the point of greatest width is at the hips or below.

There was no sun-tan vogue then. On July 1, 1919, *Vogue* admonished its readers: "If the wise woman heeds the advice of a very wise specialist, she will devote time and thought during the next two months to protecting her complexion and hair against the damaging effects of wind, sun, and salt-water bathing. This particular specialist holds that the importance of keeping the skin and hair from becoming sunburned cannot be too much stressed." And as for the status of make-up in general, an advertisement of toilet requisites in Altman's *Book of Styles* for the Fall and Winter of 1919-20 included no lipstick, no nail polish, no eye make-up, no brilliantine —only extracts, toilet water, face powder, creams, sachets, face astringents, and (presumably for really deceptive application) rouge. But when winter came around, the woman who could afford an expensive fur coat had her full chance for lavishness. The ladies above were pictured in *Vogue* for August 15, 1919, in a preview of winter fashions. The one on the left is wearing black Alaskan seal; the one in the middle, chinchilla; the one on the right, ermine with a sable collar. (Mink was not then the symbol of luxury.) *Vogue's* caption for the picture remarks, clearly without overstatement, that these furs "are somewhat indefinite as to form."

Here are "Misses' Tailored Suits" for the f
and winter of 1919-20, as shown in the ca
logue of Altman's department store in N
York. They are in navy blue and brown, t
"paramount winter shades."

Do any feminine readers of this book recall doffing their middyblouses to put on party frocks like those that these little girls are wearing, with black or white cotton stockings?

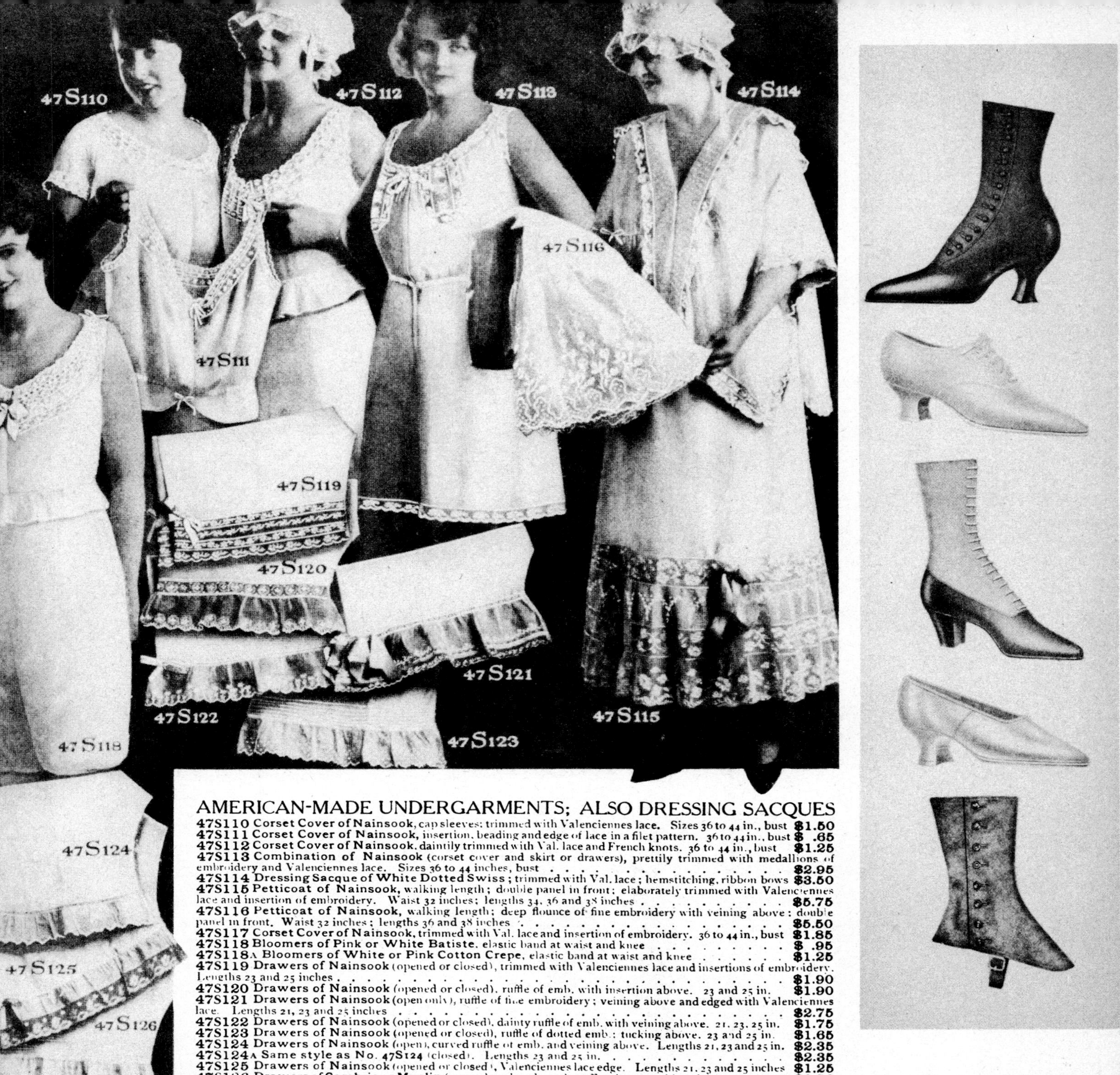


AMERICAN-MADE UNDERGARMENTS; ALSO DRESSING SACQUES

47S110 **Corset Cover of Nainsook**, cap sleeves; trimmed with Valenciennes lace. Sizes 36 to 44 in., bust **$1.50**
47S111 **Corset Cover of Nainsook**, insertion, beading and edge of lace in a filet pattern. 36 to 44 in., bust **$ .65**
47S112 **Corset Cover of Nainsook**, daintily trimmed with Val. lace and French knots. 36 to 44 in., bust **$1.25**
47S113 **Combination of Nainsook** (corset cover and skirt or drawers), prettily trimmed with medallions of embroidery and Valenciennes lace. Sizes 36 to 44 inches, bust . . . . . . . . . . . . . . . **$2.95**
47S114 **Dressing Sacque of White Dotted Swiss**; trimmed with Val. lace; hemstitching, ribbon bows **$3.50**
47S115 **Petticoat of Nainsook**, walking length; double panel in front; elaborately trimmed with Valenciennes lace and insertion of embroidery. Waist 32 inches; lengths 34, 36 and 38 inches . . . . . . . . . **$5.75**
47S116 **Petticoat of Nainsook**, walking length; deep flounce of fine embroidery with veining above; double panel in front. Waist 32 inches; lengths 36 and 38 inches . . . . . . . . . . . . . . . **$5.50**
47S117 **Corset Cover of Nainsook**, trimmed with Val. lace and insertion of embroidery. 36 to 44 in., bust **$1.85**
47S118 **Bloomers of Pink or White Batiste**, elastic band at waist and knee . . . . . . . . **$ .95**
47S118A **Bloomers of White or Pink Cotton Crepe**, elastic band at waist and knee . . . . . . **$1.25**
47S119 **Drawers of Nainsook** (opened or closed), trimmed with Valenciennes lace and insertions of embroidery. Lengths 23 and 25 inches . . . . . . . . . . . . . . . . . . . . . **$1.90**
47S120 **Drawers of Nainsook** (opened or closed), ruffle of emb. with insertion above. 23 and 25 in. **$1.90**
47S121 **Drawers of Nainsook** (open only), ruffle of fine embroidery; veining above and edged with Valenciennes lace. Lengths 21, 23 and 25 inches . . . . . . . . . . . . . . . . . . **$2.75**
47S122 **Drawers of Nainsook** (opened or closed), dainty ruffle of emb. with veining above. 21, 23, 25 in. **$1.75**
47S123 **Drawers of Nainsook** (opened or closed), ruffle of dotted emb.; tucking above. 23 and 25 in. **$1.65**
47S124 **Drawers of Nainsook** (open), curved ruffle of emb. and veining above. Lengths 21, 23 and 25 in. **$2.35**
47S124A **Same style as No.** 47S124 (closed). Lengths 23 and 25 in. . . . . . . . . **$2.35**
47S125 **Drawers of Nainsook** (opened or closed), Valenciennes lace edge. Lengths 21, 23 and 25 inches **$1.25**
47S126 **Drawers of Cambric or Muslin** (opened or closed), emb. ruffle; cluster tucking above. 23, 25, 27 in. **$1.50**
47S126A **Same style as No.** 47S126, in extra sizes. . . . . . . . . . . . . . . **$1.65**

There has been a revolution in women's underwear since the demure items pictured above appeared in Altman's Spring and Summer Catalogue for 1919. Not only did women in those days wear more layers of clothing, but the garments themselves and the terminology were different. Here are pictured "American-made undergarments" (meaning machine-made, as opposed to hand-made foreign importations) and "dressing sacques." Note the names applied to them: corset cover, combination, bloomers, petticoat, and drawers. Other garments favored at the time were the chemise, envelope chemise, camisole, bodice, and princess slip. And, naturally, the corset. You will search the advertisements of those days in vain for a girdle. It was just about this time that young girls began to shock their parents by abandoning their corsets and rolling their stockings below the knees when they went fox-trotting to the music of the barbaric saxaphone; but so far the revolution had hardly affected department store sales. On the right are some characteristic shoes of the time, from Altman's catalogues for 1919-20. In those days few women wore low shoes in winter without spats to protect their ankles from the cold; if they did not wear spats, they wore high shoes—some of them of a really noble altitude—which might have buckskin, kidskin, cloth, or suede tops in light tan or gray.

By contrast, the American man looked in 1919 very much as he does today. True, there were millions of recent immigrants, workmen, and farmers who did not possess "city clothes"; the standardization of men's attire has increased sharply since then, when the farmer on a trip to town was instantly recognizable as a "rube." But the well-dressed man of 1919 would hardly attract attention now if he were to appear on the street. The young man pictured at the right is one of the "Arrow Collar men" sketched by L. T. Lyendecker in innumerable advertisements; he represented the approved type of clean-cut good looks, vintage 1919. The collar that he wears in the picture is rather low for 1919 (and would be high for today). It was sold either starched or soft, but he would hardly have been expected to wear it soft to the office; the soft collar was still generally reserved for play.

There were differences, of course. Trousers were narrower and likely to be a little shorter than today, as you will see from the picture to the left, which is from Altman's Spring and Summer Catalogue for 1919. The man of that day was likely to wear a derby hat in winter and a cloth cap for motoring or country use, and only a few eccentrics ventured to go hatless in the city in any weather. In the evening he was more likely than now, if he had the means, to wear a tail coat with white waistcoat and white tie for formal occasions (with white gloves for dances), though the dinner coat was already invading the tail coat's territory. If he had reached man's estate he would hardly have gone without a waistcoat—or an undershirt, for that matter—except perhaps in the country or in really hot weather. He had never seen tennis shorts, and the underwear now known as shorts he called drawers or B.V.D.'s, after the name of a principal maker. His standard costume for stylish summer wear was a blue coat and white flannels. But all these 1919 items of dress are still occasionally seen; there has been no revolution in man's appearance.

*utomobiling was something 'se again.* At your right, a ımily sets out for a jaunt in new Model T Ford, 1919 Iodel. Note the narrow tires, ertical windshield, and high learance (very useful on ɔcky or muddy roads).

Other cars were longer, sleeker, more rakish. At the left is an Oldsmobile, 1920 model (with, you will notice, smooth front tires and a smooth spare for a front wheel); below is an Apperson 8, as advertised in *Town and Country* for February 1, 1919. If you are struck by the coincidence that all the cars on this page are open, remember that less than eleven per cent of the cars manufactured in 1919 were closed. The sedan had hardly begun its rush to general popularity.

The Haynes FOUR-DOOR roadster—four passengers—twelve cylinders—cord tires—five wire wheels standard equipment. Price $3250.

There were some closed cars, of course. Above is a Cadillac model 59 (1920-21); and at the left are three makes of cars now vanished: the Milburn Light Electric, the Haynes, and the (ai cooled) Franklin.

Does anybody remember also the Moon, Cleveland Six, Dor Scripps-Booth, Jordan, Grant Six, Kenworthy, Roamer, Owe Magnetic, Auburn, Bay State, Chandler, Peerless, Jewett, an Locomobile—all on the roads in 1919 and 1920?

Automobiling was spectacularly different then. There were n automatic traffic lights, no officially numbered highways, fe concrete roads, and so many bad stretches of road almost every where that the Official Automobile Blue Book (New Englan volume) for 1921 gave the following instructions as to "Wh to Take on the Tour—and How to Prepare for It": "A most im portant item is the tow line—either hempen rope, chain, or stee wire cable. . . . Tire chains should always be carried; likewi some single chains or mud hooks. There are also several aut matic 'pull-out' devices which enable one to drive through plac that might be otherwise impassable. . . . Where mountain road sandy stretches, and muddy places are to be met with, or whe the condition of the road depends on the weather, a shovel wit collapsible handle and a good camp axe often repay a hundre fold the trouble of carrying them. To some a compass may appe superfluous, but the seasoned tourist commends it."

at rural highways were like in wet weather it is almost ossible to imagine today. Above is a Ford on a road near Queen, Arkansas, before it was improved in 1918; below, e car, same man, same driver, but the road considerably proved. On the right we have reproduced for careful ection the Automobile Blue Book's description of the to drive from Columbus Circle, New York City, to ghkeepsie. The pavement is described as "macadam, k, concrete, and wood block all the way"—but that was an exceptionally well traveled route. In the same 1921 ume, the description of the route from Richford, Vermt, to Montreal, includes the warning: "Chains on all r wheels absolutely essential in wet weather." And in e 1920 the Hudson River Day Line advertised its ships he *New York Times* as follows: "No tire trouble this —run your car on the steamship and you'll really enjoy trip. No dust, no dirt, no bad roads to bother."

## Route 20—New York City to Poughkeepsie, N. Y.—74.0 m.

**For Accommodations see Index of Towns, Back of Book.**

Via Riverside drive, Yonkers, Hastings, Dobbs Ferry, Irvington, Tarrytown, Ossining, Croton, Peekskill, Fishkill Village, Wappingers Falls. Macadam, brick, concrete and wood block all the way.

This route starts from New York City along Riverside drive, affording fine view of the Hudson river and the Palisades, passing many large apartment houses and private residences. From Yonkers to Peekskill it passes many fine estates and farms. Between Peekskill and Fishkill the road goes inland from the river thru a wooded, hilly section, sparsely settled. From Peekskill to Poughkeepsie thru fine farming section, following the east side of the Hudson river, of which few views are obtainable after leaving Tarrytown.

Route 16 offers an option to Yonkers via Broadway.

| —MILEAGE— Total Mileage | Distance Between Points | For this and other exits see City Map, between pages 50-51. |
|---|---|---|
| 0.0 | 0.0 | **NEW YORK CITY, Columbus Circle, 59th St. & Broadway.** Go north on Broadway with trolley. |
| 0.7 | 0.7 | 72nd St., subway station on left; turn left. |
| 0.9 | 0.2 | Riverside drive; turn right along Hudson river. |
| 3.4 | 2.5 | Fork, Grant's tomb ahead; bear right with drive. |
| 3.6 | 0.2 | Fork; keep left. |
| | | Right downgrade leads to 130th St. ferry. |
| | | Cross long concrete viaduct 3.8. |
| 5.4 | 1.8 | 6-corners; turn left onto Riverside drive extension. |
| 8.1 | 2.7 | Broadway; meeting trolley, bear left. Elevated section of subway comes in from right 9.0. Cross iron drawbridge over Harlem river 9.2. Pass Van Cortlandt park 10.5. |
| 13.2 | 5.1 | Fork, inn in center; bear left with branch trolley onto Broadway. **Caution** for traffic regulations in Yonkers. |
| 13.7 | 0.5 | **Yonkers,** Getty square. Bear left onto N. Broadway, one long block, leaving trolley. |
| 13.8 | 0.1 | Dock St.; turn left. |
| 13.9 | 0.1 | Warburton Ave.; meeting trolley, turn right along bank of Hudson river. Cross long concrete viaduct 18.0. |
| 18.1 | 4.2 | **Hastings-on-Hudson.** Straight thru. |
| 18.3 | 0.2 | 4-corners; turn left with travel. |
| 19.2 | 0.9 | **Dobbs Ferry** (outskirts), fork. Bear right upgrade. |
| | | Left fork downgrade leads to center of town. |
| 19.9 | 0.7 | 4-corners, water-trough on right; turn left onto Broadway. |
| 21.5 | 1.6 | **Irvington.** Straight thru. |
| 24.2 | 2.7 | **Tarrytown, Broadway & Main St. Straight thru across trolley.** |
| 24.8 | 0.6 | Irregular 4-corners, church ahead; turn left downgrade. Thru **Phillipse Manor** 24.8. Cross concrete bridge 25.2. Pass Sleepy Hollow cemetery on right 25.3. Go under narrow stone arch 27.4. |
| 28.4 | 3.6 | **Scarboro,*** large stone church on right. Straight thru. |
| | | Right at Scarboro is Route 16 to Pittsfield. |
| 30.4 | 2.0 | **Ossining,*** diagonal 4-corners, bank on far right. Bear left across trolley downgrade onto Highland Ave. |
| 30.9 | 0.5 | Fork; bear left. |
| 32.1 | 1.2 | Left-hand road, brick house on left; turn left. Cross iron bridge over Croton river 32.5. Thru **Harmon*** 33.1. |
| 34.2 | 2.1 | **Croton,*** bank on left. Straight thru. Bear left at top of grade 34.7. |
| 36.9 | 2.7 | Fork; bear left. Thru **Montrose** 38.6. |
| 39.3 | 2.4 | **Buchanan,** 4-corners. Turn right with trolley. |
| 39.9 | 0.6 | Right-hand road just before RR; turn right with trolley. |
| 40.3 | 0.4 | End of street; turn left with trolley onto Washington St. |
| 41.6 | 1.3 | End of street; meeting trolley, turn right onto South St. |
| 41.8 | 0.2 | **Peekskill,** South & Division Sts., P. O. on right. Turn left with trolley onto N. Division St. |
| 42.1 | 0.3 | Fork; soldiers' monument in center; bear left onto Highland Ave., leaving trolley. |
| 46.7 | 4.6 | Fork; bear right on macadam. |
| | | Left fork leads to **West Point ferry.** |
| 49.0 | 2.3 | **Garrison,** 4-corners, at outskirts. Straight thru. Cross iron bridge 60.8. **Caution** for blind RR crossing 60.9. |
| 61.0 | 12.0 | 3-corners; bear left. |
| | | Right is **Route 58 to Pawling.** |
| 61.2 | 0.2 | **Fishkill,*** wooden church on right. Turn right. |
| | | Straight ahead before this turn is **Route 161 to Newburgh via Newburgh-Beacon ferry.** |
| 66.1 | 4.9 | 3-corners, park ahead; bear right downgrade. |
| 66.3 | 0.2 | **Wappingers Falls,*** end of road just beyond concrete bridge. Meeting trolley, turn right onto Main St. |
| 68.4 | 2.1 | 4-corners; turn left away from trolley. |
| | | Poughkeepsie City Map and Points of Interest, page 77. |
| | | Bear right at soldiers' monument onto Market St. 73.8. |
| 74.0 | 5.6 | **POUGHKEEPSIE,** Main & Market Sts., city hall on left. |

Aviation, too, was then in a rudimentary stage of development. Above is the frail-looking flying boat, the Navy's NC-4, which in May 1919 made the first perilous crossing of the Atlantic Ocean—but did it by way of a stop at the Azores. (It was in June of that year that Alcock and Browne made the first successful direct flight, from Newfoundland to Ireland, eight years ahead of Lindbergh.) At the right, you will see the personnel of the three Navy flying boats which attempted the ocean flight, including the successful NC-4. With them (in the front row, wearing straw hats) are Secretary Josephus Daniels of the Navy and the handsome young Assistant Secretary, Franklin D. Roosevelt.

If you went to the movies in 1920, you probably enjoyed seeing Douglas Fairbanks laughing and swaggering and (as at the left) leaping from roof to roof in "The Mark of Zorro."

Mary Pickford, in "Pollyanna" (below), was reminiscent of everybody's childhood sweetheart. It was in 1920 that she and Douglas Fairbanks, king and queen of the silent screen, were married, to the delight of millions. At the right is a scene from another success of 1920, "The Kid," with Charlie Chaplin, whose gift for humorous and tender pantomime was already conquering the world, and little Jackie Coogan.

Here are three other stars of the silent movies just after World War I. Above is Gloria Swanson, being a very sultry girl indeed in "Male anc Female," produced in 1919; this was some time before she marrie the Marquis de la Falaise de la Coudray. On the left is Erich von Stro heim, in a scene from "Blind Husbands," which he directed himself i 1919. And below is Pearl White, heroine of many a wild melodram and thriller serial picture, about to escape—as she did in every pictur —from black-hearted men in a 1919-20 film called "The Black Secret."

Possibly you can get just a hint, from the picture on the right, of why Rudolph Valentino, the "sheik," entranced women by the millions until he died in 1926. Here he is shown with Alice Terry in "The Four Horsemen of the Apocalypse," produced in 1921. And from the picture below you may gather that Douglas Fairbanks—here shown in "The Three Musketeers," another 1921 film—didn't even need a sword to stand off eight or ten swordsmen on a staircase. If the fight became too thick, he would probably swing himself over the staircase or up among the rafters. There have been athletic movie heroes since his heyday, but few so mightily gymnastic.

All this, as we have been suggesting, was a considerable time ago, and people whose faces have subsequently become familiar to us didn't look quite the same then. At the left is a young officer of World War I by the name of Harry S. Truman; and above you will see him posing—rather jauntily, at the left, in a gray suit—in the men's furnishing store that he operated in Kansas City with Ed Jacobson from 1919 to 1923. Below is a photograph taken at Montigny-sur-Aube, France, in 1919, showing Major General Henry T. Allen with a young officer who had made a mark for himself in our 1918 offensive: Colonel George Catlett Marshall.

It is hardly necessary to identify the young man pictured at the right, with Wilson's Secretary of the Navy, Josephus Daniels, as Assistant Secretary Franklin D. Roosevelt, still able to stand firmly on his two feet. It was in 1920 that he ran for the vice-presidency of the United States, and was snowed under in the election that brought Harding to the White House; it was in August of the next year, 1921, that he contracted poliomyelitis. From that time on, his legs were helpless and he could not even stand up without braces. Below, suitably garbed for European negotiations, are Bernard M. Baruch, Norman H. Davis, Vance McCormick, and another future president, Herbert Hoover, photographed at the King of Belgium's palace in Brussels in June, 1919, during the Peace Conference.

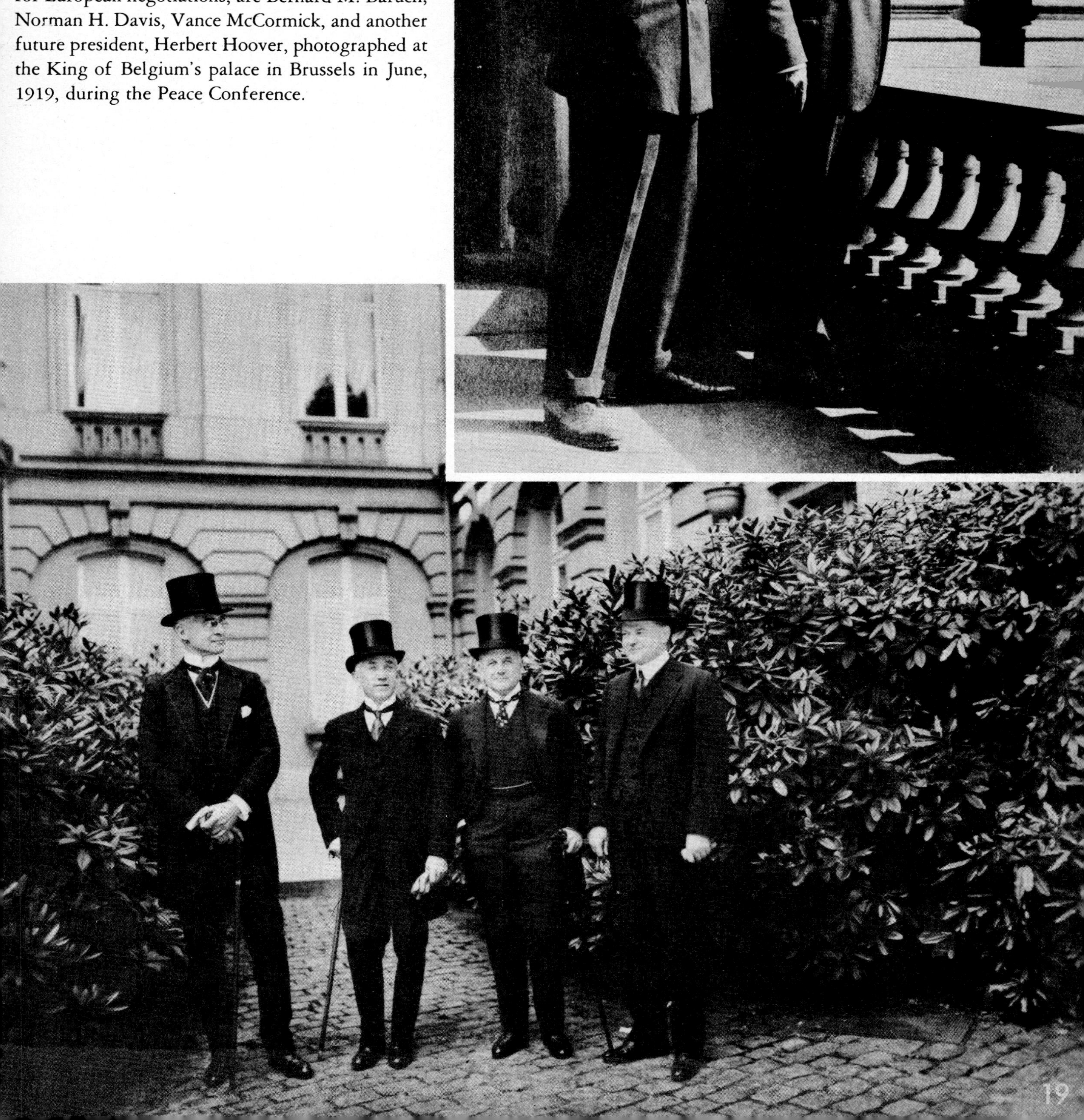

You'll have little difficulty spotting the black-haired man above, who is of course John L. Lewis, talking with Michael Gallagher, a coal operator, in 1923, when Lewis had been president of the United Mine Workers for about three years. And you will readily recognize Brigadier General Douglas MacArthur, talking with the Prince of Wales (not yet Edward VIII or the Duke of Windsor) at West Point, when MacArthur was superintendent there, 1919-1923. But the youth in the upper right hand corner? He is an undergraduate at the University of Michigan, class of 1923—Thomas E. Dewey.

One striking contrast between the first and second postwar periods is revealed in the national addiction to triumphant parades in 1919. This was a natural manifestation of the popular attitude toward World War I, as compared with that toward World War II. In the first there was far more fervor, more emotional patriotism, more intolerance toward those whose loyalty was suspect, more hopeful chanting of the slogans of democracy and future peace—and much more delight in brass bands and the sound of marching feet. When the victory was followed by disappointments, disillusionment came fast, and people in their inmost hearts felt somehow cheated. Thus it was natural that the generation which grew up after 1918 should have been conditioned to beware of military seductions. They became generally isolationist, contemptuous of the national rivalries in Europe that had bred war once and might breed it again, and suspicious of the glamour of parades. When in due course they had to go to war again, they went without illusions. War had become to them a matter of implacable necessity—a grim business to be got through with as fast as possible, with a minimum of shouting. True, they were virtually unanimous in their support of the national cause—more so than in 1917-18—but they were deadpan. And so it was natural too that in 1945-46, after the victory, there were few parades. But in 1919 there were hundreds. Below we see the Marines marching up Fifth Avenue, New York, past Madison Square, under the victory arch built as a tribute to the doughboys. (Note the hard straw hats in the crowd.)

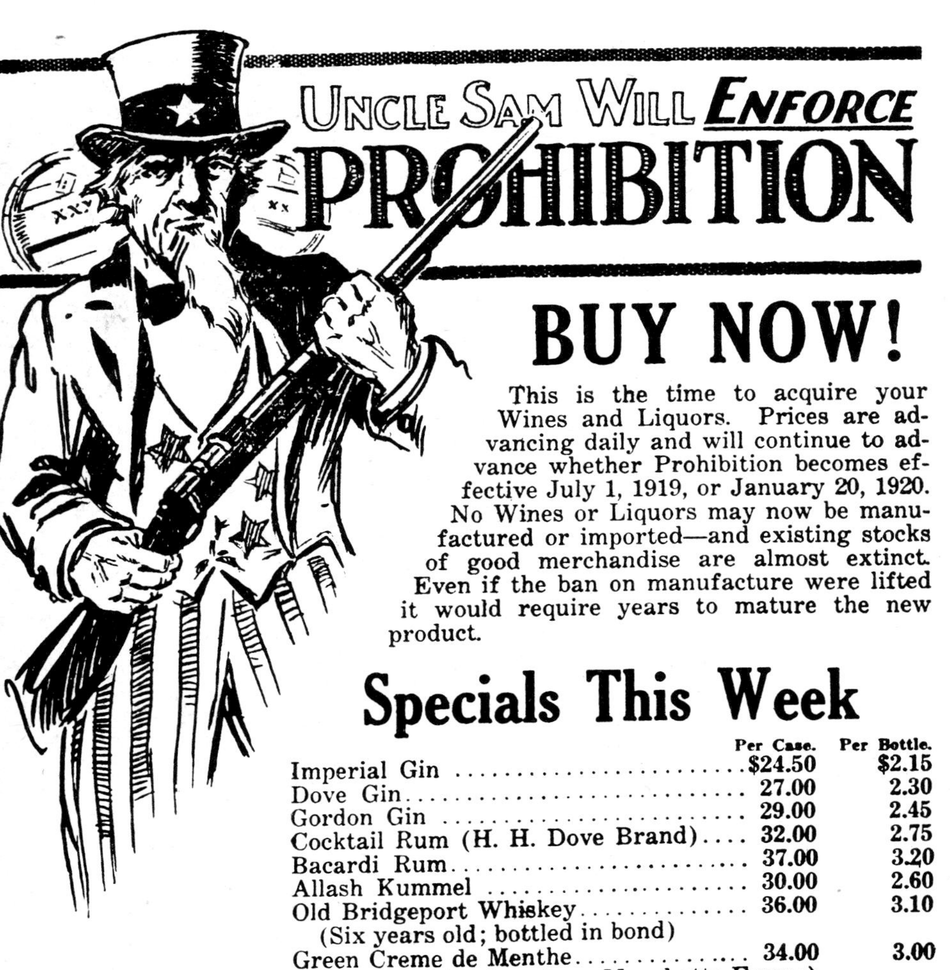


Two important reforms, generated by war fer swept into effect just after the war. The first woman suffrage, which was taken for grante soon as it had become the law of the land— made little difference in the election results th after. Above, you will see a group of San F cisco "suffragettes" (more ardent than se celebrating California's ratification of the rage amendment in November 1919.

The other reform was destined for a stor career. The wartime argument that a sober dier was a good soldier and a sober factory was a good factory hand had built up suc overwhelming public support for prohibition a "wartime" dry act had been passed, to go effect July 1, 1919; and almost without op tion an Eighteenth Amendment—to provid permanent prohibition—rushed through the stages of ratification just after the Armistic go into effect on January 20, 1920. The adve ment at the left, from the *New York Time* May 4, 1919, assumed, as did almost every then, that the country would become really

In the preceding pages of this book we have suggested some of the contrasts between the America of 1919-20 and that of 1946-47. So sharp are some of these contrasts that it may seem odd that many Americans old enough to remember those earlier days have had, again and again during the months and years since V-J Day, an odd feeling of "But I've been here before!" or "This is where I came in." For the parallels between the two periods have been absurdly close—so close that sometimes it has seemed almost as if an old and half-familiar show were being revived, with new actors, a new stage manager, new costumes and scene designs, and a few revisions and modernizations of the episodes, but essentially the same old plot.

To begin with, then as now the peace-making was difficult and accompanied by disorders, insurrections, basic disagreements, and fears of a new outbreak of war. For months in the spring of 1919 the peace-makers wrangled at Paris. (At that, they were far quicker than their counterparts a generation later.) Differences had to be battled out in conferences between the Big Four of that day. They are shown below, gathered for one of their sessions. At the left, Orlando of Italy (who walked out at one point in a dissention over Fiume, right next door to Trieste); then Lloyd George of Great Britain; then the aged Clemenceau of France; and at the right, Woodrow Wilson of the United States, whose hopes, so high when the picture on page 3 was taken, were already being shaken as the Treaty of Versailles took shape.

Above, President Wilson takes time off from the peace negotiations to review—along with General Pershing—some of the American troops still stationed in France. Below, a fragment of an advertisement of the May 1919 issue of *Current History* reminds us that after 1918, as after 1945, disorders still troubled the world.

The authentic facts of that momentous period, compiled from official records, are set forth in consecutive order in the May issue of ***Current History Magazine,*** the monthly periodical published by The New York Times Co.

The agony of the Rebirth of the Nations of the World, which forms a chapter of such thrilling yet tragic interest, is surveyed with close fidelity to facts. This one magazine covers numerous events of supreme significance, any one of which in normal times would rivet the attention of all mankind.

*The Civil War in Germany.*
*The Peril of Bolshevism.*
*The Revolution in Hungary.*
*The Conflicts in Poland.*
*The Struggle of the Czech Republic.*
*The Reforms in Rumania.*
*The Warfare in Russia.*
*The Problems of Jugoslavia.*
*The Banishment of Emperor Charles*
*The Unrest in Egypt.*

The history of each of these movements, which developed critical phases in April, is given from ***official records,*** without bias or editorial comment.

A war enforces an uneasy national unity, but when it is over, a lot of people are disposed to work off grudges built up in wartime: to say to themselves, "Now that we've licked the enemy outside, let's finish off those so-and-so's next door." In 1919 this sort of feeling led to an ugly series of race riots, of which the worst took place at Chicago. A seventeen-year-old colored boy was drowned in Lake Michigan off a Chicago bathing-beach. Whether or not he had been stoned (in the water) by whites, a lot of people thought he had—and a fight began which spread into days of rioting, at the end of which 38 people had been killed and 537 injured. Above, we see Negroes and whites leaving the beach as the trouble began; at the right, the photographer catches two whites stoning a Negro to death.

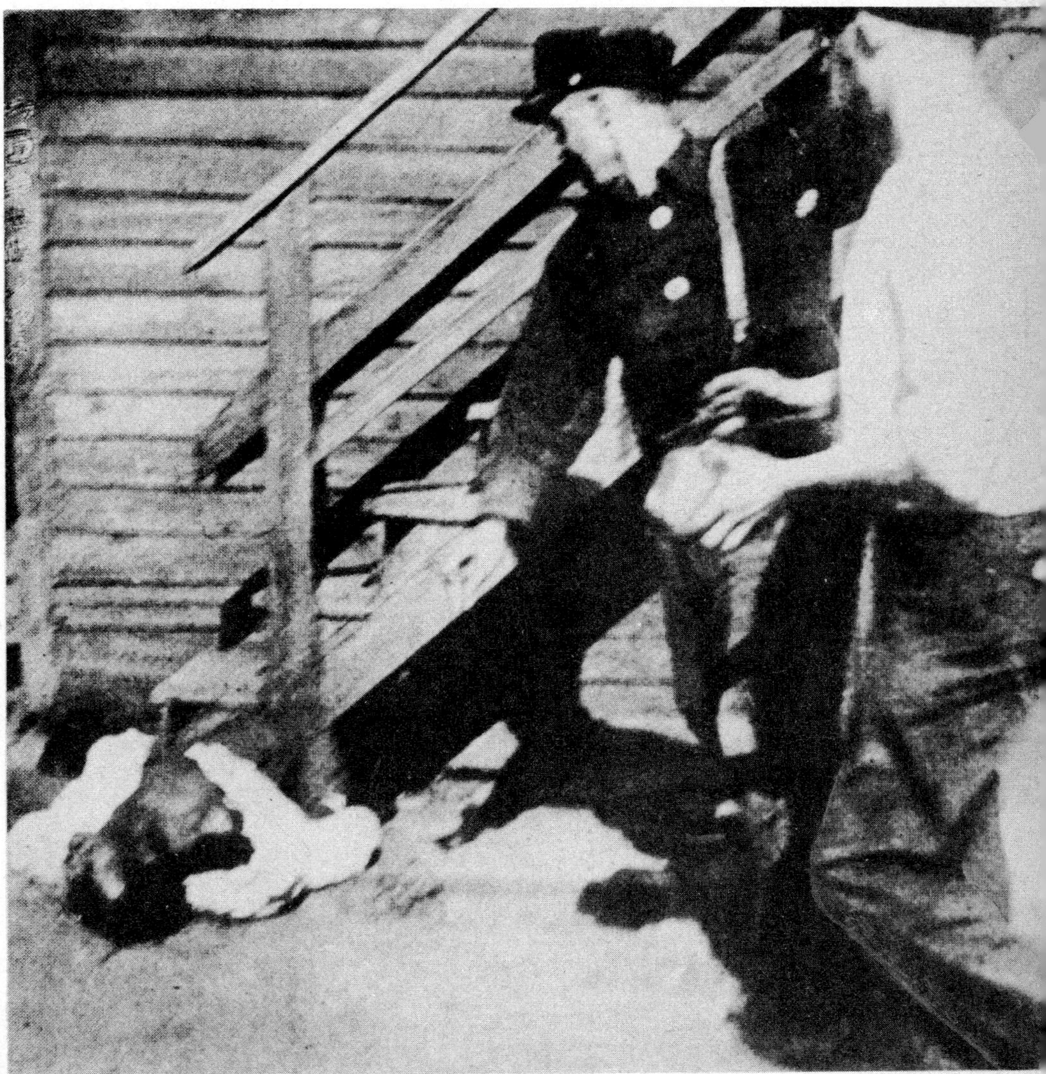

Rising prices, war fatigue, a desire to reap the much-advertised fruits of democracy, and the release of wartime tensions combined after World War I—as after World War II—to bring a terrific wave of strikes. These pictures—showing, above, telephone girls on strike in Boston, and below, actresses going on picket duty in a strike which closed nearly a dozen theaters in New York—may give a faint idea of the wide variety of workers involved in 1919.

Yes, there was a housing shortage too; and rents, uncontrolled, went sky-high. At the right, the head of the Anti-Rent League enrolls new members in a rent strike in New York at the beginning of the year 1919.

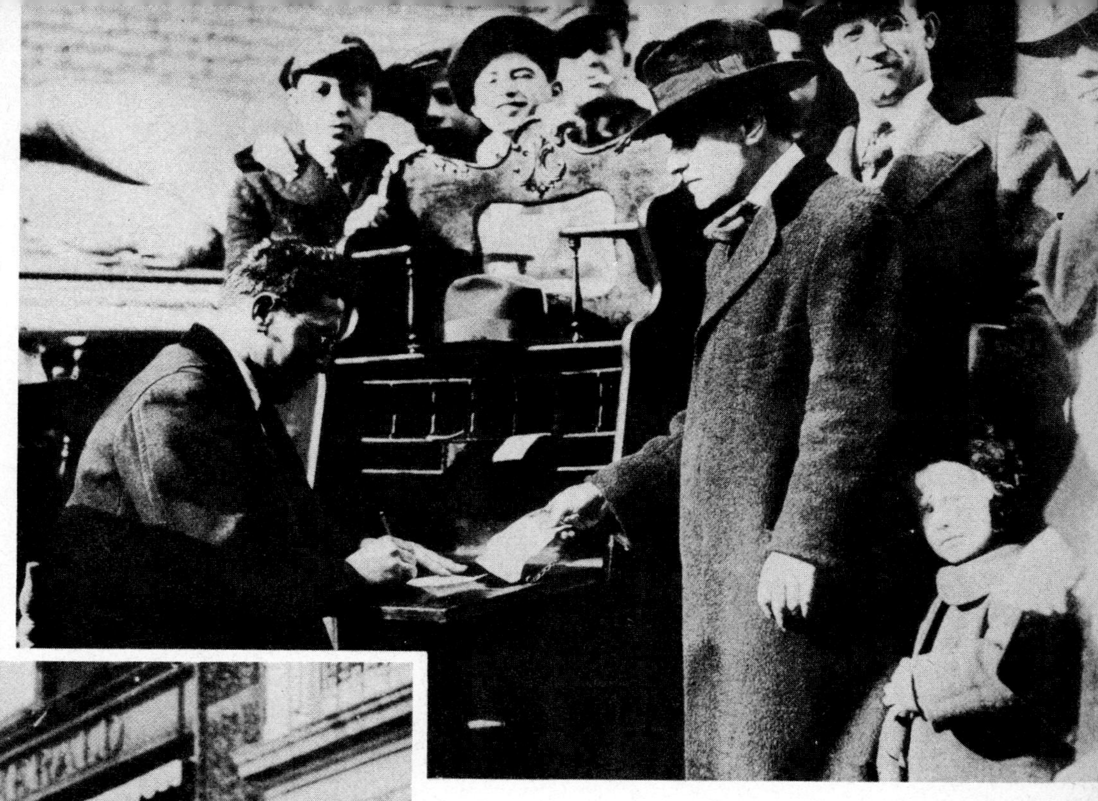

By November 1919 some people estimated that two million Americans were out on strike! But perhaps the climax of the strike wave came a little earlier, in September, when the Boston police walked out. Result: disorder, a field day for hooligans, widespread damage, and public dismay. At the left you will see a "loyal" policeman instructing a mounted State Guardsman in the preservation of public order.

A further result of the Boston Police Strike: it lifted into sudden national prominence the cautious, sandy-haired, sour-faced Governor of Massachusetts, Calvin Coolidge, who after dodging the strike issue as long as he could, issued a statement—welcomed by millions of Americans throughout the country—that there was "no right to strike against the public safety by anybody, anywhere, any time."

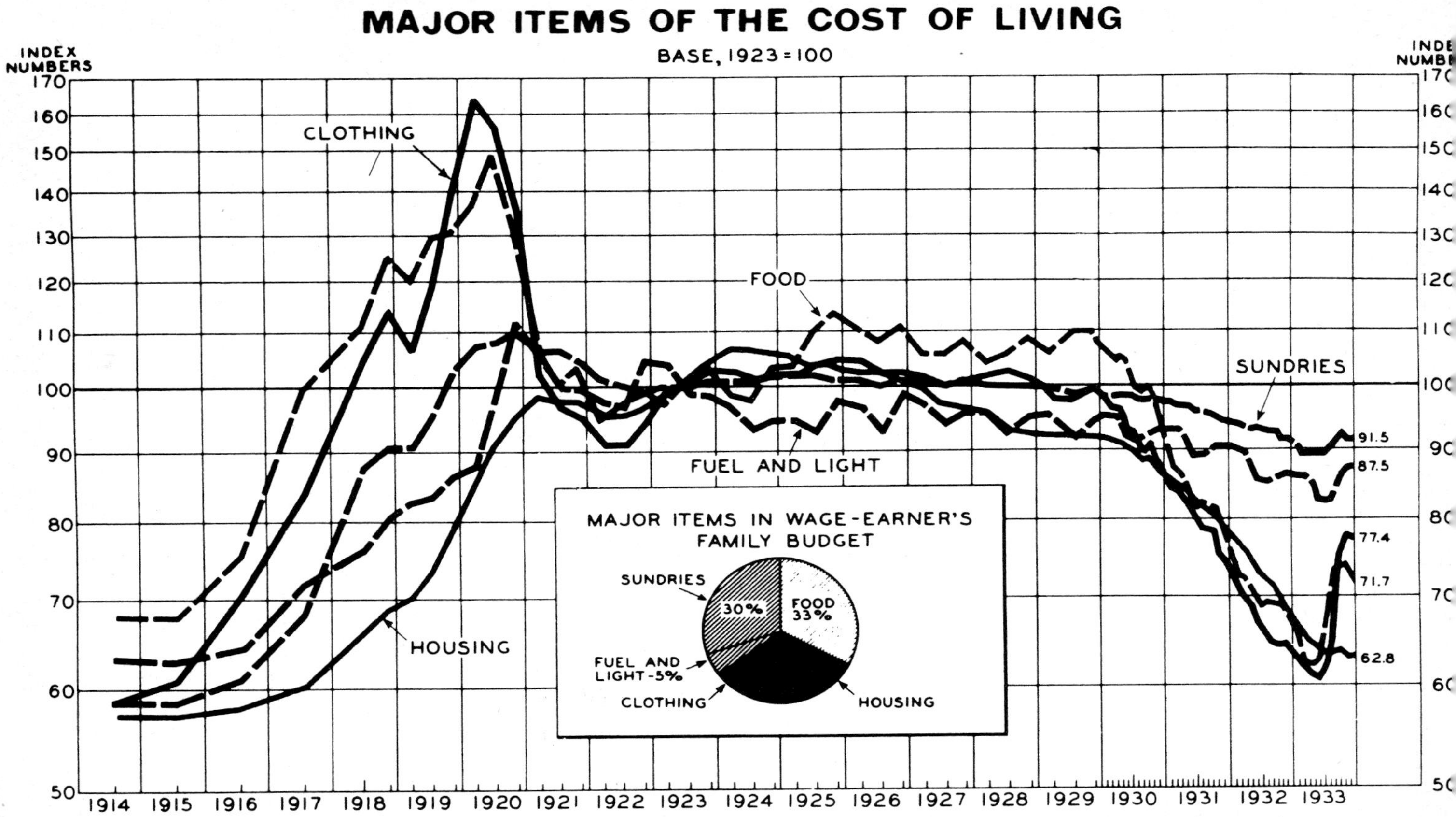

Listen to President Wilson, addressing Congress on August 8, 1919, and see whether the things he describes don't sound natural to you. He is discussing "the present cost of living":

"I need not recite the particulars of this critical matter: the prices demanded and paid at the sources of supply, at the factory, in the food markets, at the shops, in the restaurants and hotels, alike in the city and in the village. They are familiar to you. They are the talk of every domestic circle and of every group of casual acquaintances even. It is a matter of familiar knowledge, also, that a process has set in which is likely, unless something is done, to push prices and rents and the whole cost of living higher and yet higher, in a vicious cycle to which there is no logical or natural end. With the increase in the prices of the necessaries of life come demands for increases in wages. . . . Upon the increase in wages there follows close an increase in the prices of the products whose producers have been accorded the increase. . . . The laborers who do not get an increase in pay when they demand it are likely to strike, and the strike only makes matters worse. It checks production, if it affects the railways it prevents distribution and strips the markets, so that there is presently nothing to buy, and there is another excessive addition to prices resulting from the scarcity."

The chart above (Copyright, 1934, National Industrial Conference Board, Inc.) shows graphically what happened. With no adequate controls in force, prices soared throughout the war, and with the remaining controls promptly removed at the war's end, leaped still higher in 1919 and 1920—until buyers "went on strike," supply caught up with demand, merchants and manufacturers who had been doing panicky buying found themselves overloaded with goods—and in the latter part of 1920, less than two years after the Armistice, there was a violent drop in prices. To give just a couple of extreme examples of what happened then: spot cotton fell from 43¾ cents early in 1920 to 14¾ cents at the end of 1920; and rubber, from 49 cents early in the year to 19¼ cents at the year's end!

Along with the strikes, in those early postwar days, went a wave of radicalism, stimulated by the uncomfortable cost of living, the general tension of an uneasy time, and the success of the Bolsheviks in Russia. Some of it represented little more than an angry insistence by labor upon the right to organize (then denied it in many industries); some was socialist in aim; a little was communist. It was not long-lived, and perhaps its most striking result was an epidemic of red-baiting and intolerance on the part of frightened conservatives, reaching its peak in the "Red Raids" by the Department of Justice on New Year's Day, 1920. But there were a few extremists among the radicals. Packages addressed to high government officials were discovered by a post-office clerk in New York to contain lethal bombs. A bomb crashed against the front of Attorney General Palmer's house in Washington. And the climax came just before noon on September 16, 1920, while business was going on as usual in Wall Street: a terrific explosion took place just opposite the very citadel of American capitalism, the massive building of J. P. Morgan & Co.

The picture below was snapped just after the bomb went off, killing thirty people, injuring hundreds, and blowing slugs as much as thirty-four stories high. Apparently a horse-drawn wagon had carried the bomb there, and the driver had set the fuse and escaped. There was some evidence to suggest that the perpetrators were anarchists, but the crime was never solved. (Walk past the House of Morgan today and you will still see the scars on its walls.)

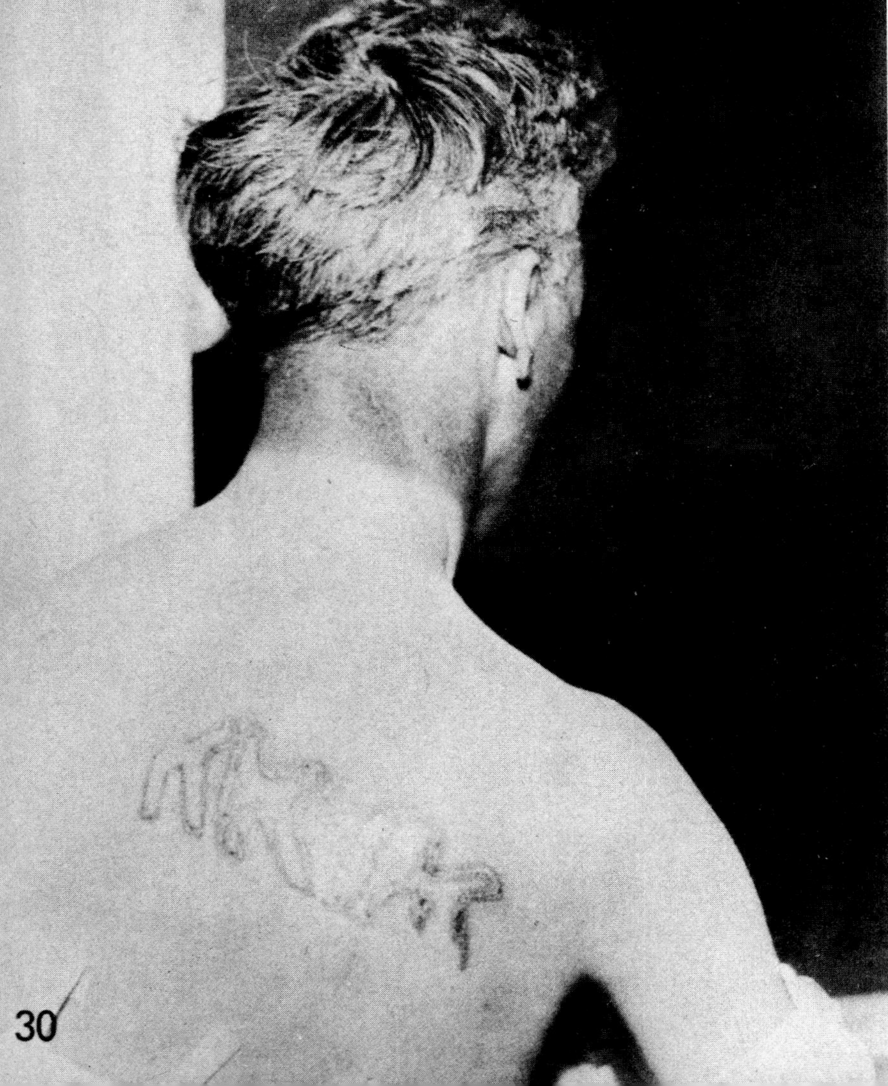

Perhaps the nastiest nucleus of postwar intolerance i the United States was the Ku Klux Klan—a secre society, started in Georgia in 1915, which spreac widely and was variously anti-Negro, anti-Jewish anti-Catholic. By 1924 it had actually got politica control of seven states. Above, you will see member being initiated near Brunswick, Maryland, under th flaming cross; at the left, the branded back of th Reverend Orrin Van Loon, pastor of a communit church near Detroit, who had displeased local Klans men and was found in a stupor with the letters KKI burned into his skin.

Above are three successful authors of those days: Booth Tarkington (left), whose *Alice Adams* was popular in 1921; James Branch Cabell (center), whose *Jurgen,* published in 1919, delighted the broad-minded and was suppressed by the narrow-minded; and Sinclair Lewis (right), whose *Main Street* topped the 1921 best sellers, and who followed it soon with another outstanding novel, *Babbitt.*

bove is Edith Wharton, whose fine *The Age of nocence* was an important book of 1920. At the right e the jackets of some leading books, and the an-ouncement of *Main Street* in Harcourt, Brace and owe's catalogue of the time. Other best sellers of ose days included *The Four Horsemen of the pocalypse,* by Ibanez (1919), *The Man of the Forest,* Zane Grey (1920), *Now It Can Be Told,* by Philip ibbs (1920), and the top non-fiction best seller for )21 and 1922, *The Outline of History,* by H. G. 'ells. Does anybody remember, too, *The Sheik,* by M. Hull, a hot number in 1921? But it was *Main reet,* with its shrewd depiction of American small-wn life, which came closest to setting the keynote American writing for the decade to come.

President Wilson came back from the Paris Conference to find the American people in no mood to accept in toto the Treaty of Versailles or the international obligations of the League of Nations. During the summer of 1919 he wearily toured the country, trying to win their support—and came back to Washington a broken man. During the rest of his term he was a half-paralyzed invalid in the White House, and the executive only half functioned. Obstinately refusing to compromise on the Treaty, Wilson saw it killed by the Senate; later the United States made a separate peace with Germany. The American people were tired—tired of war, responsibility, idealism, regulations, and duties. They wanted to relax, have a good time, make money. And in the election of 1920 they chose, in a landslide, the handsome Republican candidate who promised a return to what he called "normalcy." Above, President Wilson, with drawn face, rides to the Capitol on Inauguration Day of 1921 beside the smiling victor, the new President, Warren G. Harding.

: election of 1920 involved, ice-presidential candidates, › future Presidents. In the er picture—Calvin Coolidge, ɔ of the Boston Police Strike Republican winner, with father, wife, and sons. ow—the Democratic loser, h his wife beside him, at notification ceremony at le Park. Beyond her, in er: Secretary Daniels, Mrs. Adoo, Secretary McAdoo, mer S. Cummings, Gover- Alfred E. Smith of New ·k, and Mrs. Smith.

After the Inauguration on March 4, 1921, the defeated Wilson drove bitterly to his recently purchased house on S Street, Washington; the new President drove in triumph to the White House. All smiles, he waved his silk hat, and his wife waved a white-gloved hand, as the shiny Packard with the rococo running-boards and stylish side-lamps swung them toward what seemed then a happy future prospect. The reign of normalcy was about to begin.

# II. HIGH, WIDE, AND HANDSOME

Warren Gamaliel Harding had a magnificent face, a dignified bearing, some Washington experience as an inconspicuous senator, the affable, easy-going disposition of a small-town, poker-playing newspaper proprietor, and too many friends who regarded him as their passport to wealth. The picture below shows him at Baseball Park, Fort Benning, Georgia. Next to him is Major General Gordon; the heavily built man next to the General is John W. Weeks, Harding's Secretary of War; and the man at the right-hand end of the front row is Albert B. Fall, his Secretary of the Interior, who leased to private interests the naval oil reserves at Teapot Dome and Elk Hills, under circumstances which unfolded scandalously later. Harding lived only until 1923, dying before the full scope of the transgressions of his appointees had been disclosed. The easy-going years, the let's-forget-it-all-and-have-a-good-time years, were beginning—with corruption in Washington.

New things were coming to bedazzle the public, and not the least of these was radio. Wireless telegraphy had long existed before broadcasting for entertainment began. But in 1920 Dr. Frank Conrad, doing experimental work in a barn on his place near Pittsburgh, found that wireless enthusiasts enjoyed listening to the phonograph records which he put on the air; and the Westinghouse people set up a station to provide such entertainment and thus stimulate the sale of sets. And how the thing worked! Below, two women are listening to the first factory-built set made for entertainment (Westinghouse, 1921); above, some early entertainers are giving.

The first radio station, KDKA, was opened in time to broadcast, on November 2, 1920, the results of the Harding-Cox election. The beginnings of what was to prove a great industry were difficult. Amateur wireless operators kept objecting that the music from KDKA was a nuisance—it interfered with their important work. And what would serve as a studio? The Westinghouse people tried using a tent on the roof (shown at the right). That wasn't too good, for the tent insisted on blowing away.

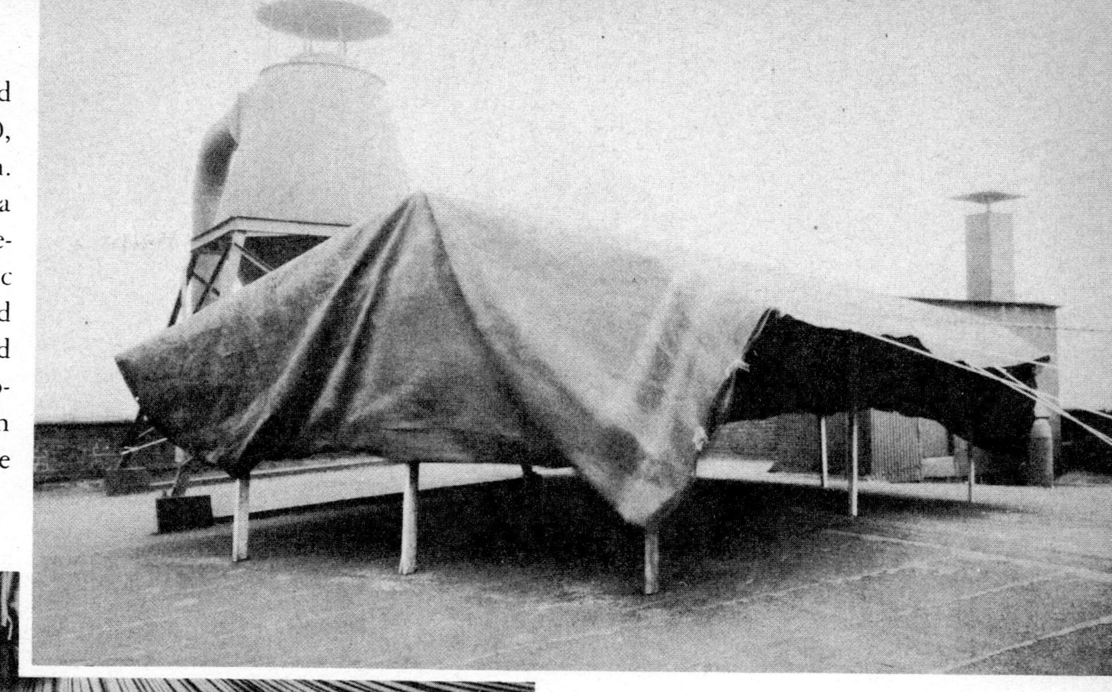

The tent was succeeded by an indoor studio; and as you can see from the photograph at the left, every effort was made to prevent reverberation by the lavish use of draperies. If you look closely at the picture you may be able to detect the microphone (generally called an "enunciator" in those days)—a disk hanging a few inches below the upper end of the slanting bar on the tripod. Most of the early listeners used crystal detectors—tubeless receiving sets; the development of the vacuum tube greatly expanded the radio audience.

Dr. Frank Conrad wasn't the first man to get the idea of using radio telephony for general entertainment. For instance, back in 1916 David Sarnoff, then assistant general manager of the Marconi Wireless Telegraph Company of America, sent a note to the general manager saying, "I have in mind a plan of development which would make radio a household utility in the same sense as a piano or phonograph. The idea is to bring music into the house by wireless." And he proposed transmitting music to a "radio music box." The plan did not go through then, and it was Dr. Conrad who actually started things going. He is pictured at the right, surrounded by apparatus which appears to the uninitiated to be anything but wireless.

Radio caught on. New stations blossomed. Thousands of people sat up late, with earphones, to pick up distant stations. By October 1923 this sort of question and answer were appearing in the *New York Times's* radio department: *Q.—Do you know of a single tube reflex circuit which if operated in Peekskill, N. Y., would pick up Chicago regularly during the winter? A.—The reflex circuit which appeared in the* New York Times *August 26, if properly constructed.* In June 1924 vast numbers of people listened to a prolonged news event, the Democratic Convention in New York, and the sale of sets boomed. In October 1926 the *Times's* front-page story on the first World's Series game reported the startling fact that some fifteen million people heard the game over "WEAF, WJZ, and 23 other stations covering the United States and Canada," and "were hearing the beginnings of plays before the announcer himself knew the conclusion." The first radio network was then being organized. Yet for a long time the small-boy appeal of hearing distant stations with earphones was strong—witness the above advertisement, which appeared in the *Saturday Evening Post* as late as January 17, 1925.

Another symptom of the changing temper of the day was the change in feminine attire. Girls were rebelling against the demure attire dictated by a puritanical convention; and there was beginning—to the delight of many and the horror of others—a sort of gradual national strip-tease. When Atlantic City held its first bathing-beauty contest in September, 1921, the spectators "gasped," according to reporters, at "skin-tight bathing suits." The winner, Miss Washington, whom you see at the right, wore—with knees daringly bare—an old-style suit, but others were less conservative. Below, you will see how far the revolution in bathing attire had got by 1923; the contestants are lined up before the judges on the boardwalk.

Above, the bathing beauties of the 1921 Atlanti City contest are gathered on the boardwalk i street dress—with the winner, little Miss Wash ington, at the extreme left. If they seem to yo to look a little matronly for such an affair, re member that in 1921 clothes were generall looser, and also that slenderness was less high prized. In those days, though the women i fashion *drawings* were exaggeratedly atten ated, nearly all the fashion *photographs* showe girls whom the model agencies of twenty o even ten years later would have rejected as ove weight. At the left, you will see the sort o bathing suit that these girls—and presently, mo American women—forsook. The miss with th long stockings, wide garters, and hat was show in *Town and Country* for August 1, 1919.

The new tight bathing suits brought joy to the hearts of rotogravure editors and the proprietors of beach resorts. The first Atlantic City pageant had been devised in a noble effort to keep summer visitors from departing right after Labor Day, and the use of the female form as the handmaiden of commerce continued with the aid of photographers. The amphibious group above were photographed in September 1922. By way of comparison, we show you (right) the 1935 winner.

Tremendous trifles, fads, and sports were winning the attention of a people tired of national and world problems. Early in 1923 Dr. Emil Coué (right) came from France to America with his magic formula, "Day by day in every way I am getting better and better." At about the same time vast numbers of people were learning to play the imported Chinese game, Mah Jongg, which in the picture above is being played — for publicity purposes — under photogenic conditions in the Wardman Park Pool, Washington.

It was the golden age of ballyhoo.
since New Yorkers, at the time o
Armistice of 1918, had learned th
was fun to throw ticker tape out of
dows, the city had delighted in sta
welcomes. At the left you will se
great metropolis exercising its sen
proportion in 1926 by welcoming
no very important reason, the attra
Queen Marie of Rumania.

Any news story of personal drama, real or phony, was a prime candidate for front-page display. In February 1925 a Kentucky boy, Floyd Collins, got stuck in an underground passage near Mammoth Cave, and for over a fortnight the attempts to rescue him (as above, where miners are at work) were banner headline stuff the country over. (Collins was found dead on the eighteenth day.)

A separation suit brought by young "Peaches" Browning against her husband, Edward W. ("Daddy") Browning (right), gave tabloids a chance to parade such items as a "composograph" showing "Daddy" saying to his bride, "Woof! Woof! Don't be a goof!"

Even a dog could become a ballyhooed hero if there was drama and suspense in his story. Below, one of these heroes sits for his picture: Balto, who brought serum to Nome, Alaska, to combat—though possibly he didn't fully grasp the idea—an influenza epidemic.

By-product of the prohibition law: a rum-running boat caught smuggling in 2,000 bottles.

On the last day before the Prohibition Amendment went into effect in January 1920, the Anti-Saloon League of New York issued an exultant statement: "At one minute past twelve tomorrow morning a new nation will be born. . . . Now for an era of clear thinking and clean living!" Two months later, at a (dry) dinner given to celebrate his sixtieth birthday, William Jennings Bryan said the liquor issue was "as dead as slavery." Extreme statements? Perhaps. But most Americans would probably have agreed with Daniel C. Roper, Commissioner of Internal Revenue, when he said: "The prohibition law will be violated—extensively at first, slightly later on; but it will, broadly speaking, be enforced and will result in a nation that knows not alcohol." They were all, of course, quite wrong.

Violation of the law began promptly and continued unabated. The boat on the opposite page had been engaged in carrying liquor from a rum-running ship at sea to the New Jersey coast, and was caught in the Rahway River, unable to land its load of liquor. The bar shown above, in a café in Camden, New Jersey, was forcibly pried up and dismantled by dry agents.

*"Here I am, old boy—in the wine cellar."*

Not only did rum-running, illicit distilling, and other organized forms of lawbreaking expand to majestic proportions, but ordinary citizens began very soon to do home brewing, making extraordinary concoctions in the cellar or the coat closet. The cartoon at the left was published in *The New Yorker* as late as June 25, 1932, but it might almost as well have appeared ten years earlier.

Take a look at the problem of enforcing prohibition. The land frontiers and coast lines of the United States total 18,700 miles in length; there were too few agents to guard them. General Lincoln C. Andrews, who was for a time in charge of enforcement, estimated that his men stopped only about five per cent of the liquor smuggled in! Industrial alcohol could still be legally manufactured—and it was so easy to divert it to use for drinking that there may have been, at the peak, some fifteen million gallons a year so diverted. Near-beer was still legal; the only way to make it was to make real beer and then remove the alcohol; what could be easier than to fail to go through this second process when nobody was looking? Illicit distilling was easy, too, and rampant everywhere; probably over a hundred millions of gallons a year were thus made. And there was so much money in selling bootleg liquor that there was plenty left over to bribe dry agents and policemen. Only one thing could have made the law effective—strong public support. And public support, in locality after locality, slowly melted away. Men such as those in the picture above—they are looking at a cache of 191 pint bottles found underneath a sailor's mattress on a steamer putting in at Norfolk, Virginia—faced a hopeless task.

The cartoon above—drawn by Fish for the May 1922 issue of *Vanity Fair*—shows a couple of tourists, returned from Bermuda, trying to fascinate a customs officer so that he won't notice the bottles bulging in their pockets. That was one phenomenon of the prohibition era. Others: the bootlegger whom you could call on the telephone and who would then deliver bottles to your office or home, warranted to be "just off the boat"; youths going to the country club dance equipped with hip flasks full of raw gin, which could be added to ginger ale provided by the management of the club, or gulped straight by the boy and girl in the parked sedan outside; coonskin-coated men at football games, cheering more and more hilariously as they drained their pint flasks; apartment dwellers making bathtub gin by a formula (distilled water, grain alcohol, and a few drops of essence of juniper) guaranteed to produce potent and unpoisonous effects; well-dressed men and women descending the steps to basement speakeasies (some of which, in New York, offered the best food in town), where they rang the bell, were examined through a grilled opening in the door by the proprietor of the place, and were admitted if they were known habitués or could establish themselves as "friends of Mr. Sweeney's"; girls drinking at the bar in these speakeasies (as depicted in *The New Yorker* cartoon by Wallace Morgan on the two following pages of this book); the courts of justice swamped with prohibition cases, and juries often refusing to bring in convictions; organized bootlegging rings running beer trucks from place to place, buying police protection to do so, holding up (or "hijacking") one another's trucks, hiring killers to protect this lucrative traffic, and thus multiplying the lawless phenomena of gangsterdom; and, in general, a saturnalia of wild drinking and rampant crime which few people would have imagined possible on January 16, 1920.

THE SALOON MUST GO! A speakeasy scene in New York City

Drawn by Wallace Morgan for *The New Yorker,* October 11, 1930

The widespread defiance of the prohibition laws was only one symptom of a pervasive change in American manners and customs during the postwar years. Great numbers of people had come out of their war experience feeling that ideals had been discredited, that those who talked about standards of conduct were old-fashioned and unrealistic, and that you might as well let the bars down and get yourself a good time whenever and wherever you could. Result: a rebellion against the puritan code of manners and morals, led by the "younger generation," who in great numbers went in for a new frankness of talk, an excited (if not obsessed) interest in sex, a tolerant acceptance of alcoholic conduct, an acceptance, too, of the permissibility of the petting-party (to use the favored term of that day), and a general lapse from gentility into rowdiness. Do not imagine that the change was universal, for it was not. In many a circle the old code held firmly. The change was rooted, of course, in the sort of world-weariness satirized in the cartoon above, by Fish, from *Vanity Fair* for April 1922, of a fashionable cabaret scene.

The most successful caricaturist of the wide-trousered, coonskin-coated cake-eaters of the mid-twenties, and the short-skirted, long-legged flappers, was John Held, Jr. His two cartoons on this page are both from the old *Life* (at the right, October 8, 1925; below, April 1, 1926). The photograph is a scene from the movie, "Our Dancing Daughters," which portrayed in 1928 the wild conduct of the young; the blonde dancer, believe it or not, is none other than Joan Crawford.

"BILL! SHE'S GOT *two* SETS OF GARTERS ON!"
"SURE, THEY'RE ALL WEARING 'EM NOW—ONE PAIR TO HOLD UP THEIR STOCKINGS AND THE OTHER TO HOLD UP TRAFFIC."

ONE MOTHER, ONE FATHER, ONE TONSIL-EXPERT, FOUR GENERAL PRACTITIONERS, THREE TRAINED NURSES, FIVE GOVERNESSES, FIFTY-SIX ORDINARY TEACHERS, THIRTY-TWO PROFESSORS, AND THREE ATHLETIC TRAINERS COMBINED THEIR EFFORTS TO PRODUCE THIS.

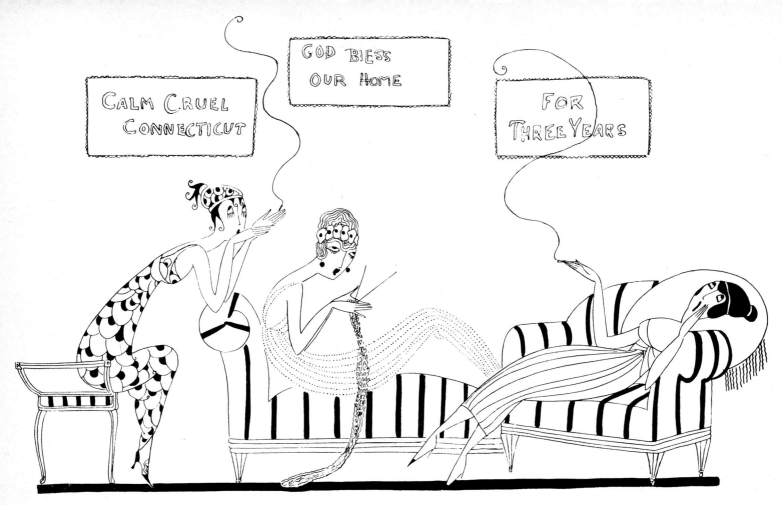

The growing acceptance of divorce, in well-to-do circles, as a quite-to-be-expected thing, not tragic but boresome and rather amusing, was hit off by Fish in these two cartoons (from *Vanity Fair,* January 1920). Above, three ladies are waiting in Reno; below, a young woman is introducing her newest husband to his predecessors.

The abandonment of ballroom decorum was typified by the vogue of the Charleston, caricatured above for the cover of *Life* by John Held, Jr. This dance was a furious, knock-kneed, foot-twisting antic which had originated among Southern Negroes, was imported from Harlem into white society, and became briefly popular about 1926 —along with another dance of similar ancestry, the Black Bottom.

"Not at all - the aroma is delightful"
Chesterfield
CIGARETTES


At the end of World War I, very few American women smoked cigarettes. Within a few years, millions of them had taken it up, and the number increased steadily. This was one reason why annual sales leaped from 47 billion cigarettes in 1920 to 125 billion in 1930, and 217 billion in 1941. But the number of people who disapproved of women smoking remained formidable so long that for many years tobacco manufacturers hesitated to go farther than to suggest—as in the advertisement at the left, from *Life,* for June 10, 1926—that a woman might like the smell of smoke.

Another Fish cartoon reminds us that not until after World War I did psychoanalysis become familiar to a wide public. Then it became fashionable for the prosperous to resort to psychiatric treatment, which brought to many of them the lovely news that they ought to subdue their inhibitions. The husband and wife in Fish's sketch (from *Vanity Fair,* May 1921) are thinking of their respective psychiatrists.

With the drastic change in manners and customs went an equally drastic change in the appearance of the female of the species. Gone were ankle-length skirts; the skirt-hem, which had climbed a few inches between 1919 and 1920, and then had descended again, began in 1923 an ascent which by 1927 was to take it all the way to the knee and even above. Gone were black stockings, white stockings, brown stockings; they had been displaced by the approximately flesh-colored stocking, which made its advent early in the nineteen-twenties and was to remain a virtually unchanging item of fashion for at least twenty-five years. Gone—or going—was long hair; by 1926, when the picture above appeared, nearly all girls were wearing their hair short, older women were fast following them (usually after a period of agonizing indecision), the most fashionable version was the shingle, and the ladies' hairdressing business, stimulated by the acceptance of the permanent wave, was booming. And the waistline had moved down to the hips. The picture above, from *Vogue* for April 15, 1926, represents "a frock of canary yellow chiffon . . . ideal for dancing on a warm evening at Palm Beach. . . ."

To point the violent change which took place in the aspect of women in the few years between 1919 and 1926, we show on this page two contrasting pictures from catalogues of Altman's department store in New York. At the left are some women in evening dresses sketched for the September 1926 editions; below are their counterparts in the edition for fall and winter, 1919-20. By 1926 the line from shoulder to hip was supposed to be straight, in spite of nature, and the general effect was supposed to be pencil-slim. That double ambition caused anguish to many a matron; for the style of the middle and late nineteen-twenties was remarkably unkind to all but the unnaturally slender.

Another striking contrast between the Altman catalogue women of September 1926 (above) and of Fall and Winter 1919-20 (right) is in the fashion artist's idea of what a woman should look like. No longer, in 1926, did he try to make her look gentle, maidenly, rosebud-like; she must now look sleek and world-weary. This change was not, of course, confined to the catalogues of any one store; it was very general, and was reflected also in the changed demeanor of shop-window manikins, which must now no longer simper but appear very experienced and very, very hard to astonish.

The small cloche hat had now arrived—to the dismay of makers of milliners' materials. Above, some characteristic 1926 headgear.

Above, a young woman illustrates for the readers of *Vogue* for May 15, 1926, "the newest version of the décolletage"—the deep U shape in the back. Note the contrast between this shingled lady and her counterparts as pictured (at the left) in *Vogue* for May 1, 1919—the difference in hair, yardage of costume material, and general aspect. The original caption for the 1919 picture speaks of "the lightsomeness of youth"; the woman in the 1926 Chanel dress above wants to be worldly, not lightsome.

No. 120 Spring and Summer 1919

CORSETS AND BRASSIERES FOR WOMEN, MISSES AND SMALL WOMEN ALSO CORSET ACCESSORIES

45S26 Corset of Pink Broche; low bust with elastic band at bust and under arm; two pairs of hose supporters. Sizes 19 to 28 . . . . . $3.50

45S27 Maternity Corset of White Coutil; length of front steel 10½ inches; extremely soft elastic section at each side of front steel; lacing at sides, also at back; low at top; hooks and eyes below front steel; three pairs of hose supporters. Sizes 22 to 34 . . . . . $5.00

45S28 Misses' Corset of Pink Striped Batiste; elastic gusset at each side of front; low top; medium length; front steel 4½ ins.; four pearl buttons and buttonholes above; lace trimmed; satin bow; two pairs of hose supporters. Sizes 21 to 26 $3.75

45S29 Corset of Pink Broche; for medium and stout figures; full and medium low back and [illegible]; long over hips; well-boned throughout; insert of elastic on hips; hooks and eyes below front steel; trimmed with lace and satin ribbon; three pairs of hose supporters. 20 to 30 $6.00

45S31 Sports Corset of Pink Tricot, [illegible] back and front only; very low top; eyelets below front steel; [illegible] pink batiste; two pairs of hose supporters. Sizes 20 to 27 $4.00

45S30 Brassiere of White Tape and Lace; opens in front with hooks and eyes; lace in back. Sizes 32 to 40 . . . . . $1.50

45S32 Corset, White Batiste, for misses and small women; low top, long hips; well-boned; [illegible] 2 pairs supporters. [illegible] $2.00

45S33 Laced Front Corset of Pink Coutil; low at top with band of strong elastic; long skirt; suitable for [illegible] figures; three pairs of hose supporters. Sizes [illegible] $4.00

45S34 Round Garters, made of [illegible] [illegible] ribbon with hand-made [illegible] [illegible] . . . . . $1.25

Coutil Corsets can be altered for nursing purposes (with laps) at an additional charge of $2.00.

Special attention is given to all correspondence; individual requirements are carefully considered, and corsets are selected by expert corsetieres.



And how was that severely rectangular effect achieved? The essentials of the feminine physique had not changed in six or seven years; nor—impossible as it may seem—have they changed since 1926. What has changed has been feminine aspiration—and underpinnings. On these two pages you will find all the evidence as to the latter that the corset and brassière pages of two Altman catalogues will vouchsafe. On this page, the exhibit for Spring and Summer 1919; on the right-hand page, ditto for Spring and Summer 1926.

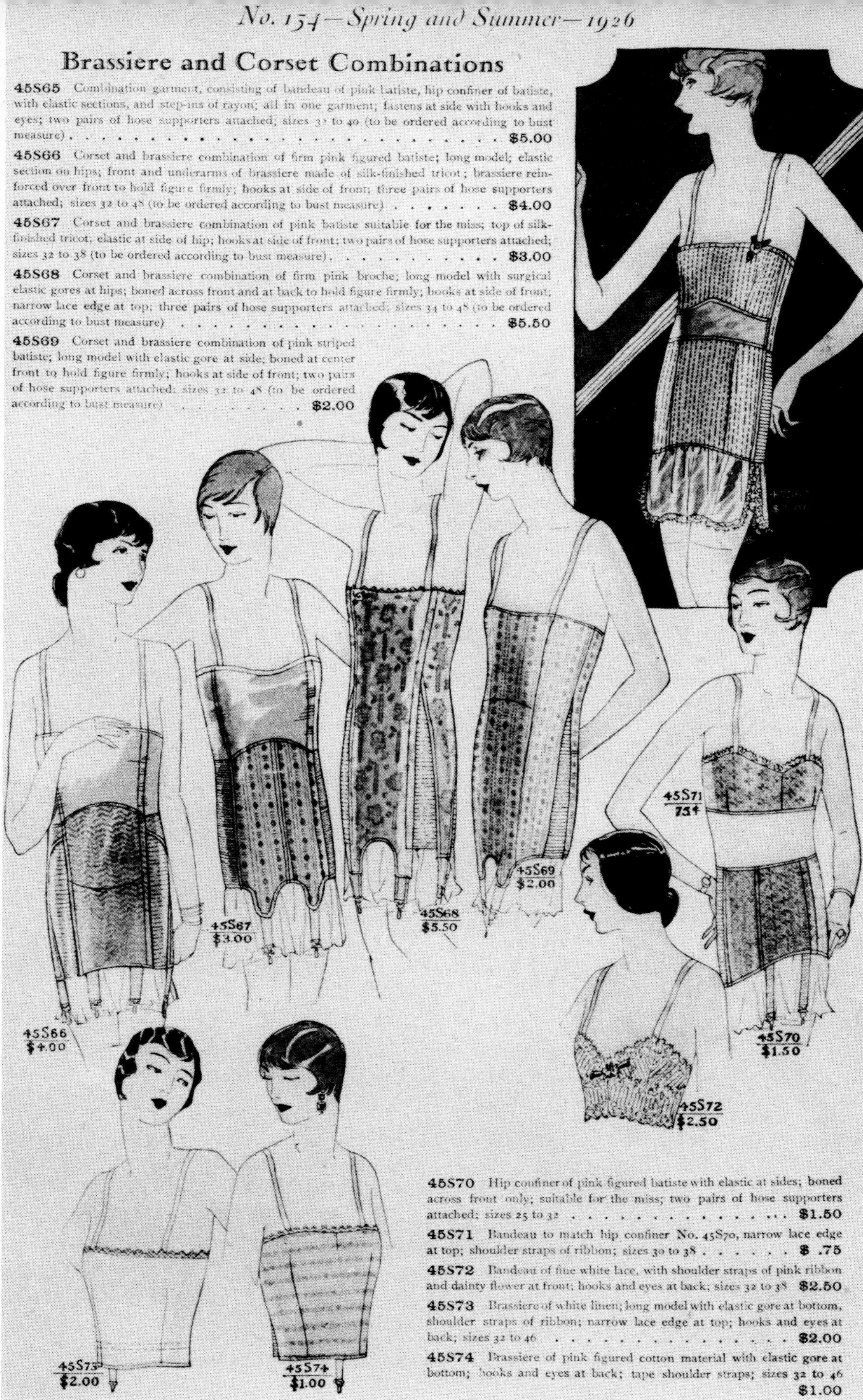

No. 154—Spring and Summer—1926

## Brassiere and Corset Combinations

**45S65** Combination garment, consisting of bandeau of pink batiste, hip confiner of batiste, with elastic sections, and step-ins of rayon; all in one garment; fastens at side with hooks and eyes; two pairs of hose supporters attached; sizes 32 to 40 (to be ordered according to bust measure) . . . . . . . . . . . . . . . . . . . . . . . . . **$5.00**

**45S66** Corset and brassiere combination of firm pink figured batiste; long model; elastic section on hips; front and underarms of brassiere made of silk-finished tricot; brassiere reinforced over front to hold figure firmly; hooks at side of front; three pairs of hose supporters attached; sizes 32 to 48 (to be ordered according to bust measure) . . . . . . . . **$4.00**

**45S67** Corset and brassiere combination of pink batiste suitable for the miss; top of silk-finished tricot; elastic at side of hip; hooks at side of front; two pairs of hose supporters attached; sizes 32 to 38 (to be ordered according to bust measure). . . . . . . . . . . . **$3.00**

**45S68** Corset and brassiere combination of firm pink broche; long model with surgical elastic gores at hips; boned across front and at back to hold figure firmly; hooks at side of front; narrow lace edge at top; three pairs of hose supporters attached; sizes 34 to 48 (to be ordered according to bust measure) . . . . . . . . . . . . . . . . . . . . . . **$5.50**

**45S69** Corset and brassiere combination of pink striped batiste; long model with elastic gore at side; boned at center front to hold figure firmly; hooks at side of front; two pairs of hose supporters attached; sizes 32 to 48 (to be ordered according to bust measure) . . . . . . . . . **$2.00**

45S71 75¢

45S69 $2.00

45S67 $3.00

45S68 $5.50

45S86 $4.00

45S70 $1.50

45S72 $2.50

45S73 $2.00

45S74 $1.00

**45S70** Hip confiner of pink figured batiste with elastic at sides; boned across front only; suitable for the miss; two pairs of hose supporters attached; sizes 25 to 32 . . . . . . . . . . . . . . . . . **$1.50**

**45S71** Bandeau to match hip confiner No. 45S70, narrow lace edge at top; shoulder straps of ribbon; sizes 30 to 38 . . . . . . . **$ .75**

**45S72** Bandeau of fine white lace, with shoulder straps of pink ribbon and dainty flower at front; hooks and eyes at back; sizes 32 to 38 **$2.50**

**45S73** Brassiere of white linen; long model with elastic gore at bottom, shoulder straps of ribbon; narrow lace edge at top; hooks and eyes at back; sizes 32 to 46 . . . . . . . . . . . . . . . **$2.00**

**45S74** Brassiere of pink figured cotton material with elastic gore at bottom; hooks and eyes at back; tape shoulder straps; sizes 32 to 46 **$1.00**

These were the kinds of undergarments with the aid of which, in 1926, the boyish form was achieved by American women—or, if not achieved, was yearned after. The popular discovery of the vitamin was not the only reason for the increased sale of fruit juices, tomato juice, and fresh vegetables; the ladies were reducing as never before.

No such radical transformation took place in the aspect of the male. But "plus fours," like those adorning the young man in the upper left-hand corner of this page, were a novelty. (The name meant that they were four inches longer than knickerbockers had previously been.) That picture is from a Finchley advertisement in *The New Yorker* for June 16, 1928. There was a huge boom in the popularity of golf and of country club life in general during the nineteen-twenties, and plus fours became standard wear for men on the links, although some still preferred long flannels and a picture in *Vanity Fair* in 1926 showed a golfer attired in what the magazine called "somewhat startling golfing 'shorts.' " The picture above, from *Vanity Fair* for January 1926, will remind you that the man's bathing-suit top had not yet been discarded; and the sketch at the left, from a Finchley advertisement in *The New Yorker* for July 2, 1927, that striped flannels were smart.

When President Harding died in San Francisco in the summer of 1923, the vast burdens of the Presidency of the United States fell upon the shoulders of the cautious, laconic Vice President, Calvin Coolidge. During five and a half years (for he was elected to succeed himself in 1924) he provided just the sort of administration that most Americans seemed to want: he did and said just as little as it was possible for a President to do and say, and kept assiduously out of the limelight. On the rare occasions when he felt he had to do a little play-acting for the photographers, he always looked embarrassed—as above, where he is dressed up in full cowboy attire for a Fourth of July celebration at Rapid City, South Dakota, in 1927. His function was to provide an honest administration, to muffle as best he could the reverberations from the Harding scandals, and to smile silently upon "Coolidge prosperity."

Each horse-and-carriage represents 10 million horses
Each motor vehicle represents 3 million motor vehicles
Distance between milestones represents 500,000 miles of road—surfaced portion dark

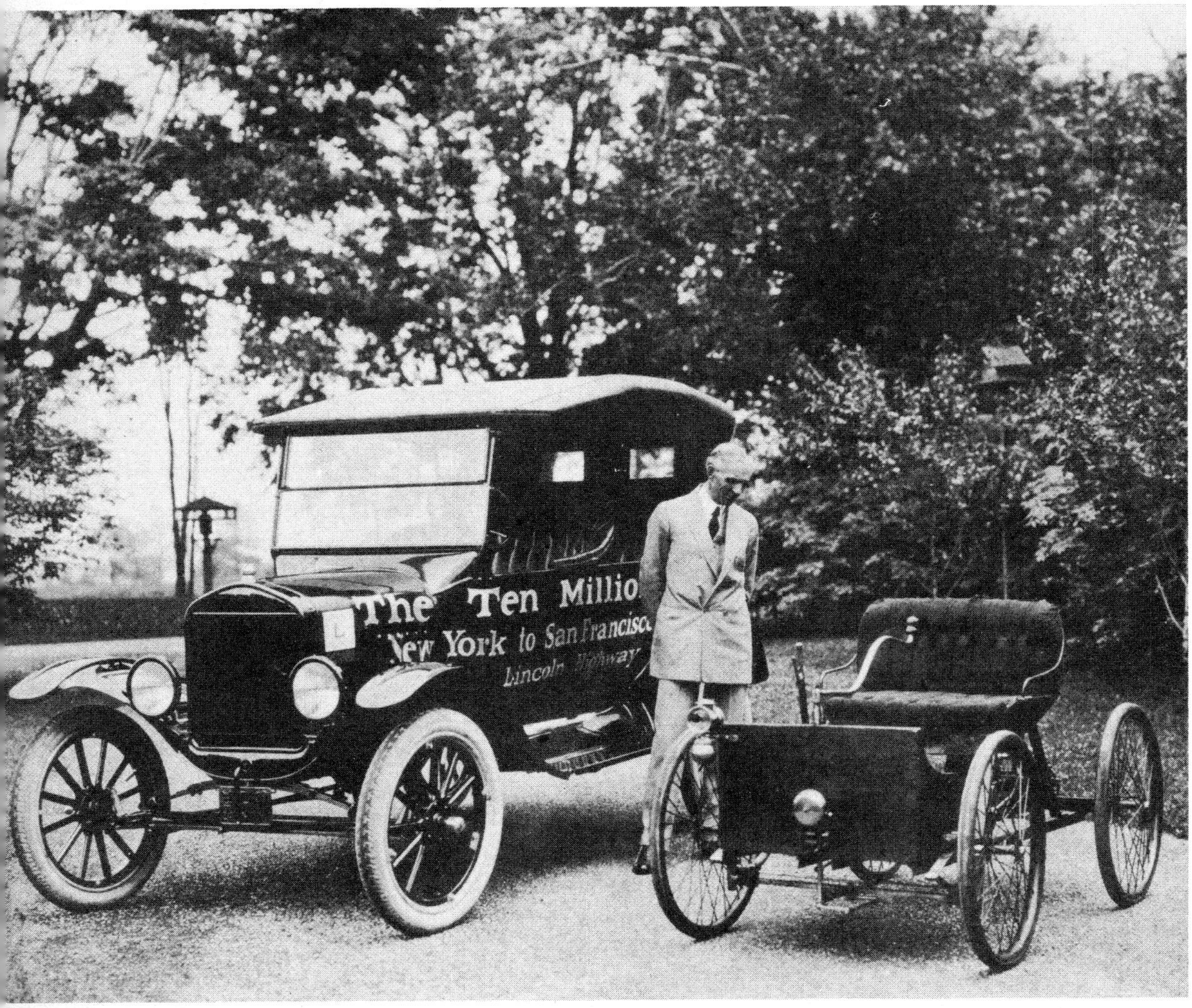

The chief presiding genius of automobile boom of the ni teen-twenties was Henry Fo who is here shown with his f car and his ten millionth. It h taken him seven years to ma his first million cars; the te million took only 132 work days to build. The car at the l is, of course, a Model T.

At the heart of Coolidge prosperity was the automobile, which in the nineteen-twenties became for the first time a utility and plaything to be used and enjoyed by the average American. The graph at the top of this page shows how the number of cars leaped during that period. Not only did car-making expand enormously, but also the industries associated with road-building, filling stations, bus lines, trucking, suburban expansion, and all the other manifold and familiar phenomena of the automobile age.

re, for the nostalgic, are three cars 1924, the year when Coolidge be- ne President in his own right. At right, a Ford Model T coupé, high l square; below, the first Chrysler r built (it had a six-cylinder en- e); and below that, a 1924 Buick ring car, model 6-45. No stream- ng in those days; the horizontal e dominated all motordom.

Above is an old Ford publicity picture of the delights of picnicking with a Model T roadster in 1926—the year before it was dropped for Model A. At the right, the long Cadillac V-16 of 1929, the lush and climactic year of the Big Bull Market.

As the years went by, Model T, with its three f pedals (high and low speeds, reverse, and brake), its planetary gears, and its sturdy ugliness, bega look more and more like an antique beside the o cars on the road; and in 1927 Henry Ford at last the plunge, closed down production, and afte interval of mystery unveiled on December 2 his Model A, shown at the left. Vast crowds thro to see this new wonder; a million people, it was mated, tried to get into the showroom in New Y and other millions elsewhere. For this new car wa just another automobile to the American peop was an exciting symbol of American progress.

s hard for us nowadays to realize v drastically the extensive road-lding and road-resurfacing that ac-npanied and aided the expansion the automobile industry trans-med the conditions of American ng. But the pictures on this page y at least suggest the extent of the nge. At the top is a view of the *in highway* between Washington, C., and Richmond, Virginia, in 9. Next is the same stretch of road er it was resurfaced in 1920. At bottom is the identical scene in 7, after it had become a three-lane cadam road. Since then it has been verted into a four-lane concrete d which by-passes Dumfries, Vir-ia, where these pictures were taken.

# Genesee Isles

## "Florida's Venice DeLuxe"

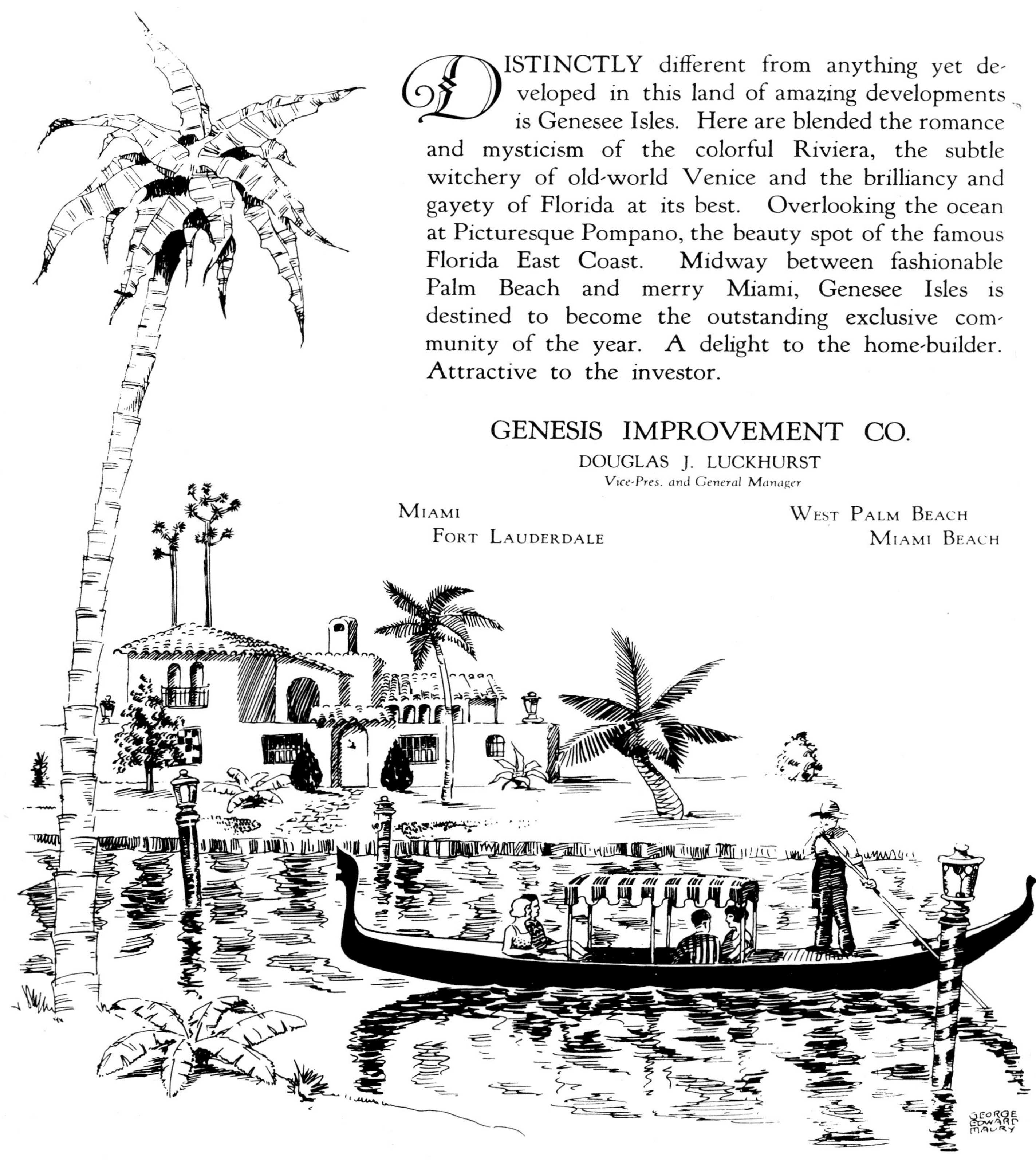


DISTINCTLY different from anything yet developed in this land of amazing developments is Genesee Isles. Here are blended the romance and mysticism of the colorful Riviera, the subtle witchery of old-world Venice and the brilliancy and gayety of Florida at its best. Overlooking the ocean at Picturesque Pompano, the beauty spot of the famous Florida East Coast. Midway between fashionable Palm Beach and merry Miami, Genesee Isles is destined to become the outstanding exclusive community of the year. A delight to the home-builder. Attractive to the investor.

GENESIS IMPROVEMENT CO.

DOUGLAS J. LUCKHURST

*Vice-Pres. and General Manager*

MIAMI
FORT LAUDERDALE

WEST PALM BEACH
MIAMI BEACH

The Florida boom reached its peak late in 1925, by which time houselots in remote swamps were selling for ten or twenty times their pre-boom value and Miami was a storm-center of wild speculation. It weakened in 1926 and then collapsed with the aid of hurricanes. But by that time the Big Bull Market was rising, and Coolidge prosperity roared right on. Meanwhile California did not slacken in promoting its own rival climate. We present at the left one of California's cozier displays of its attractions—a photograph of some "personality girls," selected "for their character, personality, and charm" to tour the United States on California's behalf.

Another potent factor in Coolidge prosperity was building construction — of mighty office buildings, apartment houses, suburban dwellings, and resorts. The boom in building and real estate went on its wildest jamboree in southern Florida in the mid-twenties, when speculation in land—based on the captivating idea that the country's rising gods, its business executives, would bask by the millions in Florida's winter climate —reached fantastic heights. On the page to the left is an advertisement from *Town and Country* for November 1, 1925, with old-world gondolas for new-world golfers. At the right is a sketch of Miami's new skyline, with the building of the Miami *News* in the foreground. It is from *Vanity Fair* for April 1926.

In sports, too, the old order had yielded place to new. Ty Cobb, above, led the American League in batting every year from 1907 through 1919, with the single exception of 1916!

By 1920 Babe Ruth had taken over the spotlight. In that year baseball was hit hard by scandal, when the Chicago White Sox were indicted for "throwing" the World Series of 1919. The players were acquitted, but so besmirched with suspicion had the game become that a federal judge, Kenesaw Mountain Landis, was invited by the major-league owners to become "czar" of organized baseball. At the right is Judge Landis, snapped in a characteristic pose a great many years later—in 1939.

abe Ruth, the Bambino, the Sultan of Swat, as the undisputed king of the ball parks all rough the ballyhoo years. Above, he is bundled after a workout; at the right, he is putting his rmidable weight behind a hit.

After the nineteen-twenties, Ruth's annual collection of home runs began to diminish. In the picture at the left he is talking, bat in hand, with Lou Gehrig, another idol of the Yankee fans, who from 1925 until he left the lineup because of a fatal illness in 1939, played 2,130 consecutive games for that one club.

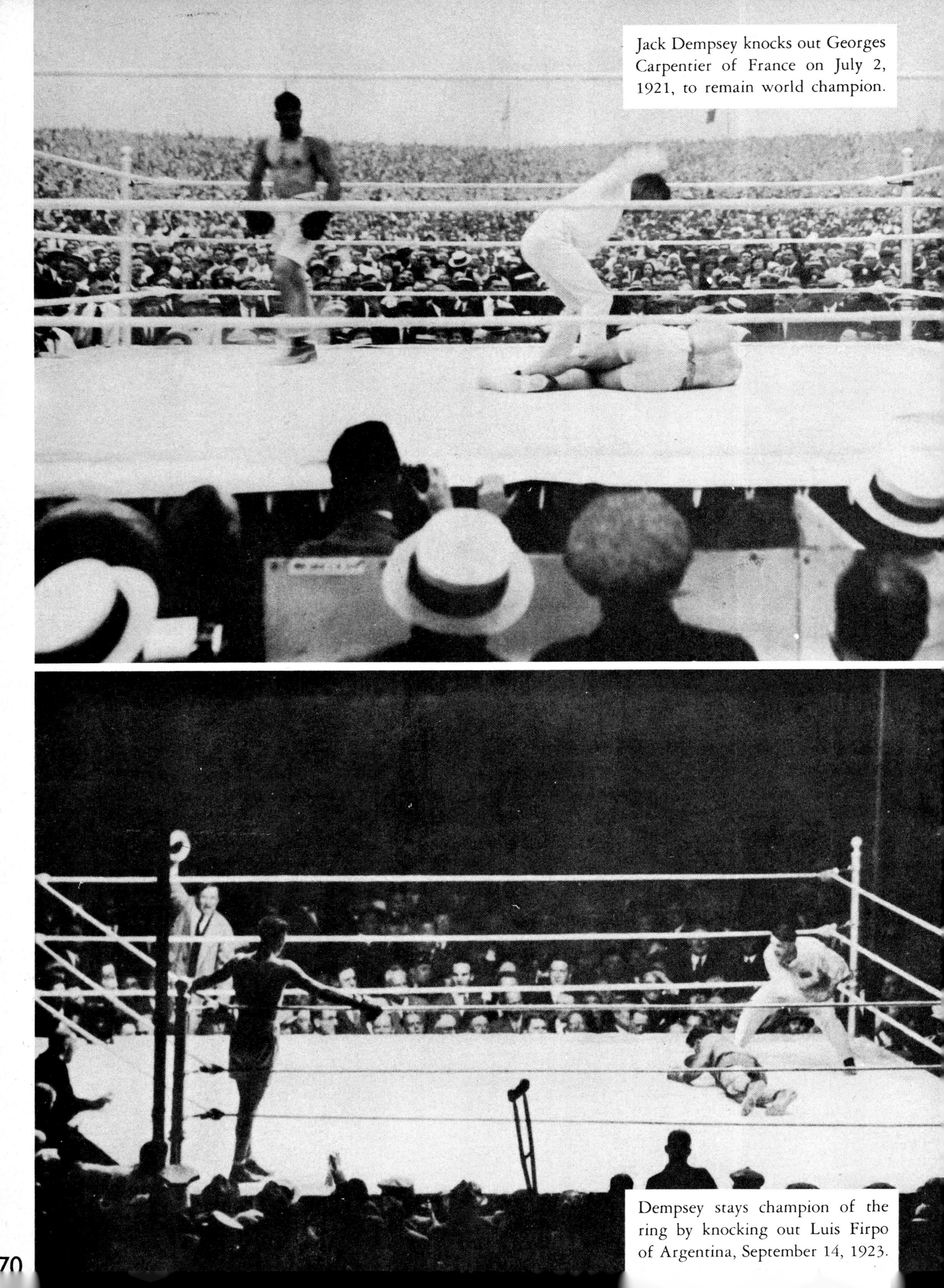

Jack Dempsey knocks out Georges Carpentier of France on July 2, 1921, to remain world champion.

Dempsey stays champion of the ring by knocking out Luis Firpo of Argentina, September 14, 1923.

High among the heroes of sport stood Jack Dempsey, who took the world boxing championship in 1919 by defeating the lofty Jess Willard at Toledo, and held the title against all comers until 1926, when he lost to Gene Tunney by decision of the judges at Philadelphia. The next year, 1927, the two men fought again at Chicago; and in the seventh round, Tunney fell. Because the referee delayed beginning his count, Tunney had thirteen seconds to recover—and he subsequently won. The picture above shows him going down for that famous "long count." Tunney did not hold the championship long; after beating Tom Heeney in 1928 he announced his retirement from the ring, having acquired more intellectual ambitions—and went for a walking trip abroad with the novelist and playwright, Thornton Wilder.

At the left, the two meet again in World War II: Commander Tunney, left; Commander Dempsey, right.

The first woman to swim the English Channel was Gertrude Ederle, the stalwart nineteen-year-old daughter of an Amsterdam Avenue butcher in New York. Battling against tricky tides, she made better time than her masculine predecessors—14 hours, 31 minutes. At the left you will see her entering the water, in a costume permissible then only for long-distance swimmers, and well smeared with grease. Below, she is on her way; her head is bobbing in the water alongside the accompanying tug. It was a great feat; and characteristic of the spirit of 1926 was the fact that when Miss Ederle got back to New York, her ship was met by an official yacht, by circling planes, and by a Fire Department band; fifteen thousand people were at the Battery to greet her; she was given an official welcome with ticker tape; and Mayor Walker likened her exploit to Moses' crossing of the Red Sea and Caesar's crossing of the Rubicon.

Still another great figure in sport was William T. Tilden, 2nd, whose cannon-ball serve and all-round mastery of tennis made him champion every year from 1920 through 1925, and then—after a lapse during which the Frenchmen Lacoste and Cochet won—again in 1929. At the right, you see him in his heyday on the court; below he is shown with the other members of the Davis Cup team of 1921—Watson M. Washburn (with glasses) and R. Norris Williams and William M. Johnston, previous champions. Tilden later turned professional, and so well retained his skill that even after World War II he was a player well worth seeing in action.

The feminine counterpart to Bill Tilden was Helen Wills of California, who first won the women's national tennis championship in 1923, when she was not yet seventeen, and took it again in 1924, 1925, 1927, 1928, and 1931—by which time she had become Mrs. Moody. The picture above was taken in 1924, when she was still very young—and burdened with a costume that would seem a little hampering to a contemporary tennis star. At the right is a portrait taken considerably later; again she is wearing her usual eye-shade.

What was most remarkable about the sports of the nineteen-twenties was not the prowess of the stars, though this was noteworthy, but the vast publicity that surrounded them, the adulation they received, and the hugely increased amount of money taken in at sporting events. In the mid-twenties college football aroused such excitement that Harold E. ("Red") Grange of the University of Illinois (who appears above), affectionately known as the "Wheaton iceman," at the close of his senior season was offered $120,000 a year by a real estate firm, took in $12,000 at his first professional game and $30,000 at a subsequent one, signed a $300,000 movie contract, and was the subject of a petition nominating him for Congress.

That any one player should have been able to dominate a game so beset with uncertainties as golf for as long a time as did Bobby Jones was extraordinary. He was five times national amateur champion, four times national open champion; and in 1930 he performed the feat of winning four major titles in a single season—the American and British amateur and open championships. Above, left, he is shaking hands with Alexa Sterling after winning his first open title in 1923; at the right, he is finishing his effortless swing.

When the depression came, Jones turned professional. At the left, a later glimpse: Captain Jones is reporting for duty in World War II.

No American track stars of the twenties—not even Charlie Paddock or Joie Ray—attracted so much attention as did Paavo Nurmi, the "Flying Finn," when he came to the United States early in 1925 and showed astonished crowds that it was possible to run two miles in less than nine minutes. In the picture at the right he is carrying in his right hand the stopwatch with which he regulated his speed.

Add to the heroes of sport the great Man o' War, whose money winnings in 1920, when he was a three-year-old, were much the biggest up to that time. Later, as racing grew more popular, his total was beaten by Zev (1923), Gallant Fox (1930), and many another; but he remained a creature of legend—and his offspring won over three million dollars. Our picture shows him in 1924.

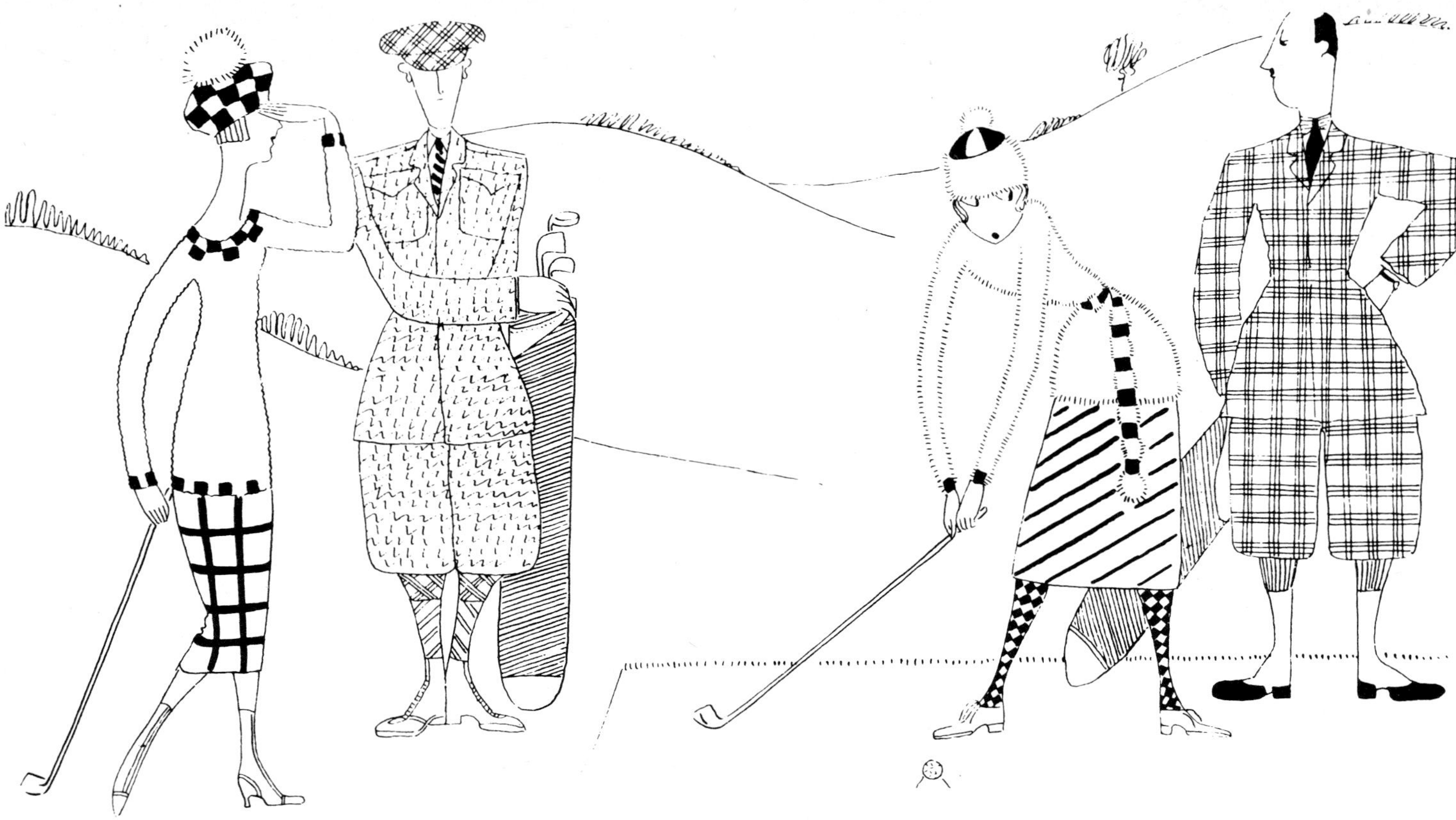

Let us look for a moment at spor costumes. Above, Fish's notion of golfing scene at Palm Beach, fro *Vanity Fair,* February 1920. At th left, a photograph taken at Vass a little earlier, showing Preside MacCracken catching behind a b wielded by a surprising batter.

Regard the bloomers worn by the sturdy Vassar sprinters at the right, snapped on Field Day, 1919, and you will see why women were ready for new ideas in sports wear in the twenties. Before long, about the only victims of the bloomer were to be found at girls' camps. (For the winner's ankle we offer no explanation.)

Track athletics as well as basketball and field hockey, once dear to the hardier students at women's colleges, have virtually disappeared since those days in favor of the more socially useful tennis and golf.

No bloomers for these Vassar figure skaters at the 1922 ice carnival, who represented one phase of the impulse toward art in physical exertion. Another phase is illustrated by the picture below—still another Vassar number—showing aesthetic (at least in intention) dancers.

Along with the recklessness and glorified commercialism of the nineteen-twenties went an outburst of another sort—a lively awakening in the arts. Nowhere was this more exciting than in the theatre. Aided by the enthusiasm of the Provincetown Players and the young Theatre Guild, a gifted group of playwrights, scene designers, and actors gave the production of plays a new coherence and vitality. (Consider the playwrights alone: those who first made their mark then included Eugene O'Neill, Philip Barry, Sidney Howard, George S. Kaufman and Marc Connelly, Robert E. Sherwood, Elmer Rice, and Maxwell Anderson.)

Don't think, however, that such distinguished artists had things all their own way. The theatre-going public gave its most spontaneous and sustained support to the play whose wedding scene is pictured above—"Abie's Irish Rose," an obvious comedy of Irish-Jewish relationships. Opening on May 25, 1922, and slighted by the critics, "Abie" ran on and on until 1927, for a record run of 2,327 performances—while such meritorious plays as "The Adding Machine," "Rain," "The Show-Off," "Beggar on Horseback," "Desire Under the Elms," and "What Price Glory?" came and went. This record stood until "Tobacco Road" at last broke it.

In the theatre, as well as in the novel, a favorite topic was the hopeless and tragic decadence of the "lost generation." This was the theme of Michael Arlen's "The Green Hat," in which the rising actress Katharine Cornell, pictured at the right, played the part of Iris March with such moving intensity that many a bouncing outdoor girl of 1925 became convinced that she too was a lost but gallant sophisticate. Below are the three stars of the delightfully intimate importation, "Charlot's Revue," as they looked when they were pleasing New York audiences in 1924: Beatrice Lillie, Jack Buchanan, and Gertrude Lawrence (whom you will see again on page 85, subtly changed).

The stage of the twenties is closer to us today than one might suppose, for it brought out many a talent since made familiar to millions by Hollywood, and its popular tunes are still heard constantly on the radio. Here are Fred and Adele Astaire in "The Band Wagon." Their greatest Broadway hit was perhaps their appearance as the stars of "Lady Be Good," in 1924 (music by George Gershwin).

Earl Carroll, who according to Stanley Walker "always had a song in his heart and a keen eye for nakedness," is here shown watching the work of what, in the caption of the 1925 photograph that we reproduce above, are described as "Boston Beauties to appear in 'Vanities.' " Let it go at that. At the right he is greeting Countess Vera Cathcart in 1926, after she had been detained by immigration authorities on charges involving alleged "moral turpitude." Carroll gave a party for her at his theatre at which Joyce Hawley, a seventeen-year-old girl, took a bath in a tub said to be full of wine—an event which led to Carroll's subsequently going to prison for perjury.

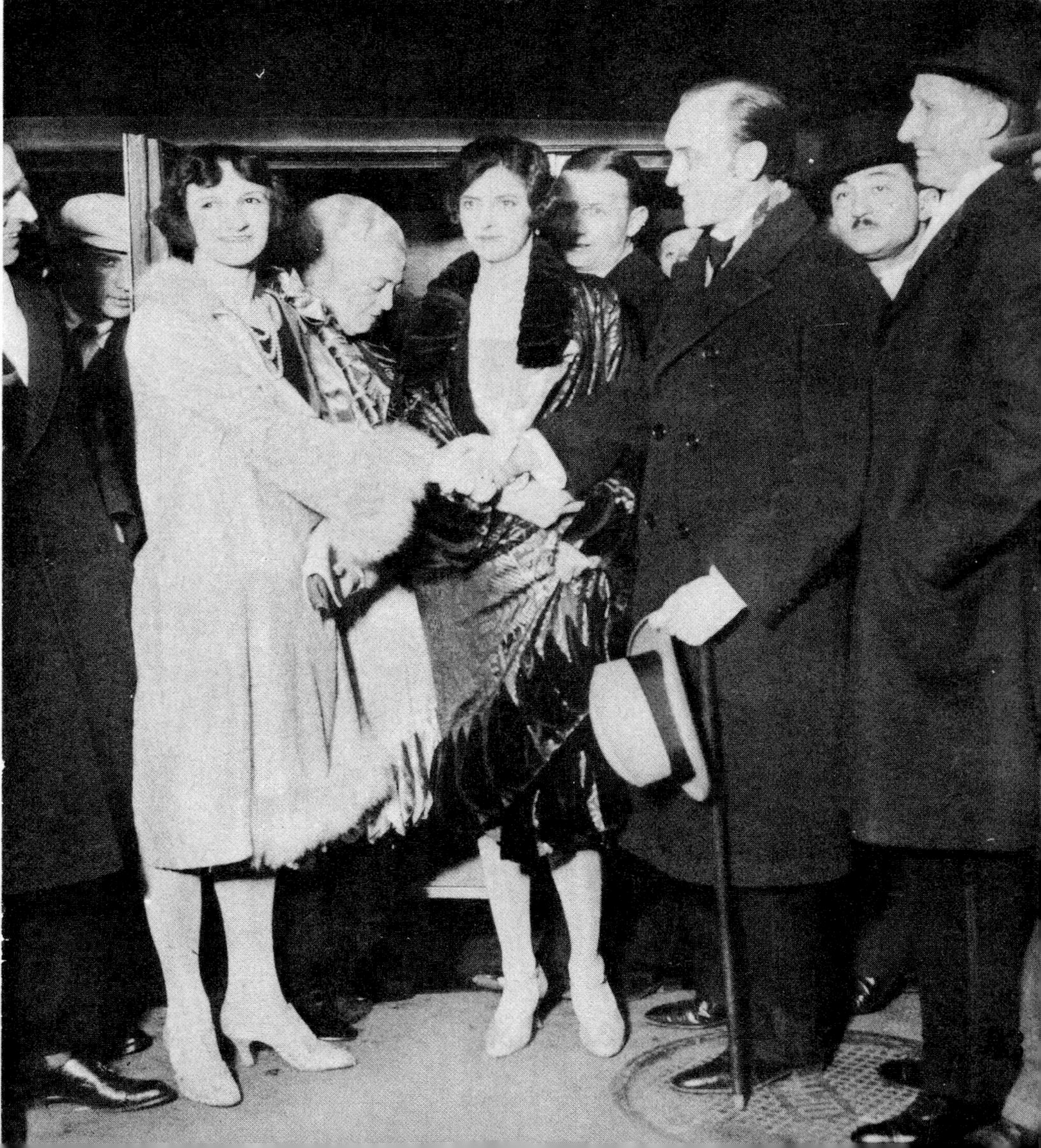

Though World War I had been given uncompromising treatment soon after its close in books such as Dos Passos' *Three Soldiers* and E. E. Cummings' *The Enormous Room,* it was not presented on the stage with whole-hearted realism until the appearance in September 1924 of "What Price Glory?" by Maxwell Anderson and Laurence Stallings —a play which presented the Rabelaisian talk of Captain Flagg and Sergeant Quirt so boldly that the tender-minded were horrified. And the presentations of the horrors of warfare that made the deepest impression on a wide public came still later—over ten years after the Armistice. These were the novel, *All Quiet on the Western Front,* published in 1929, and the play pictured below: "Journey's End," by an Englishman, R. C. Sherriff. "Journey's End" reached the New York stage in March 1929, when the Big Bull Market was about to go into its last crescendo.

The cult of fashionable sophistication did not end with the postwar decade; "Private Lives," by Noel Coward, did not appear in New York until 1931, when the depression was deepening. Above are the author-actor and Gertrude Lawrence in a scene from that play.

The latter nineteen-twenties, being years of riotous spending, were the heyday of the expensive night club, where prohibition could be forgotten and the profits of a speculation in Montgomery Ward or Mike Meehan's Radio common could be tossed away in a night. At the right is one of the most spectacular of night club figures, already canonized by Hollywood: Mary Louise Cecilia ("Texas") Guinan, darling of the butter-and-egg men.

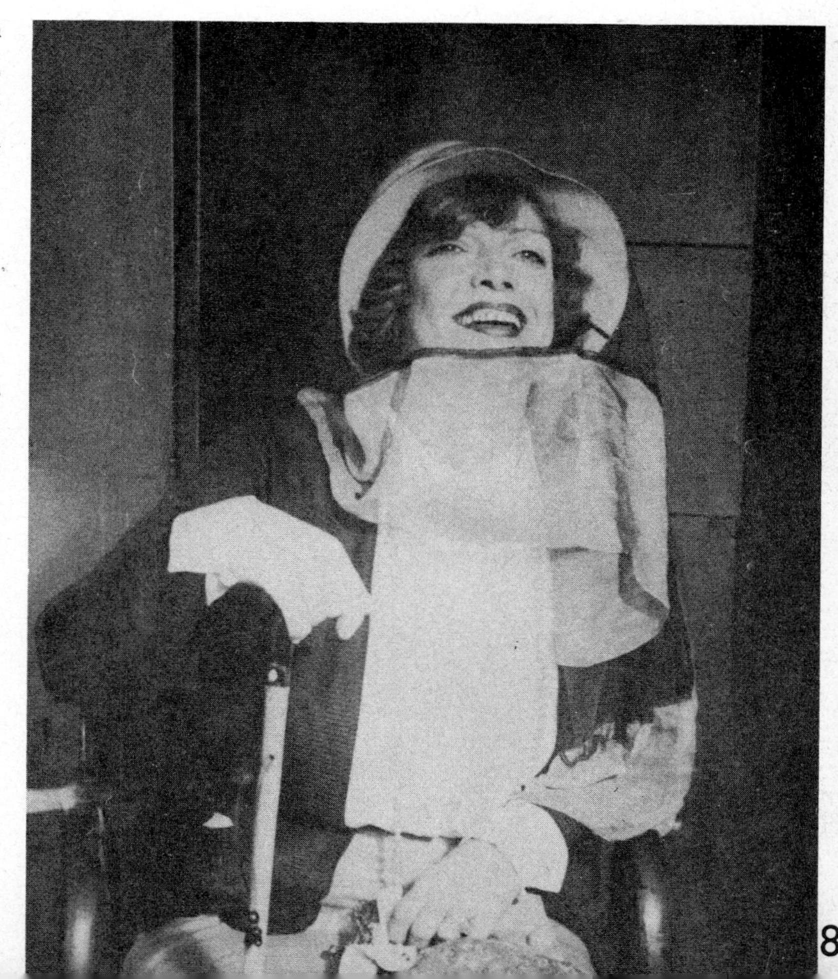

Speaking of canonization, it was not until motion-picture audiences had been laughing for years at the screen antics of Charlie Chaplin that the intellectuals began referring to him, with bated breath, as (to quote Gilbert Seldes in *The Seven Lively Arts*) "the man who, of all the men of our time, seems most assured of immortality." But when, after long preparation, Chaplin produced "The Gold Rush" in 1925—a picture which included a wonderful tilting-floor scene when a house teetered on the edge of a precipice in an Alaskan storm, and a still more hilarious scene in which Charlie nibbled with the air of a gourmet at some cooked shoe-leather—everybody took delight. At the left is Charlie, shivering in that picture. Below is Harold Lloyd, the comedian with the horn-rimmed glasses, in a scene from "Safety Last," produced in 1923.

Limited in many ways as were the movies before the advent of sound, they gave ample scope for the skill of actors who, like Chaplin and Lloyd, were essentially pantomimists. No words were needed to supplement such humorous effects as were offered by Buster Keaton (at the right), who brought to the movies from his vaudeville beginnings what Gilbert Seldes described as "an enormous, incorruptible gravity." And the actors could get along pretty well without words in such huge, expensive, romantic spectacles as "Ben Hur," produced in 1926, from which we select a chariot-race scene, with Francis X. Bushman and Ramon Novarro at the controls.

Greta Garbo and the late John Gilbert at work in "Flesh and the Devil." The date was 1927.

"Beau Geste," 1926 (with William Powell, left, and Ronald Colman, center).

A great change was coming to Hollywood—a change which would end many a star's career, make many another's, strike Broadway a body blow by drawing some of its ablest actors and dramatists to the Coast, and turn Hollywood into a gold mine for writers too. Late in 1926, while silent films like "Beau Geste" were attracting great crowds, this sort of announcement was to be found here and there among the theatre advertisements:

"Warner Brothers and Vitaphone Corporation, by arrangement with Western Electric Company and Bell Telephone Laboratories, PRESENT The Greatest Broadway Talent Ever Assembled, personalizing in voice, music, and action, AL JOLSON, ELSIE JANIS, GEORGE JESSEL." And you could read among the motion-picture notes: "Mr. Jolson's appearance will be in blackface . . . singing 'April Showers,' 'Rocka-bye Baby,' and other melodies." This picture was a short; but the next year, 1927, Jolson appeared (as below) in a more ambitious effort, "The Jazz Singer."

Properly speaking, this was not a talkie but a silent film with sound sequences; it contained only 291 words of spoken dialogue. And even after "The Jazz Singer" the change was slow, for the early talking pictures were crude and cacophanous. In May 1929 an irate movie-goer was writing to the *New York Times,* "One has to elongate one's ears and try to unravel from a concatenation of sounds what it's all about. . . . Do give us one delightful, quiet theatre until the infant grows up." But by 1930 the talkies commanded the field.

A major sport of the high, wide, and handsome years was following murder trials; and the most fascinating murder case of all was the Hall-Mills case. What made it remarkable was the extent to which it captured national attention, thrusting temporarily into the background foreign affairs, national politics, and everything else; and also the fact that it illustrated the power of a sensation-hungry press.

On September 16, 1922, the Reverend Edward Wheeler Hall and Mrs. James Mills, the choir leader in his church, were found shot to death near New Brunswick, New Jersey—their bodies lying side by side under a crab-apple tree on an abandoned farm. The mystery was not solved and the case died down—until, four long years later, it was re-opened through the influence of a tabloid that claimed to have new evidence —and wanted new circulation. Mrs. Hall, the clergyman's widow, was arrested and in November 1926 she and her two brothers and cousin went on trial for murder. As you can gather from the picture of her at the left, she was a person of great respectability — which made the sensation all the greater. Below, she is shown with the other defendants: at the left, the slow-witted Willie Stevens; at the right, Henry Stevens and her cousin, Henry Carpender.

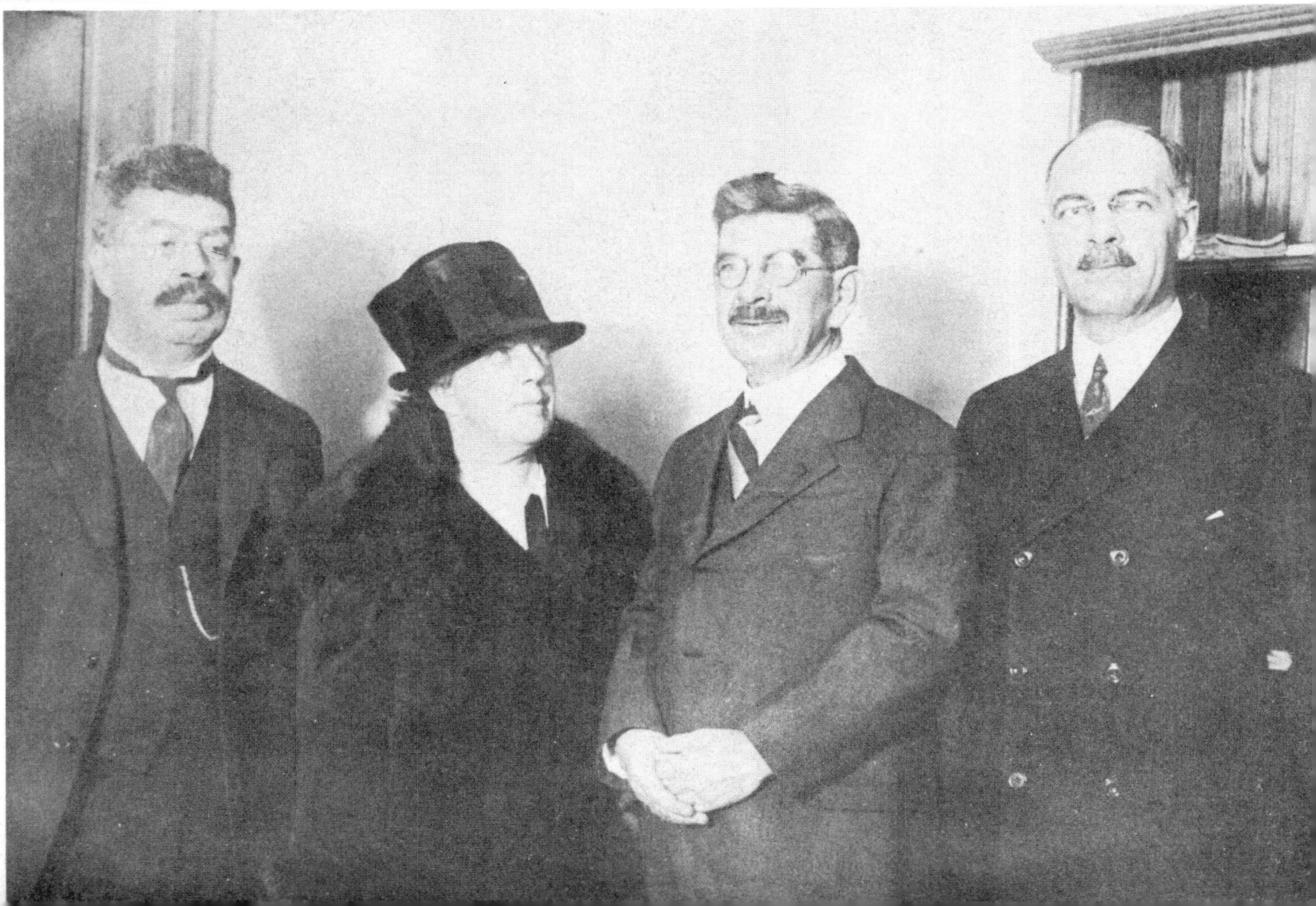

A swarm of star reporters, including such unwonted journalists as Billy Sunday, the revivalist, and James Mills (above), the husband of the murdered woman, sent out five million words from Somerville, New Jersey, during the first eleven days of the Hall-Mills trial; and the whole country became familiar with DeRussey's Lane, and with Willie Stevens's innocently earnest aspect as he stood up to his cross-examination, and with the peculiar testimony—given from a hospital bed in the courtroom—of Jane Gibson, the "pig woman," who had been out on the fatal night with Jennie, her mule (shown with her above, right).

Even Charlotte Mills, the young daughter of the murdered choir-singer, was pressed into service as a reporter. At last the defendants were acquitted—but not until they had gone through a horrible ordeal in the production of bigger and better headlines. And the mystery remained unsolved.

Another horror took place somewhat earlier in Chicago, when Nathan Leopold and Richard Loeb, two brilliant youths, both postgraduate students at the University of Chicago and both members of rich and prominent Chicago families, were tried for the peculiarly cold-blooded and revolting murder of a child named Bobby Franks. The young men, eloquently defended by the gnarled old trial lawyer, Clarence Darrow, were given life sentences. (The picture below shows young Loeb at the time of the trial.)

With its appetite for scandalous crime well whetted, the pu leaped with avidity upon the details of the Gray-Snyder case, wh went to trial in the spring of 1927. There was little mystery subtlety to this sordid murder: Albert Snyder, an art editor in a L Island suburb, had been killed with a sash-weight by his wife, R Snyder, and her lover, a corset salesman named Henry Judd G (At the left, Mrs. Snyder is listening to the reading of Gray's fession; below is Gray himself, with his mother, during the tri. But this affair, too, commanded mighty headlines.

American journalism and press-agentry set some low-water m during the year or so, in 1926 and 1927, which witnessed the J Hawley bathtub incident (page 83), the extravagant funera Rudolph Valentino, the disproportionately publicized welcom Queen Marie (page 42), the Hall-Mills trial (pages 90-91), charges growing out of the mysterious disappearance of the evang Aimee Semple McPherson, and the Gray-Snyder case; but few lower than the feat of one New York tabloid in getting a sneak ph graph (not shown here) of Mrs. Ruth Gray's electrocution at Sing S

There was one trial in the mid-twenties which involved neither murder nor sex and yet riveted the attention of the country. Tennessee had passed a state law forbidding the teaching of the doctrine of evolution; and a young high-school biology teacher in Dayton, Tennessee, named John Thomas Scopes, let himself be tried for defying it. Clarence Darrow, who had defended Leopold and Loeb, was chief lawyer for the defense; and old William Jennings Bryan, the famous former Secretary of State, led the prosecution. Scopes was found guilty (and later freed on a technicality) after as strange a trial, in the blazing heat of July 1925, as ever took place in America—with Bryan insisting that the world was literally created in the year 4004 B.C. and that Eve was literally made out of Adam's rib. Above, Bryan with some of his Dayton admirers; at the left, Scopes; below, a playful sign hung out by a local merchant, J. R. Darwin.

Lawless gangs were no novelty to America, but prohibition and public cynicism lifted them to unprecedented power, wealth, and violence in the late nineteen-twenties. At the right, mid-page, is the face of Al Capone, who seized Chicago's illicit liquor trade and became the super-boss of organized crime in that city. At the right, above, he is at the races, laughing with two women, during the federal proceedings in 1931 which were to send him at last to Alcatraz. Below, you may see what happened to the O'Banion gang when it warred with the Capone forces in 1929: the "St. Valentine's Day Massacre," in which seven men were machine-gunned to death in a Chicago garage.

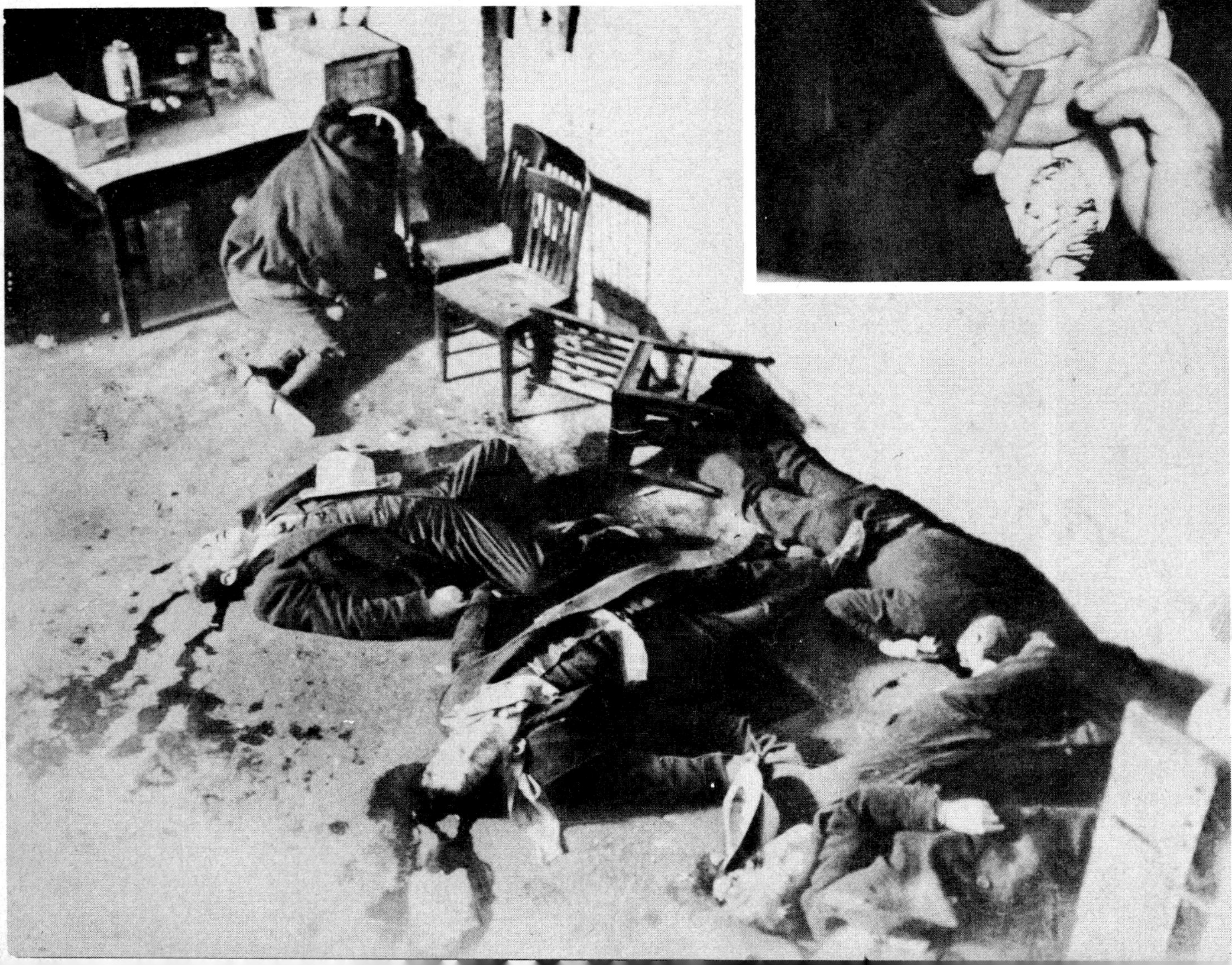

ne criminal case of those days set itself part from all others by arousing fierce olitical loyalties all over the world. In pril 1920, a paymaster in South Braintree, Iassachusetts, was shot by hold-up men; id two Italian-American radicals, Nicola acco and Bartolomeo Vanzetti, were ar-sted and soon convicted of the crime. But any people thought they had been rail-aded; the case was re-investigated and ebated everywhere; the demeanor of Van-tti in particular was admirable and his atements most impressive; and even after e two men were at last electrocuted on ugust 22, 1927, millions believed them have been innocent. You see them at the ght (Vanzetti with the mustache); below e some Sacco-Vanzetti sympathizers who ve been arrested by Boston police.

The progress of aviation during the early nineteen-twenties was exciting—with the Post Office running a hazardous airmail service and with records for speed and endurance being constantly broken—but those records look a little unimpressive today. When the first triumphant round-the-world flight was made in 1924 by U. S. Army Air Force planes (four starters, two finishers), their flying time was over 15 days and their elapsed time, owing to delays at intermediate points, was no less than 5 months and 22 days! Above are those Army planes: Douglas biplane cruisers with single Liberty motors. When Charles A. Lindbergh made his sensational point-to-point transatlantic flight in May 1927, public interest in long-distance flying and its possibilities became really intense. Below is young Lindbergh with his plane; we shall see more of him on pages 112-119.

Lindbergh's triumph set off a procession of would-be trans-ocean flyers—Chamberlin and Levine, Byrd, Brock and Schlee, Ruth Elder, and the first woman to turn the trick, the engaging Amelia Earhart. Above, Miss Earhart is getting a City Hall welcome at New York in July 1928, with her flying mates, Wilmer Stultz and Louis Gordon, flanking her. Acting Mayor McKee is at the extreme right; Commander Richard E. Byrd at the extreme left. The picture at the right shows Miss Earhart with her husband, George Palmer Putnam, planning the Pacific flight in the course of which she was lost nine years later, in 1937.

On this page are four contrasting authors of the time. Above, Willa Cather, who was then perhaps the most deeply admired American novelist. Below, the Englishman, A. S. M. Hutchinson; his *If Winter Comes* was the big 1922 best seller.

Above, another English writer whose work was very popu here: Margaret Kennedy, author of *The Constant Nymph*, 1924 favorite; below, the German, Erich Maria Remarque, auth of *All Quiet on the Western Front,* published in 1929.

IF WINTER
COMES

By
**A. S. M. HUTCHINSON**
**Author of "The Happy Warrior," etc.**

*William Lyon Phelps in The New York Times says:*
"'If Winter Comes' is not only a thrilling tale, it is an important work of art. . . . I do not know when I have had more continuous enjoyment in reading a new book. . . . 'If Winter Comes' is one of the best books of our times."

*Edwin Francis Edgett in The Boston Transcript says:*
"No review, no amount of comment or praise can reveal the warm humanity of this story. . . . if ever the mirror were held up to nature, it is held up by Mr. Hutchinson in 'If Winter Comes'; if ever man were re-created in a literary image that man is his Mark Sabre.'

*Robert E. Sherwood in Life, New York, says:*
"'If Winter Comes' is more than a mere novel, it is an epic poem of very great beauty. It will last long after most other literary products of this age have gone to an obscure and unlamented grave."

FOUR HUNDRED AND SEVENTH THOUSAND

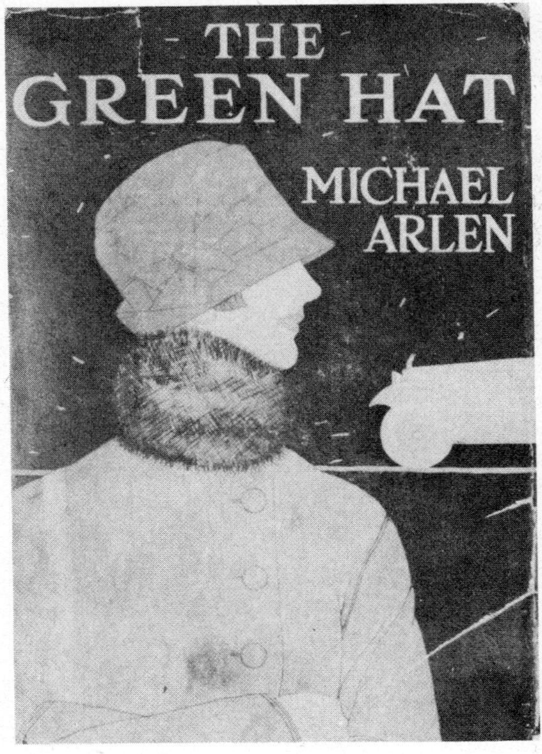

ıe riotous twenties were a time of ferment and resurgence in American :iting (cf. the theatre, page 80). Sinclair Lewis, Willa Cather, John Dos .ssos, F. Scott Fitzgerald, Theodore Dreiser, Ernest Hemingway, and hers were breaking new ground in fiction. Young literati hied themselves Montparnasse, got excited over Joyce, and scorned the American Babbitt om abroad while H. L. Mencken's *American Mercury* walloped him at me. New writers, publishing houses, magazines, ideas burgeoned; even ok design was livened (compare the jacket of *If Winter Comes* with ter ones shown on this page). As for the taste of the wider audience, re are the best sellers, fiction and non-fiction, 1921-29. Readers with ng memories may detect in the list hints of the public temper: the battle er the proprieties, the concern over calories and vitamins, the worship business men, the zeal of the materially successful to acquire a background:

·21—*Main Street,* Sinclair Lewis; *The Outline of History,* Wells.
·22—*If Winter Comes,* Hutchinson; again *The Outline of History.*
·23—*Black Oxen,* Gertrude Atherton; *Etiquette,* Emily Post.
·24—*So Big,* Edna Ferber; *Diet and Health,* Lulu Hunt Peters.
·25—*Soundings,* A. Hamilton Gibbs; again *Diet and Health.*
·26—*The Private Life of Helen of Troy,* John Erskine; *The Man Nobody Knows,* Bruce Barton.
·27—*Elmer Gantry,* Lewis; *The Story of Philosophy,* Will Durant.
·28—*The Bridge of San Luis Rey,* Wilder; *Disraeli,* Maurois.
·29—*All Quiet on the Western Front,* Remarque; *The Art of Thinking,* Ernest Dimnet

Among the political leaders during an era when politics was neglected, none more attractively combined friendliness, practicality, and principle than Alfred E. Smith of New York—the boy from Oliver Street who became governor of New York State for four two-year terms, was almost nominated for the Presidency in 1924, and was actually nominated in 1928, to run against Herbert Hoover when Calvin Coolidge chose not to run. In '24 and '28 his name was presented at the party convention by the admirer who is comparing notes with him in the picture at the left—and who is now wearing leg-braces.

ove, Governor Smith is accepting the Democratic nomination for the ·sidency in a speech in the Assembly chamber at Albany in August ·28. It was a bold speech; instead of straddling on the still ticklish ·hibition issue, Smith declared that the Eighteenth Amendment must amended. But he waged a losing campaign; for not only did many ·ers knife him because of his Catholicism, but prosperity was in full ·d while the stock market boomed, and Hoover was therefore invin- ·e when he said, "Given a chance to go forward with the policies of last eight years, we shall soon, with the help of God, be in sight of day when poverty will be banished from this nation." It didn't help ·th at the time that this statement made sorry reading later. He was ·eated; took over the management of the Empire State Building in ·v York; fell out with his old friend who had been wont to call him "happy warrior," and ended his days a conservative. At the right, ·ernor and Mrs. Smith are leaving St. Patrick's Cathedral on Easter · of 1943; within two years thereafter both of them were dead.

We turn now to Wall Street, which during the last two or three years of Coolidge-Hoover prosperity was the blow-torch that kept it at white heat. But first let us glance back to the financial district of New York as it appeared at the time this chronicle opens. Here is a photograph taken looking up Broad Street toward Wall in about 1918 (can sharp eyes distinguish Allied flags and service flags of World War I?) In those days, as you see, the Curb Market actually operated on the curb, outdoors in Broad Street itself. (Incidentally, the buildings shown in this picture have hardly changed since those days, over a quarter-century ago.)

# INDIVIDUAL INCOME TAX RETURN

FOR NET INCOMES FROM SALARIES OR WAGES OF MORE THAN $5,000

OR INCOMES, REGARDLESS OF AMOUNT, FROM BUSINESS, PROFESSION, RENTS, OR SALE OF PROPERTY

... Calendar Year 1927

...ternal Revenue for Your District on or Before March 15, 1928

The prosperity of the nineteen-twenties was not complete. Much dire poverty, by any humane standard, remained. But after prices dropped in 1920-21, throwing many a company into bankruptcy and gripping many another with fear, the resulting depression and unemployment were short-lived. Business roared ahead, with the automobile industry (and its allied trades), the radio industry, the construction industry, and others ranging from cosmetics to movie theatres as its bellwethers. Business men were in the saddle; the labor unions had weakened after their outburst of 1919-20, the penny-saving President kept interference from Washington in check, and the brakes were off. The Florida boom gave this prosperity a brief (and unhealthy) shot in the arm, and when this boom collapsed and construction generally slowed up, unbridled finance provided another and bigger stimulant. Mergers, stock split-ups, holding-company empires, and speculation went into high gear. By this time the banker and broker were scarcely fallible; Wall Street was the center of economic learning, it was GHQ, it was Mecca. In March 1928, stock prices, which had seemed to most shrewd observers to be already dangerously high, began really to leap; and the Big Bull Market was off on its fatal binge.

**SURTAX RATES FOR 1927**

| Amount of net income | Rate per cent | Surtax | Total surtax on each amount | Amount of net income | Rate per cent | Surtax | Total surtax on each amount |
|---|---|---|---|---|---|---|---|
| A | B | C | D | A | B | C | D |
| $10, 000 | | | | $44, 000 | 11 | $440 | $2, 240 |
| 14, 000 | 1 | $40 | $40 | 48, 000 | 12 | 480 | 2, 720 |
| 16, 000 | 2 | 40 | 80 | 52, 000 | 13 | 520 | 3, 240 |
| 18, 000 | 3 | 60 | 140 | 56, 000 | 14 | 560 | 3, 800 |
| 20, 000 | 4 | 80 | 220 | 60, 000 | 15 | 600 | 4, 400 |
| 22, 000 | 5 | 100 | 320 | 64, 000 | 16 | 640 | 5, 040 |
| 24, 000 | 6 | 120 | 440 | 70, 000 | 17 | 1, 020 | 6, 060 |
| 28, 000 | 7 | 280 | 720 | 80, 000 | 18 | 1, 800 | 7, 860 |
| 32, 000 | 8 | 320 | 1, 040 | 100, 000 | 19 | 3, 800 | 11, 660 |
| 36, 000 | 9 | 360 | 1, 400 | 100, 000+ | 20 | | |
| 40, 000 | 10 | 400 | 1, 800 | | | | |

It is perhaps unkind to print here excerpts from the Federal Income Tax form for 1927 (payable in 1928, just as General Motors and Radio began to go through the roof); but if you are in an experimental mood, you can enter your present net income as Item 31 in the Computation below, and use the surtax form at the left, and after a little figuring you'll get the idea—which is that things were different then. But unless you're feeling strong, don't even think of it.

**COMPUTATION OF TAX** (See Instruction 21)

...ed Net Income (not over $20,000) $
... Personal Exemption and Credit ... Dependents (see Instruction 20)
...nce (Item 19 minus 20) $
...unt taxable at 1½% (not over the ...st $4,000 of Item 21) $
...unt taxable at 3% (not over the ...cond $4,000 of Item 21)
...unt taxable at 5% (balance over ...,000 of Item 21)
...nal Tax (1½% of Item 22) $
...nal Tax (3% of Item 23)
...nal Tax (5% of Item 24)
...x on Item 19 (see Instruction 21)
...n Earned Net Income (total of ...ms 25, 26, 27, and 28) $
...t of 25% of Item 29 (not over ...% of Items 28, 42, 43, and 44) $

31. Net Income (Item 18 above) $
32. Less Dividends (Item 7 above) $
33. Interest on Liberty Bonds, etc. (Item 8)
34. Personal Exemption
35. Credit for Dependents
36. Total of Items 32, 33, 34, and 35
37. Balance (Item 31 minus 36) $
38. Amount taxable at 1½% (not over the first $4,000 of Item 37)
39. Balance (Item 37 minus 38) $
40. Amount taxable at 3% (not over the second $4,000 of Item 37)
41. Amount taxable at 5% (balance over $8,000 of Item 37) $
42. Normal Tax (1½% of Item 38) $
43. Normal Tax (3% of Item 40)
44. Normal Tax (5% of Item 41)
45. Surtax on Item 18 (see Instruction 21)
46. Tax on Net Income (total of Items 42, 43, 44, and 45) $
47. Less Credit of 25% of Tax on Earned Net Income (Item 30)
48. Balance (Item 46 minus 47) $
49. Adjustment for Capital Gain or Loss (12½% of Column 9, Schedule D)
50. Total Tax (total of or difference between Items 48 and 49) $
51. Less Income Tax Paid at Source
52. Income and Profits Taxes paid to a foreign country or U. S. possession
53. Balance of Tax (Item 50 minus Items 51 and 52) $

Scarcely exaggerated at all is Carl Rose's drawing at the right from *The New Yorker,* September 10, 1927, which illustrates the prevalent custom of buying on margin.

*"Say, Doc, do me a favor. Just keep your eye on Consolidated Can Common, and if she goes bearish tell my broker to sell and get four thousand shares of P. & Q. Rails Preferred on the usual margin. Thanks."*

## STOCK PRICES AND TRADING

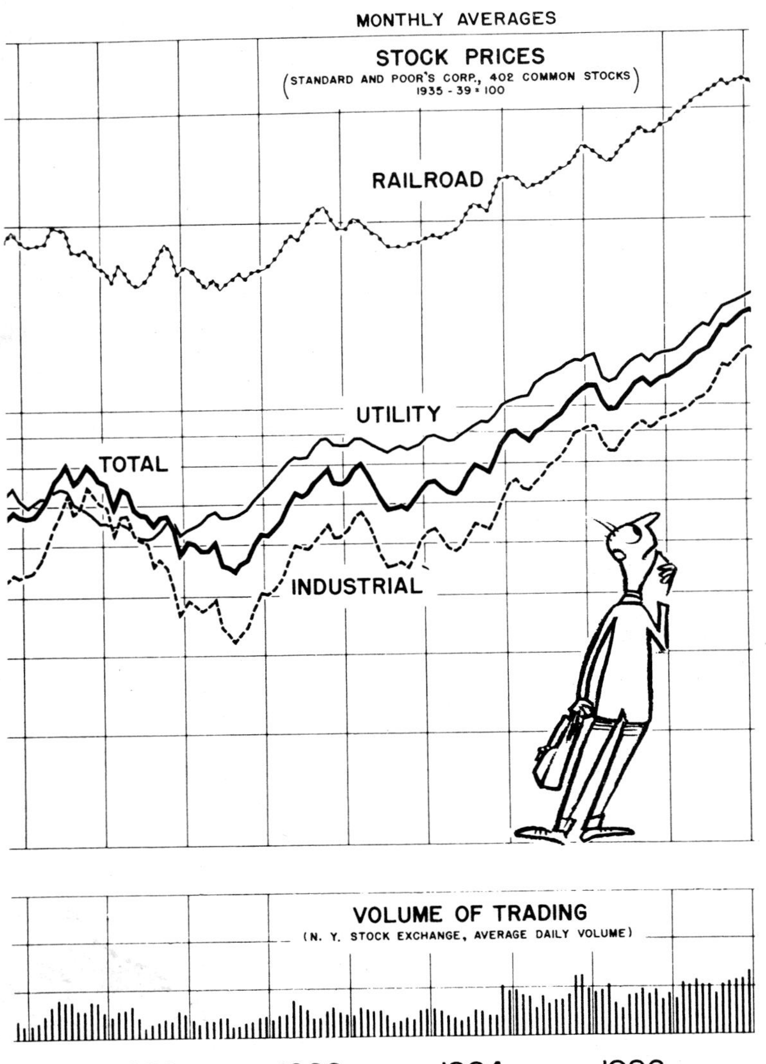


The trouble with history is that decisions look so easy in re spect. You know what happened afterwards, and you natur think any dope ought to have been able to foresee it.

Take the Big Bull Market, for instance. If we look, today, graph which shows the course of stock prices in the late ninete twenties and early nineteen-thirties, and see the curve going hill pretty steadily until September 1929 and then slanting do hill steeply, we are likely to imagine that almost anybody wit little ready money ought to have had sense enough to buy stc early, hold on to them until the summer of 1929, and then them. What could be simpler?

But it wasn't like that. We present on this page and the following pages some graphs which may make the actual un tainty a little clearer.

The skeptical gentleman at the left is looking at a graph of course of stock-market prices as it looked at the end of 1927: he is very naturally saying, "They've gone pretty high. Shoul I sell?"

In the graph immediately to the right, on the opposite page, have reached the end of 1928; and the man with the brief ca —again naturally—saying, "This bull market is getting too g to miss."

The third graph shows how things looked in the summe 1929; the man with the brief case is shouting, "We have ent a new era!"

Turn over the page and you will see what was invisible to on any of the previous occasions.

The story is told of a young man who went in 1928 to a leading economist for advice as to how he could best learn about finance. Said the economist, "Well, if you can scare up a few hundred dollars, you might learn something by buying some stock on a good safe margin and seeing what happens," and he named a good buy. A couple of weeks later the young man came in and cried ecstatically, "How long has this been going on?"

That illustrates what happened, in 1928 and 1929, to hundreds of thousands—perhaps millions—of people who had never before speculated. Business men big and little, housewives, farmers, professors, factory hands followed excitedly the price gyrations of General Motors, Radio, Wright Aeronautical, Montgomery Ward, Electric Bond & Share, Cities Service. Suburbanites going to the city on the 8:14 studied and restudied the financial pages; talked earnestly about the prospect that Samuel Insull or the Van Sweringens or Associated Gas & Electric would buy up the shares of this or that company at "attractive prices"; mentioned with awe the names of John J. Raskob, Albert H. Wiggin, Charles E. Mitchell, Mike Meehan; argued as to whether or not it was wise to confine one's attention to the "blue chips" that the new investment trusts were concentrating upon; but agreed that prices had reached a "permanently high plateau."

Meanwhile, the profits from stock speculation poured into the marts of trade, poured into the building of bigger and better country clubs, enriched the steamship companies as the successful went on round-the-world cruises, gratified hotel proprietors at Paris, London, Biarritz, Deauville, Nice, Cannes, Venice, St. Moritz, Honolulu, Bermuda, Nassau.

To people accustomed to inflated price levels since World War II, most of the prices of goods in the latter nineteen-twenties do not seem extravagant. But a few, as one looks back now over the newspaper and magazine advertisements of those years, bring one up with a start. Saks Fifth Avenue advertising sets of flasks (so useful in prohibition days) at prices up to $375 . . . and men's walking sticks up to $90 each . . . Black Starr and Frost quoting fitted traveling bags at prices from $200 to $4,000 . . . Douglas Elliman publicizing a triplex roof apartment on Fifth Avenue for sale on a co-operative basis at $150,000, with maintenance at 11 per cent . . . and this item: "Where, save at Peck and Peck's, can one buy silk stockings for as much as $500 a pair?"

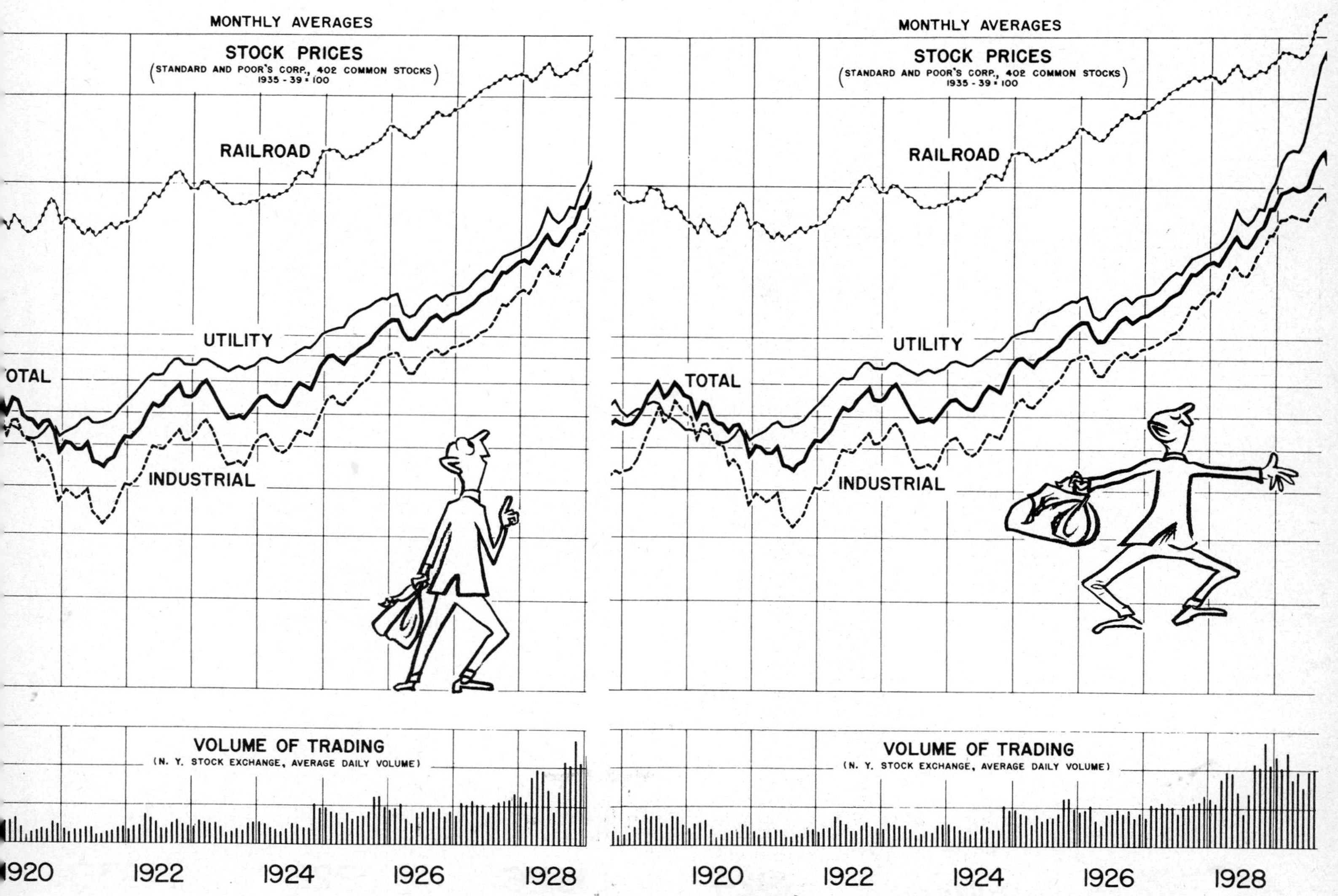

Below, you will see what happened after September 1929 to those stock-market price levels that the man with the brief case was following on the two preceding pages. But the downward slope from the statistical peak was still quite invisible in the summer of 1929—that summer when serious-minded readers were discussing Walter Lippmann's *A Preface to Morals,* and theatre-goers were comparing notes on "Street Scene," and the talkies still made outrageous noises but were outrunning the silent films in popularity; when women's hats completely covered the head from the nape of the neck to the eyebrows; when Bobby Jones, Bill Tilden, and Babe Ruth were still the top men in their respective sports; when the Wickersham Commission, appointed by President Hoover to investigate prohibition and law enforcement, was beginning its labors; when emissaries from Wall Street were selling South American bonds, the Van Sweringens were the miracle men of Cleveland, Insull Utilities Investments was the best buy in Chicago, the wise men of Wall Street were launching the Blue Ridge investment trust, brokers' loans totaled eight billion dollars, and the sky was the limit.

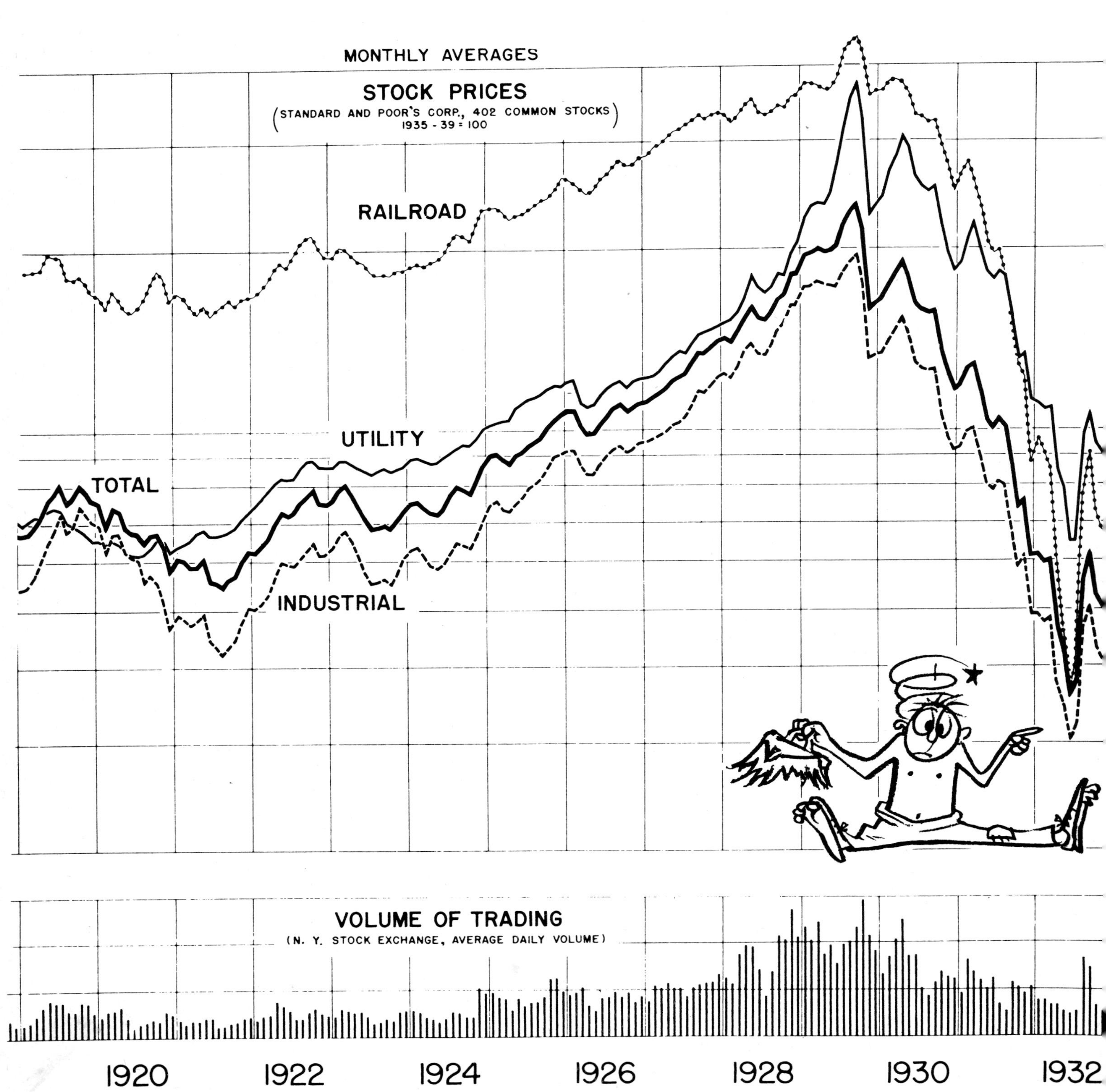

*"Oh, just a summer toy."*

Stately were the mansions built by the plus-foured princes of finance and industry. The cartoon above, by Barlow, is from *The New Yorker* for June 29, 1929. Although modern architectural ideas were making headway in the profession, few of the builders of such houses would have any traffic with them; and it was with full approval that *Town and Country*, in 1929, described a Long Island country house as "an affectionate materialization of an architect's appreciation for details remembered from here and there in France."

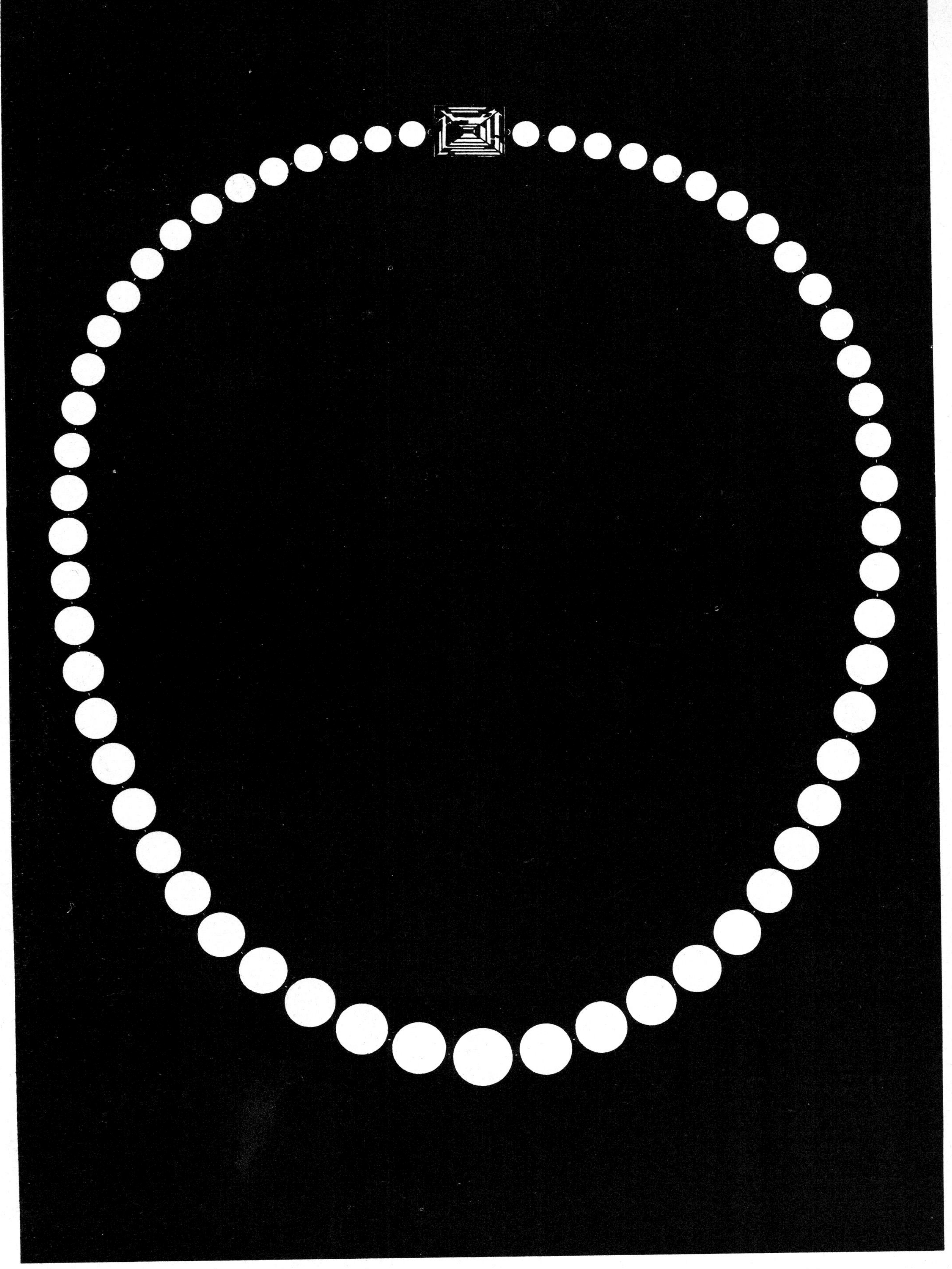

The advertisement reproduced on these two pages appeared in *The New Yorker* for November 3, 1928.

*For more than one hundred years this house has collected pearls . . . for more than one hundred years it was believed impossible to assemble a large single necklace in which each individual pearl would have the highest lustre and be perfectly, exquisitely matched . . . and now, as the culminating achievement of our history, we have reached this goal.*

*This necklace is conceded by experts and connoisseurs to be the finest in existence • • • • Price $685,000*

THE NECKLACE ILLUSTRATED ON THE OPPOSITE PAGE IS APPROXIMATELY DRAWN TO THE ACTUAL SIZE . . . EACH PEARL IS ROSE PINK, OF THE DEEPEST HUE AND THE HIGHEST LUSTRE

# BLACK STARR & FROST

*JEWELERS IN NEW YORK FOR 118 YEARS*

FIFTH AVE., COR. 48TH ST., NEW YORK • • • PARIS • PALM BEACH

The pearls, described as "approximately drawn to the actual size," appear here in that same size.

We are always tempted, when we read about an earlier day and its excesses, to feel that everybody must have been more or less crazy then. Of course that isn't true. We are just about as crazy now as in 1929, and no crazier—our dementia simply takes different forms. But it does seem as if, as the boom era ended, the enthusiasm for daft publicity stunts was especially frenzied. Above, you see "Shipwreck" Kelly, noted flagpole-sitter, atop a theatre.

Marathon dancing still goes on here and there, but its vogue was for a time remarkable. The girls at the left are having their feet looked after during a $5,000 prize contest at Madison Square Garden, New York, in June 1928, in which 135 couples entered.

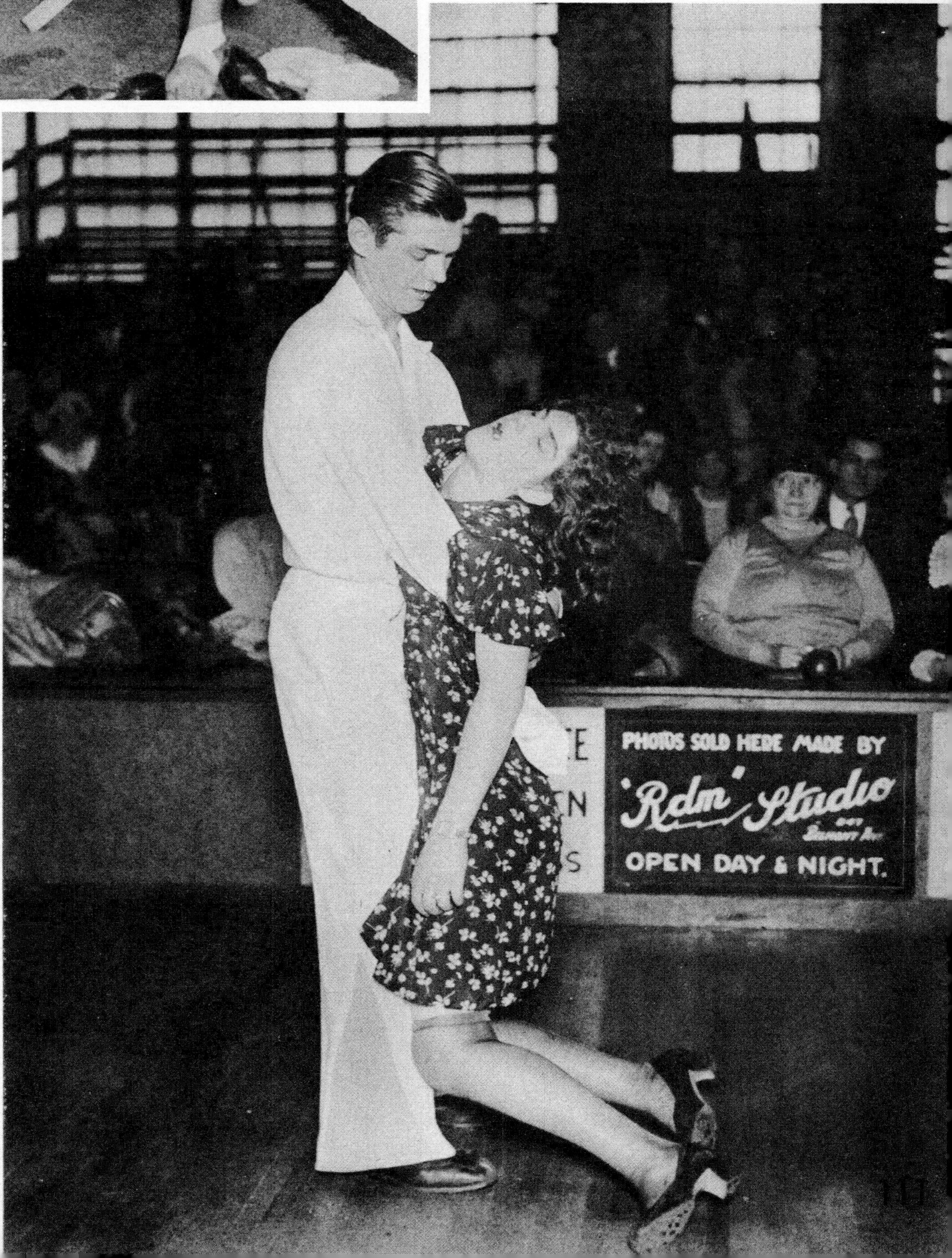

Dance marathon contests originated in England and Scotland, it is said; at any rate the first American contest was held March 31, 1923. On April 19 of that year a record of 90 hours 10 minutes was set. It did not last. The picture at the right was taken in the 3,327th hour of a dance marathon held in Chicago in 1930—or rather, beginning on August 29, 1930, and lasting (with intervals of time for sleep) into 1931! The girl who has fallen asleep is dancing with her brother as partner.

Section 1 | "All the News That's Fit to Print." | **The New York Times.** | THE WEATHER Generally fair today and tomorrow; moderate to fresh southerly winds.

VOL. LXXVI....No. 25,320. NEW YORK, SUNDAY, MAY 22, 1927. FIVE CENTS

# LINDBERGH DOES IT! TO PARIS IN 33½ HOURS; FLIES 1,000 MILES THROUGH SNOW AND SLEET; CHEERING FRENCH CARRY HIM OFF FIEL

## COULD HAVE GONE 500 MILES FARTHER

### Gasoline for at Least That Much More Flew at Times From 10 Feet to 10,000 Feet Above Water.

### ATE ONLY ONE AND A HALF OF HIS FIVE SANDWICHES

### Fell Asleep at Times but Quickly Awoke—Glimpses of His Adventure in Brief Interview at the Embassy.

**LINDBERGH'S OWN STORY TOMORROW.**

*Captain Charles A. Lindbergh was too exhausted after his arrival in Paris late last night to do more than indicate, as told below, his experiences during his flight. After he awakes today, he will narrate the full story of his remarkable exploit for readers of Monday's New York Times.*

By CARLYLE MACDONALD.

Copyright, 1927, by The New York Times Company. Special Cable to THE NEW YORK TIMES.

PARIS, Sunday, May 22.—Captain Lindbergh was discovered at the American Embassy at 2:30 o'clock this morning. Attired in a pair of Ambassador Herrick's pajamas, he sat on the edge of a bed and talked of his flight. At the last moment Ambassador Herrick had canceled the plans of the reception committee and, by unanimous consent, took the flier to the embassy in the Place d'Iena.

A staff of American doctors who had arrived at Le Bourget Field early to minister to an "exhausted" aviator found instead a bright-eyed, smiling youth who refused to be examined.

"Oh, don't bother; I am all right," he said.

"I'd like to have a bath and a glass of milk. I would feel better," Lindbergh replied when the Ambassador asked him what he would like to have.

A bath was drawn immediately and in less than five minutes the youth had disrobed in one of the embassy guest rooms, taken his bath and was out again drinking a bottle of milk and eating a roll.

**"No Use Worrying," He Tells Envoy.**

"There is no use worrying about me, Mr. Ambassador," Lindbergh insisted when Mr. Herrick and members of the embassy staff wanted him to be examined by doctors and then go to bed immediately.

It was apparent that the young man was too full of his experiences to want sleep and he sat on the bed and chatted with the Ambassador, his son and daughter-in-law.

By this time a corps of frantic newspaper men who had been madly chasing the airman, following one false scent after another, had finally tracked him to the embassy. In a body they descended upon the Ambassador, who received them in the salon and informed them that he had just left Lindbergh with strict instructions to go to sleep.

As Mr. Herrick was talking with the reporters his son-in-law came downstairs and said that Lindbergh had rung and announced that he did not care to go to sleep just yet and that he would be glad to see the newspaper men for a few minutes. A cheer went up from the group who dashed by Mr. Herrick and rushed upstairs.

**Expected Trouble Over Newfoundland.**

In the blue and gold room, with a soft light glowing, sat the conqueror of the Atlantic. He immediately stood up and held out his hands to greet his callers. THE NEW YORK TIMES cor-

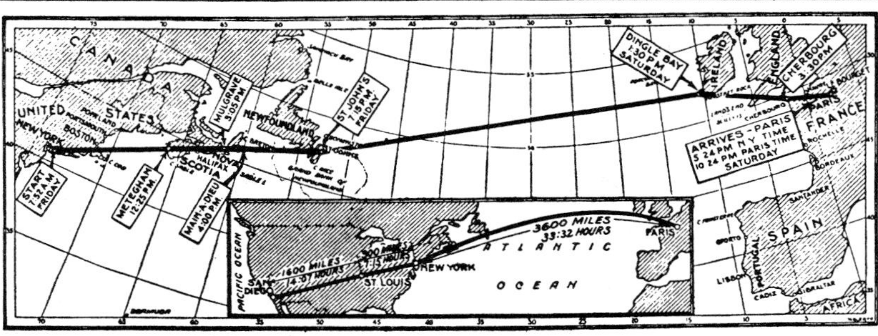


MAP OF LINDBERGH'S TRANSATLANTIC ROUTE, SHOWING THE SPEED OF HIS TRIP.

## LEVINE ABANDONS BELLANCA FLIGHT

### Venture Given Up as Designer Splits With Him—Plane Narrowly Escapes Burning.

### BYRD'S CRAFT IS NAMED

### Lindbergh Cheered at Ceremony—Commander, Now Last in Field, Waits on Weather.

Through no fault of his own, Clarence D. Chamberlin, who with Bert Acosta established a world's non-stop flying record a few weeks ago, will not fly the record-breaking monoplane in an attempt to establish a second New York-Paris non-stop flight.

G. M. Bellanca, designer of the plane, and Charles S. Levine of the Columbia Aircraft Company, owner of the ship, came to the parting of the ways last night and the designer finally severed his connection with the promoter. Then Levine issued a statement that the proposed flight, which has been talked of for weeks, was off.

The statement said:

"Due to the crowning blow of Mr. Bellanca's resignation, the plane will be placed in the hangar. Mr. Bellanca's resignation causes us to abandon plans for the New York-Paris flight for the present."

At the very moment that the statement was issued the plane was near the runway at Roosevelt Field with gas tanks filled and oil and equipment aboard ready for the start for Paris.

**Plane Threatened by Fire.**

A few minutes later, as it was being wheeled off, preparatory to being housed for the night, it narrowly escaped being destroyed by fire. When the word came to the field that the flight was definitely off mechanics were ordered to empty one gasoline tank to lighten the machine. The gasoline spilled on the ground and while the ship was being towed away a careless spectator threw the stub of a lighted cigarette down.

Times Wide World Photo.

CAPTAIN CHARLES A. LINDBERGH,
Who Flew Alone Across the Atlantic, New York to Paris, in Thirty-three and One-half Hours.

## *New York Stages Big Celebration After Hours of Anxious Waiting*

### *Harbor Craft, Factories, Fire Sirens and Radio Carry Message of the Flier's Victory Throughout the City—Theatres Halt While Audiences Cheer.*

New York bubbled all day yesterday with excitement and expectancy, first yearning for word of Captain Lindbergh, then half-doubting, gaining confidence as the afternoon progressed and finally acclaiming the victory of the young aviator with street demonstrations where the crowds were thickest, in which the ancient phrase, "I told you so," was often repeated. It was evident dur-

She said it with an air which signified: "I don't mean maybe." A surprising number of persons insisted that the difference in time was three hours.

Early in the day, even before there was any good reason why there should be definite news, the interest of the people was demonstrated in two ways. At every news stand there were little groups scanning the head-

## LINDBERGH TRIUMPH THRILLS COOLIDGE

### President Cables Praise to "Heroic Flier" and Concern for Nungesser and Coli.

### CAPITAL THROBS WITH JOY

### Kellogg, New, MacNider, Patrick and Many More Join in Paying Tribute to Daring Youth.

*Special to The New York Times.*

WASHINGTON, May 21.—The triumph of Captain Charles A. Lindbergh in flying from New York to Paris without a stop created a tremendous sensation in the national capital and found immediate response in a host of official messages and statements congratulating the daring aviator upon his achievement.

President Coolidge expressed his admiration in a message transmitted through Ambassador Herrick in Paris for delivery to the young flier in person.

With a single possible exception, this city has never been more thrilled since the armistice, when Woodrow Wilson mingled with noisy thousands in celebrating the end of the war. The exception was when Walter Johnson arose from apparent defeat and won the deciding world series baseball game in 1924.

"The American people," the President said, "rejoice with me at the brilliant termination of your heroic flight. The first non-stop flight of a lone aviator across the Atlantic crowns the record of American aviation, and in bringing the greetings of the American people to France you likewise carry the assurance of our admiration of those intrepid Frenchmen, Nungesser and Coli, whose bold spirits first ventured on your exploit, and likewise a message of our continued anxiety concerning their fate."

Secretary Kellogg, in a message similarly transmitted, said:

"I heartily congratulate you on the success of your great adventure in accomplishing a non-stop flight from New York to Paris. It is a great step in the advancement of

## CROWD ROARS THUNDEROUS WEL

### Breaks Through Lines of Soldiers Police and Surging to Plane Li Weary Flier from His Cockpit

### AVIATORS RESCUE HIM FROM FRENZIED MOB OF

### Paris Boulevards Ring With Celebration Afte and Night Watch—American Flag Is Call For and Wildly Acclaimed.

By EDWIN L. JAMES.

Copyright, 1927, by The New York Times Company. Special Cable to THE NEW YORK TIMES.

PARIS, May 21.—Lindbergh did it. Twenty minute 10 o'clock tonight suddenly and softly there slipped out darkness a gray-white airplane as 25,000 pairs of eyes s toward it. At 10:24 the Spirit of St. Louis landed and soldiers, ranks of policemen and stout steel fences wer before a mad rush as irresistible as the tides of the ocean

"Well, I made it," smiled Lindbergh, as the little monoplane came to a half in the middle of the field and t vanguard reached the plane. Lindbergh made a move t out. Twenty hands reached for him and lifted him out were a baby. Several thousands in a minute were arou plane. Thousands more broke the barriers of iron rails the field, cheering wildly.

**Lifted From His Cockpit.**

As he was lifted to the ground Lindbergh was pa with his hair unkempt, he looked completely worn out. strength enough, however, to smile, and waved his hand crowd. Soldiers with fixed bayonets were unable to ke the crowd.

United States Ambassador Herrick was among the welcome and congratulate the hero.

A NEW YORK TIMES man was one of the first to re machine after its graceful descent to the field. Thos to arrive at the plane had a picture that will live i minds for the rest of their lives. His cap off, his famou falling in disarray around his eyes, "Lucky Lindy" sat out over over the rim of the little cockpit of his machine

**Dramatic Scene at the Field.**

It was high drama. Picture the scene. Twenty to five thousand people were massed on the east side of Le air field. Some of them had been there six and seven

Off to the left the giant phare lighthouse of Mou rien flashed its guiding light 300 miles into the air. on the left Le Bourget Lighthouse twinkled, and off right another giant revolving phare sent its beams h the heavens.

Big arc lights on all sides with enormous electri were flooding the landing field. From time to time rose and burst in varied lights over the field.

Seven thirty, the hour anounced for the arrival, h and gone. Then 8 o'clock came, and no Lindbergh: at the sun had set but then came reports that Lindbergh h seen over Cork. Then he had been seen over Valentis land and then over Plymouth.

Suddenly a message spread like lightning, the avi been seen over Cherbourg. However, remembering t sages telling of Captain Nungesser's flight, the cro skeptical.

"One chance in a thousand!" "Oh, he cannot do it navigating instruments!" "It's a pity, because he was boy." Pessimism had spread over the great thron

The easiest way to grasp how Lindbergh's great flight from New York to Paris instantly monopolized national attention is to see how the *New York Times* reported it on the morning of May 22, 1927. If such a newspaper gave it the entire front page and a triple banner headline, you can guess how more excitable papers went overboard. Ever since the young man from the West—"Lucky Lindy," they called him—had taken off from Roosevelt Field on the morning of May 20, the whole country had been hoping and praying that he would succeed; and it greeted the news of his landing at Le Bourget with a miraculously united cheer.

The personal drama which reached its first climax when the young barnstorming pilot in the "Spirit of St. Louis" flew the Atlantic was to continue into other acts; and so we interrupt the chronological sequence of this book to look briefly ahead at them. But first, a glimpse of Lindbergh's triumph after that 1927 flight, for it was incredible.

In the picture above, he has returned from Paris to Washington (traveling on the cruiser *Memphis,* sent by President Coolidge especially to fetch him and his plane), and before a vast crowd at the Washington Monument is accepting the Distinguished Flying Cross, just bestowed on him by the President. (Mr. Coolidge is hidden behind him, but Mrs. Coolidge, with a big hat, is to be seen just to the left of the microphones; Secretary of War Dwight F. Davis, hand on hip, is to the right of Lindbergh.)

This was only a single incident in an enormous and continuing welcome. On his arrival in this country he received 55,000 telegrams of congratulation. When he went to New York, 200 vessels, 75 planes, and 10,000 troops took part in the ovation; and after it was over the street-cleaners gathered up over ten times as much torn paper as had been tossed from windows at the time of the Armistice. As he went about the country, front-page headlines followed him, medals and decorations were showered on him. He had become a god.

These demonstrations celebrated a great stunt and something more: a modesty and charm doubly admired at a moment when the country had had its fill of the blatant and the sordid.

In 1929 Lindbergh married Anne Morrow, daughter of the Morgan partner who had become Ambassador to Mexico; and thereafter she flew with him. This picture was taken on their flight to Japan, 1931.

The adulation continued—and continued all the more intensely because Colonel Lindbergh, frequently angered at the relentless way in which the crowds pursued him and the newspapermen pestered him, tried—sometimes with a short temper—to dodge the limelight. He was caught in a paradoxical situation: publicity had had a great part in making him, publicity was in a sense his chief job, and yet he hated the way it enslaved him. But he continued, as a matter of duty, to forward aviation by taking goodwill flights and participating in air celebrations. In the picture below, he and Mrs. Lindbergh are standing on either side of Mary Pickford at the opening, in July 1929, of the Transcontinental Air Transport's flight service, which was to carry passengers across the country in forty-eight hours, flying during the daytime and continuing by railroad sleeper at night. Of course it was Lindbergh's function to pilot the first plane to set out from the airport near Los Angeles. He engaged in research, too, with Dr. Alexis Carrel; in 1931 he and Mrs. Lindbergh made the trip which she described later so movingly in *Flight to the Orient* (the picture on the opposite page was taken at Churchill, Canada); they built a house at Hopewell, New Jersey, intended as a remote retreat from an importunate and interfering public; and here their first child was born.

Then came tragedy. On the evening of March 1, 1932, the Lindbergh baby was kidnapped: removed from his bed on the second story of the new house at Hopewell, and spirited away.

The event would have been grim enough if it had happened to an ordinary family; it was additionally grim because instantly, because of Lindbergh's renown, it was headlined and discussed and argued about from one end of the country to the other, while reporters, detectives, photographers, and rumor-mongers surrounded the unfortunate parents. Lindbergh was even the victim of a brutal hoax: taken off on a boat-trip to meet some supposed kidnappers who did not even exist.

After some ten weeks of this torture, the baby's body was found dead in a thicket beside a road a few miles from the Lindbergh home. So familiar was the tragedy to everybody that one tabloid ran a headline which declared simply, in huge type, "BABY DEAD."

Nor was this the end of the ordeal. For the investigations went on and on; after over two years, on September 19, 1934, the kidnapper was arrested; early in 1935 he was tried at Flemington, New Jersey, and convicted; on April 3, 1936, he was electrocuted—and all through those years the Lindberghs' distress was public property. The kidnapper was a fugitive felon from Germany by the name of Bruno Richard Hauptmann. The picture above shows newspapermen in the press room across the street from the death house at the New Jersey State Prison, waiting for the moment of the Hauptmann execution in 1936.

The dramatis personae of the Lindbergh case became familiar figures to all newspaper readers: Dr. John F. Condon ("Jafsie"), the elderly welfare worker in the Bronx, New York City, who got a message from the kidnapper, made contact with Lindbergh, and was given $50,000 in ransom money, which he handed to the kidnapper in a Bronx cemetery; Colonel Schwartzkopf of the New Jersey State Police; Mr. and Mrs. Oliver Whateley, the Lindberghs' butler and his wife; Betty Gow, the baby's nurse, who is shown in the picture at the left as she came to testify at the trial of Hauptmann early in 1935.

And here is Hauptmann, the kidnapper, whose arrest was facilitated by an odd circumstance — the fact that between 1932 and 1934 the country had gone off the gold standard. The ransom money had been paid to him in (marked) gold certificates. By 1934 these had become scarce, so that when the criminal spent them they attracted attention, thus locating him and leading to his capture.

We come now to the third act of the drama. Still in search of seclusion from press and public, Lindbergh (after a flight reconnaissance of transatlantic airways, recorded in his wife's book, *Listen, The Wind*) moved to England, moved to France, traveled in Germany, reported fully on the prowess of the German *Luftwaffe,* and returned to the United States to become not simply a leader of the isolationist forces of the country in 1940-41, but one of the harshest American foes of the countries that had given him asylum. In the picture above, he is testifying against the Lend-Lease Bill in February 1941, before the Senate Foreign Relations Committee; in the picture below, he is sitting on the platform at a huge "peace rally" held in Madison Square Garden, New York, in May 1941. At the left, in a white suit, listening to Lindbergh, is Senator Burton K. Wheeler; beyond Lindbergh are Kathleen Norris, the novelist, and Norman Thomas, Socialist leader.

After Pearl Harbor, Lindbergh went to work for Henry Ford at the big bomber plant at Willow Run. This picture of the two men was taken in April 1942, when the greatest of the early exponents of mass production was seventy-nine, and the man who had become a national idol at twenty-five was still no more than forty.

# III. NOSEDIVE

It was on the morning of Thursday, October 24, 1929, that the bottom dropped out of the stock market, as the result of heavy selling and severe losses on preceding days. The picture above shows the panic crowds that collected that morning outside the majestic Stock Exchange building at Broad and Wall Streets, New York. The big bankers came to the rescue and the avalanche was briefly stayed, but soon it was under way again; and on the following Tuesday, October 29, came the great liquidation, the famous sixteen-million-share day. On the opposite page we reproduce, from the next morning's *New York Times,* a part of the stock-market table that recorded the unparalleled disaster. (You might glance at what happened *on that single day* to Auburn, Allied Chemical & Dye, Electric Auto-Lite—remembering that it was only one day among many.)

# TRANSACTIONS ON THE NEW YORK STOCK

## TUESDAY, OCTOBER 29, 1929.

| Day's Sales. | Monday. | Saturday. | A Year Ago. | Two Years Ago. |
|---|---|---|---|---|
| 16,410,030 | 9,212,800 | 2,087,660 | 3,483,770 | 1,676,570 |

| Year to Date. | Same Period 1928. | 1927. | 1926. | 1925. |
|---|---|---|---|---|
| 950,797,190 | 708,649,607 | 464,944,575 | 376,924,360 | 363,084,123 |

| Stock and Dividend Rate. | First. | High. | Low. | Last. | Net Ch'ge. | Closing Bid. | Ask. | Sales. |
|---|---|---|---|---|---|---|---|---|
| Abitibi Power & Paper | 40 | 40 | 38 | 38 | −6¾ | 38 | 40 | 1,800 |
| Abraham & S. pf. (7)* | 107¼ | 107¼ | 107¼ | 107¼ | −2¾ | 106 | 108¼ | 20 |
| Adams Express pf. (5) | 87⅛ | 87⅛ | 87⅛ | 87⅛ | +⅛ | 87⅛ | 88 | 200 |
| Adams Millis (2) | 26 | 26 | 24¾ | 24¾ | −2¾ | 20 | 25 | 700 |
| Advance Rumely | 8¼ | 8¼ | 7 | 7 | −6¾ | 7 | 9 | 2,600 |
| Advance Rumely pf. | 20 | 20 | 15 | 16 | −7 | .. | 16 | 1,300 |
| Ahumada Lead | 1 | 1 | ¾ | ¾ | −⅜ | ¾ | 1 | 6,500 |
| Air Reduction (†4½) | 125⅛ | 128 | 100¼ | 120 | −25 | 118 | 120 | 23,500 |
| Air Way El. Appl. (2½) | 25 | 25 | 25 | 25 | −3½ | 25 | 27 | 3,000 |
| Ajax Rubber | 2½ | 2½ | 2½ | 2½ | −¼ | 2½ | 2¾ | 7,200 |
| Alaska Juneau | 5¼ | 5⅞ | 5 | 5⅞ | .. | 5⅝ | 5⅞ | 14,600 |
| Albany Perf. W. Paper | 5 | 7 | 5 | 7 | −1 | 6 | 7 | 2,400 |
| Alleghany Corporation | 24¼ | 24¾ | 18⅛ | 20⅝ | −8½ | 20½ | 21 | 224,100 |
| Alleg. Corp pf. x w (5½) | 88⅝ | 88⅝ | 88½ | 88½ | −1¼ | | | 600 |
| Allied Chem. & Dye (6) | 205 | 218 | 204¾ | 210 | −35 | 210 | 215 | 32,100 |
| Allied Chem. & D pf. (7) | 122 | 122 | 121 | 121 | −¼ | 120½ | 124 | 400 |
| Allis-Chalmers Mfg. (2) | 46½ | 47½ | 37¼ | 41 | −5 | 41 | 44 | 15,500 |
| Alpha Port. Cement (3) | 30 | 30 | 30 | 30 | −¼ | 29¼ | 30 | 400 |
| Amalgamated Leather | 3⅞ | 3⅞ | 3⅞ | 3⅞ | −⅝ | 3 | 4 | 700 |
| Amerada Corp. (2) | 20¼ | 21 | 17½ | 17½ | −4 | 17½ | 19 | 11,000 |
| Am. Agricult. Chemical | 7¼ | 7⅞ | 4 | 4 | −3¾ | 4 | 5 | 5,700 |
| Am. Agricult. Chem. pf. | 26 | 28½ | 25½ | 25½ | −5¾ | 25½ | 29 | 2,400 |
| Am. Beet Sugar pf. | 49 | 49 | 49 | 49 | .. | 45 | 50⅞ | 200 |
| Am. Bosch Magneto | 30 | 30 | 30 | 30 | −5 | 19 | 30 | 2,000 |
| Am. Br. S. & F. (2.40) | 49 | 49½ | 44½ | 44½ | −5½ | 44 | 46 | 8,200 |
| Am. Brown Bov. Elec | 4¼ | 5½ | 4⅛ | 4⅛ | −6⅞ | 4⅛ | 7 | 11,100 |
| Am. Br. Bov. E. pf. (7)* | 64 | 64 | 64 | 64 | −1 | 52 | 65 | 30 |
| Am. Can (†5) | 130¼ | 134 | 110 | 120 | −16 | 116 | 120 | 140,100 |
| Am. Can pf. (7) | 136⅞ | 136⅞ | 136⅞ | 136⅞ | −1⅜ | .. | 137 | 200 |
| Am. Car & Fdy. (6) | 81⅛ | 87½ | 76 | 87 | +6⅞ | 87 | 89 | 10,100 |
| Am. Car & Fdy. pf. (7) | 113 | 113 | 113 | 113 | .. | 113 | 114½ | 200 |
| Am. Chicle (2) | 38½ | 38½ | 35 | 35 | −9 | 35 | 37 | 2,900 |
| Am. Com. Alco. (k1.60) | 20 | 30 | 20 | 30 | −¾ | 29 | 30 | 17,100 |
| Am. & Foreign Power | 68 | 73 | 50 | 55 | −22½ | 54½ | 57 | 89,500 |
| Am. & F. Pwr. pf. (7) | 106½ | 106½ | 106 | 106 | −1 | 105½ | 107 | 1,400 |
| Am. & F. Pw. 2d pf. (7) | 89½ | 90 | 87 | 90 | −2½ | 89 | 90 | 2,000 |
| Am. Hawaiian S. S. (1) | 21½ | 21½ | 21½ | 21½ | −1½ | .. | 21½ | 500 |
| Am. Hide & Leather | 5 | 5 | 5 | 5 | −1 | 5 | 6 | 500 |
| Am. Hide & Leath. pf. | 32⅞ | 32⅞ | 31 | 31 | −4⅛ | 31 | 32 | 300 |
| Am. Home Prod. (3.60) | 46¼ | 49 | 43½ | 47 | −3 | 45 | 47 | 9,500 |
| Am. Ice (3) | 33 | 3[illegible] | 30 | 35 | −2½ | 34½ | 37 | 8,200 |
| Am. Ice pf. (6) | 90 | 90 | 90 | 90 | .. | 90 | 93 | 600 |
| Am. International (‡2) | 30 | 41½ | 30 | 41½ | −2½ | 41 | 42 | 71,400 |
| Am. La F. & Foamite | 3 | 3 | 2½ | 2½ | −⅞ | .. | 2½ | 900 |
| Am. Locomotive (8) | 101 | 101½ | 99 | 100 | −½ | 100 | 101 | 10,500 |
| Am. Locomotive pf. (7) | 115 | 115¼ | 115 | 115 | −⅜ | 114½ | 115 | 500 |
| Am. Mach. & Fdy. (†5) | 185 | 185 | 175¼ | 175¼ | −25¾ | 175 | 183 | 1,000 |
| Am. Metal (3) | 41⅛ | 46 | 41⅛ | 46 | −7 | 45 | 50 | 16,000 |
| Am. Nat. Gas pf. (7)* | 78¼ | 78¼ | 78¼ | 78¼ | −1¾ | .. | 80 | 50 |
| Am. Piano | 4 | 4 | 3½ | 3½ | −1½ | 3 | 5½ | 300 |
| Am. Piano pf.* | 19 | 19 | 18 | 18 | −1 | .. | 20 | 100 |
| Am. Pwr. & Lgt. (†1) | 75¼ | 76¼ | 73¾ | 73¾ | −5¼ | 73¾ | 74 | 58,400 |
| Am. P. & L. pf. (6) | 98⅛ | 98⅛ | 92¼ | 92¼ | −5¾ | 92 | 95 | 800 |
| Am. P.&L. pf. A sta (5) | 82⅛ | 82¼ | 80 | 80 | −2 | 79⅜ | 80 | 1,000 |
| Am. Rad.&Sd. San. (1½) | 30 | 32 | 29 | 32 | +4 | 31½ | 32½ | 141,000 |
| Am. Republics | 15 | 20⅛ | 15 | 17⅞ | −4¼ | 15 | 18 | 7,100 |
| Am. Rolling Mill (c2) | 85⅛ | 89¾ | 72 | 72 | −13 | 70½ | 71 | 22,800 |
| Am. Safety Razor (†5) | 56⅞ | 56⅞ | 52 | 53¾ | −4¼ | 53½ | 54 | 4,100 |
| Am. Seating (2) | 30 | 30 | 29½ | 29½ | −½ | 29 | 30 | 3,400 |
| Am. Ship & Commerce | 1 | 1 | ⅜ | ⅜ | −1¾ | ¼ | 1 | 1,800 |
| Am. Shipbuilding (8)* | 70 | 78 | 70 | 70 | −10 | .. | 75 | 630 |
| Am. Smelt. & Ref. (4) | 81 | 84¾ | 81 | 84 | −6 | .. | 85 | 14,500 |
| Am. Snuff (3) | 40⅛ | 40½ | 39 | 39 | −2 | 38½ | 40 | 2,300 |
| Am. Steel Found. (3) | 42½ | 43 | 35¾ | 40 | −5¼ | 39½ | 40 | 23,200 |
| Am. Stl. Found. pf. (7)* | 111 | 111 | 110½ | 110½ | −½ | 111 | 112 | 160 |
| Am. Stores (2½) | 45 | 47 | 40 | 47 | −13 | 47½ | 58 | 6,000 |
| Am. Sugar Refining (5) | 70 | 70 | 66 | 66 | −6¾ | 66 | 68 | 7,500 |
| Am. Sugar Ref. pf. (7) | 103⅞ | 103⅞ | 102 | 103⅞ | −⅛ | 102 | 104 | 1,100 |
| Am. Sumatra Tob. (3) | 32 | 33 | 28 | 29¾ | −3¼ | 29½ | 30 | 4,200 |
| Am. Tel. & Tel. (9) | 225 | 230 | 204 | 204 | −28 | 204 | 205 | 131,100 |
| Am. Tobacco (8) | 190 | 194½ | 182 | 191 | −5 | 189 | 192 | 10,100 |
| Am. Tobacco, B (8) | 190 | 194¾ | 182 | 186 | −9¼ | 185 | 188 | 41,800 |
| Am. Tobacco pf. (6) | 117 | 117 | 117 | 117 | −1 | 117 | 118 | 200 |
| Am. Type Fdrs. pf. (7)* | 109 | 109 | 108½ | 108½ | −1½ | 108½ | 109 | 60 |
| Am. Water Works (c1) | 70 | 71 | 65 | 68 | −12 | 68 | 70 | 38,600 |
| Am. Wat. W. 1st pf. (6) | 102⅝ | 102⅝ | 102⅝ | 102⅝ | −⅜ | 102⅝ | 103 | 400 |
| Am. Woolen | 10⅛ | 10⅛ | 8 | 8⅛ | −3 | 9 | 10 | 4,200 |
| Am. Woolen pf. | 25⅛ | 26 | 24 | 26 | −2⅛ | 20 | 26 | 1,500 |
| Am. Writ. Paper pf. (3) | 37½ | 37½ | 37½ | 37½ | −1½ | 34½ | 37½ | 100 |
| Am. Zinc, L. & S. | 8⅛ | 8⅛ | 6⅛ | 8⅛ | −2⅞ | 8½ | 10 | 6,300 |
| Anaconda Copper (7) | 82 | 90½ | 75½ | 85 | −8½ | 84 | 85 | 381,500 |
| Anchor Cap (2.40) | 40 | 40 | 25 | 35 | −16 | 34 | 36 | 8,500 |
| Anchor Cap pf. (6½) | 111 | 111 | 111 | 111 | −1 | 102 | 110 | 100 |
| Andes Copper (3) | 34 | 38½ | 30 | 35 | −5¼ | 37 | 40 | 11,700 |
| Archer-Dan.-M. (2) | 30 | 31 | 22¾ | 24½ | −5¾ | 22½ | 25 | 11,200 |
| Archer-Dan.-M. pf. (7)* | 104¼ | 104¼ | 104¼ | 104¼ | −¼ | 104 | 104¼ | 50 |
| Armour of Del. pf. (7) | 82¾ | 82¾ | 75 | 75 | −8 | 75 | 80 | 1,000 |
| Armour of Ill., A | 5⅞ | 5⅞ | 5⅛ | 5⅞ | −1⅛ | 5½ | 5⅞ | 19,300 |
| Armour of Ill., B | 3½ | 3⅞ | 3½ | 3½ | −⅝ | 3½ | 3¾ | 32,000 |
| Arnold, Constable & Co. | 12¼ | 13 | 12 | 12⅛ | −3¼ | 12 | 14 | 8,700 |
| Artloom (2) | 22 | 22 | 22 | 22 | −1 | 20 | 25 | 300 |
| Art Metal Constr. (1½) | 25½ | 26½ | 25 | 26½ | +1¾ | 26 | 27 | 500 |
| Assoc. App. Ind. (4) | 40 | 42 | 35 | 37 | −6 | 37 | 39 | 2,900 |
| Assoc. D. G. (2½) | 28 | 28 | 28 | 28 | −9¼ | .. | 28 | 22,000 |
| Assoc. D. G. 1st pf. (6) | 91 | 93 | 91 | 93 | +½ | 93½ | 95 | 400 |
| Assoc. Oil (2)* | 43¾ | 43¾ | 43¾ | 43¾ | −¾ | 40 | 44½ | 10 |
| At., T. & S. Fe (10) | 242½ | 244 | 221 | 234 | −17 | 230 | 235 | 25,000 |
| At., T. & S. Fe pf. (5) | 102⅞ | 102⅞ | 101⅝ | 101⅝ | −1½ | 101 | 102 | 1,400 |
| Atl. Coast Line (†10) | 169½ | 169½ | 165 | 165 | −7 | 165 | 166 | 4,000 |
| Atl., G. & W. I. | 70 | 70⅞ | 67 | 67½ | −4⅜ | 67½ | 69 | 5,800 |
| Atl., G. & W. I. pf. (4) | 54¾ | 54¾ | 54½ | 54½ | −½ | 54¼ | 55 | 1,700 |
| Atl. Refining (†2) | 30 | 38¾ | 30 | 35 | −5⅝ | 35 | 35½ | 131,300 |
| Atlas Powder (4) | 91¼ | 93½ | 80 | 80 | −5 | 79 | 85 | 4,300 |
| Atlas Powder pf. (6)* | 100 | 100 | 99 | 99 | −4 | 99 | 105 | 110 |
| Auburn Auto (j4) | 130 | 175 | 120 | 130 | −60 | 135 | 150 | 3,300 |
| Austin, Nichols | 5 | 5 | 4 | 4 | −1½ | .. | 4½ | 4,500 |
| Austin, Nichols pf. | 32 | 32 | 32 | 32 | −3 | .. | 32 | 100 |
| Austr. Cr. Anst. (4.49) | 53¾ | 53¾ | 52½ | 52½ | −2 | 52 | 54 | 200 |
| Autosales | 25½ | 25½ | 24 | 24 | −2½ | 24 | 25 | 11,400 |
| Autosales pf. (3) | 38 | 38 | 36½ | 36½ | −2 | 38 | 38½ | 500 |
| Auto-St. S. Razor, A (3) | 37⅞ | 37⅞ | 37⅞ | 37⅞ | −1⅛ | 37¾ | 38 | 300 |
| Aviation Corp. of Del. | 7⅝ | 8 | 6 | 6¼ | −2¼ | 6⅛ | 6½ | 44,300 |
| Baldwin Loco. new | 20 | 25 | 19 | 25 | .. | 25 | 25½ | 20,800 |
| Baldwin Loco. pf. (7)* | 117¾ | 117¾ | 117½ | 117½ | −2¼ | 117 | 117½ | 40 |
| Baltimore & Ohio (7) | 115¼ | 117¼ | 112 | 114½ | −¾ | 113 | 115 | 85,900 |
| Baltimore & O. pf. (4) | 78½ | 78½ | 78½ | 78½ | −1⅝ | 78 | 79½ | 200 |
| Bamberger pf. (6½)* | 107 | 107 | 107 | 107 | −½ | 105 | 106 | 80 |
| Bang. & Aroos. (3½) | 63 | 63 | 55 | 60 | −7 | 60 | 61 | 3,600 |
| Bang. & Aroos. pf. (7)* | 110 | 110 | 105¾ | 105¾ | −4¼ | 110 | 110½ | 300 |
| Barker Bros. (2)* | 25¼ | 25¼ | 25 | 25 | −½ | 24½ | 25½ | 130 |
| Barnsdall, Cl. A (†2¼) | 22 | 23 | 20 | 20⅞ | −1¼ | 20¼ | 20½ | 61,000 |
| Bayuk Cig. 1st pf. (7)* | 97½ | 97½ | 97½ | 97½ | +½ | 97 | 100 | 80 |
| Beacon Oil | 17 | 17 | 17 | 17 | −5 | 17 | 20 | 5,700 |
| Beatrice Creamery (4) | 92⅛ | 92⅛ | 80 | 80 | −20 | 80 | 90 | 2,500 |
| Beech-Nut Packing (3) | 68¼ | 68¼ | 67 | 67 | −5 | 67 | 68 | 3,500 |
| Belding-Heminway | 7 | 8¼ | 7 | 8¼ | −¾ | 7 | 8½ | 2,900 |
| Bendix Aviation (2) | 38⅛ | 39⅞ | 28¼ | 35 | −7 | 33 | 35 | 55,800 |
| Best & Co. | 32¼ | 35 | 32¼ | 35 | −5⅝ | 32 | 36 | 3,600 |
| Bethlehem Steel (6) | 90¼ | 91 | 80 | 84 | −10¼ | 83 | 84 | 103,600 |
| Bethlehem Steel pf. (7) | 126 | 126 | 126 | 126 | −⅛ | 125½ | 126 | 2,400 |
| Bloomingdale Bros | 35 | 35 | 30 | 30 | −10 | 30 | 37 | 4,100 |
| Bloomingdale pf. (7)* | 100¼ | 100¼ | 100¼ | 100¼ | −5 | 100¼ | 108 | 30 |
| Blumenthl. & Co. pf. (7)* | 85 | 85 | 85 | 85 | −5¼ | .. | 90 | 10 |
| Bohn Al. & Brass (†5) | 60¼ | 60¼ | 47¾ | 49¾ | −15¼ | 49½ | 50 | 4,100 |
| Bon Ami, Class A (†5) | 70 | 70 | 70 | 70 | −7 | 70 | 74 | 400 |

| 1929 High. | 1929 Low. | Stock and Dividend Rate. | First. | High. | Low. | Last. | Net Ch'ge. | Closing Bid. | Ask. | Sales. |
|---|---|---|---|---|---|---|---|---|---|---|
| 90 | 25¼ | Cont'l Baking, A | 35 | 35 | 25¼ | 25¾ | −9¼ | 25½ | 35 | 17,200 |
| 63¾ | 45 | Cont'l Bank N. Y. (1.20) | 45 | 45 | 45 | 45 | −4 | 45 | 48 | 1,000 |
| 92 | 40½ | Cont'l Can (2½) | 48 | 49 | 40½ | 44⅛ | −14⅛ | 44 | 45 | 56,100 |
| 110¼ | 50 | Cont'l Insurance (2) | 61 | 69½ | 50 | 59 | −11 | 58 | 60 | 17,500 |
| 28⅜ | 6½ | Cont'l Motors (80c) | 8¼ | 8⅞ | 7½ | 8¼ | −¾ | 8 | 8⅛ | 49,500 |
| 47⅛ | 25 | Cont'l Oil of Del. | 25 | 25¾ | 25 | 25¾ | −1⅜ | .. | 25¼ | 34,000 |
| 126⅝ | 82 | Corn Prod. Refin. (†3½) | 95⅛ | 98¾ | 90 | 94 | −5⅞ | 94 | 94½ | 35,600 |
| 144¾ | 138¼ | Corn Prod. Ref. pf. (7)* | 140½ | 140½ | 140½ | 140½ | −½ | 139¾ | 140 | 760 |
| 82¼ | 20⅛ | Coty, Inc. (g2) | 21 | 27 | 20⅛ | 23 | −10 | 23 | 24 | 31,600 |
| 125 | 25 | Crosley Radio (‡1) | 25 | 29¾ | 25 | 28 | −11½ | 28 | 30 | 9,100 |
| 79 | 40 | Crown Cork & Seal | 42 | 42 | 40 | 40 | −12 | 38 | 52 | 1,600 |
| 121¾ | 80 | Crucible Steel (5) | 86¼ | 89 | 80 | 80 | −6 | 80 | 83 | 4,200 |
| 116¾ | 109 | Crucible Steel pf. (7) | 109⅞ | 109⅞ | 109⅞ | 109⅞ | −⅛ | 109¾ | 112 | 200 |
| 5½ | ¾ | Cuba Cane Sugar | ¾ | 1⅛ | ¾ | 1⅛ | +⅜ | .. | .. | 400 |
| 17 | 9 | Cuban-Amer. Sugar | 10 | 10 | 9 | 9 | −1¼ | 9 | 10 | 3,200 |
| 95 | 60⅛ | Cuban-Amer. Sug. pf.* | 66 | 66 | 65 | 65 | −2 | 66 | 67 | 170 |
| 67⅞ | 40 | Cudahy Packing (4) | 40⅛ | 41⅜ | 40 | 40 | −3½ | 40⅛ | 41 | 5,100 |
| 118 | 112½ | Curtis Publish. pf. (7) | 113 | 113 | 113 | 113 | .. | 112⅝ | 113⅛ | 100 |
| 30⅛ | 7⅞ | Curtiss-Wright | 10⅝ | 11⅞ | 7⅞ | 9⅜ | −3½ | 9⅜ | 9½ | 159,100 |
| 37⅞ | 14 | Curtiss-Wright, A | 16⅛ | 18¾ | 14 | 18 | −1⅝ | 18 | 19 | 34,000 |
| 115¼ | 108½ | Cushman's Sons pf. (8)* | 110½ | 110½ | 110½ | 110½ | .. | 110½ | 114 | 40 |
| 121¼ | 58⅛ | Cutler-Hammer (3½) | 73 | 76 | 60⅝ | 71 | −18 | 71 | 75 | 300 |
| 126½ | 63 | Cuyamel Fruit | 100½ | 100½ | 94 | 94 | −11¼ | .. | 95 | 1,700 |
| 69⅛ | 21¼ | Davison Chemical | 33¾ | 33⅞ | 21⅛ | 25 | −10⅛ | 25 | 28 | 15,600 |
| 46⅞ | 27½ | Debenhams Sec. (a2.31) | 29¼ | 29¼ | 28⅝ | 28⅝ | −½ | 28¼ | 30 | 500 |
| 128 | 116 | Deere & Co. pf. (7)* | 119 | 119 | 117½ | 117½ | −2 | 117½ | 119 | 270 |
| 226 | 141½ | Delaware & Hudson (9) | 152 | 152 | 141½ | 144¾ | −25¼ | 144 | 145 | 5,800 |
| 169¾ | 120¼ | Del., Lack. & W. (†7) | 138¼ | 145½ | 138¼ | 145½ | +8½ | 145½ | 150½ | 10,200 |
| 77¾ | 54 | Denver & R. Gde. W. pf. | 56 | 56 | 54 | 54 | −3 | 45 | 54 | 600 |
| 64⅞ | 33 | Devoe & R., A (†3) | 33 | 33 | 33 | 33 | −3¼ | 32 | 38 | 1,500 |
| 115½ | 112 | Devoe & R. 1st pf. (7)* | 113 | 113 | 113 | 113 | .. | 100 | 112 | 40 |
| 164 | 125⅛ | Diamond Match (8)* | 126 | 137 | 125⅛ | 135⅛ | +6⅝ | 135⅛ | 136 | 860 |
| 11¼ | 6½ | Dome Mines (1) | 8 | 8 | 6½ | 7 | −1 | 7 | 7½ | 3,800 |
| 54¾ | 12 | Dominion Stores (1.20) | 22½ | 23 | 12 | 14 | −11 | 16 | 25 | 8,200 |
| 126⅛ | 71 | Drug, Inc. (4) | 71 | 72¼ | 71 | 72¼ | −19 | 72 | 80 | 12,100 |
| 4⅞ | 2⅜ | Duluth, S. S. & Atl. | 2½ | 2½ | 2½ | 2½ | .. | 2⅜ | 2½ | 100 |
| 7½ | 3¾ | Duluth, S. S. & Atl. pf. | 3¾ | 3¾ | 3¾ | 3¾ | .. | 3¾ | 4 | 100 |
| 92 | 25 | Dunhill Internatl. (‡4) | 27½ | 32 | 25 | 32 | −7 | 32 | 36 | 4,200 |
| 28⅞ | 14 | Duplan Silk (1) | 14 | 14 | 14 | 14 | −2 | .. | 13 | 500 |
| 102 | 92 | Duplan Silk pf. (8) | 95 | 95 | 95 | 95 | −1 | 95½ | 98⅞ | 10 |
| 231 | 80 | Du Pont de Nem. (†4½) | 138 | 138 | 80 | 116 | −34¼ | 115 | 120 | 103,600 |
| 119¾ | 112 | Du Pont de N. deb. (6) | 115 | 115 | 112¾ | 112¾ | −1½ | 111 | 113 | 1,800 |
| 39½ | 19 | Eastern Roll. Mill (1½) | 23 | 23 | 19 | 19 | −8 | 18 | 24 | 1,000 |
| 264¾ | 162 | Eastman Kodak (†8) | 183½ | 186 | 162 | 170 | −11½ | 170 | 180 | 27,800 |
| 76¾ | 28 | Eaton Axle & Spring (3) | 29 | 33 | 28 | 30 | −5 | 30 | 30½ | 9,300 |
| 39¾ | 11⅜ | Eitingon-Schild (2½) | 11⅜ | 11⅜ | 11⅜ | 11⅜ | −5⅝ | 11⅜ | 17 | 1,500 |
| 112½ | 61 | Eitingon-Schild pf. (6½) | 61 | 61 | 61 | 61 | −8⅞ | 61 | 66 | 300 |
| 174 | 50 | Electric Auto-Lite (6) | 75 | 78½ | 50 | 50 | −45 | 50 | 60 | 28,300 |
| 115 | 106¾ | Elec. Auto-Lite pf. (7)* | 107 | 107 | 107 | 107 | +⅛ | 106¾ | 110¾ | 20 |
| 18⅜ | 3¼ | Electric Boat | 4⅝ | 4⅞ | 3¼ | 4⅛ | −1⅜ | 4⅛ | 5 | 9,500 |
| 86⅝ | 32½ | Elec. Power & Lt. (1) | 34 | 35⅞ | 32½ | 34⅞ | −⅞ | 34⅝ | 34⅞ | 96,200 |
| 109¼ | 103 | Elec. Pow. & Lt. pf. (7) | 106½ | 107⅜ | 106 | 106 | −1½ | 106 | 107 | 3,300 |
| 104½ | 73 | Elec. Storage Bat. (5) | 80¼ | 84½ | 73 | 80 | −3⅞ | 80 | 80¼ | 15,200 |
| 10½ | 3½ | Elk Horn Coal | 6 | 6 | 6 | 6 | −⅝ | 6 | 8 | 100 |
| 24 | 7¾ | Elk Horn Coal pf.* | 13 | 13 | 12½ | 12½ | −1½ | 12 | 13⅞ | 250 |
| 22½ | 3½ | Emerson-Brant., A | 4¼ | 4¼ | 3½ | 3½ | −2¼ | 3¼ | 5 | 700 |
| 13 | 2⅝ | Emerson-Brant., B | 3 | 3 | 3 | 3 | −1 | 2½ | 2¾ | 100 |
| 79⅝ | 31 | Eng. Pub. Service (¶1) | 36 | 38½ | 31 | 34 | −9 | 33 | 36 | 26,100 |
| 123¼ | 90 | Eng. Pub. S. pf. (5) | 97 | 97 | 93 | 93 | −3⅛ | 90¼ | 93 | 600 |
| 109 | 84¾ | Eng. Pub. S. pf. (5½) | 84¾ | 85 | 84¾ | 85 | −8 | .. | 85 | 200 |
| 41 | 31¼ | Equit. Off. Bdg. (2½) | 37¾ | 37¾ | 36¾ | 37 | −1⅛ | 36⅞ | 37 | 6,400 |
| 93½ | 43 | Erie R. R. | 50 | 53 | 43 | 45¼ | −9¾ | 45¼ | 46½ | 60,600 |
| 66¼ | 57 | Erie R. R. 1st pf. (4) | 62 | 62 | 57⅛ | 57⅛ | −4⅞ | 53 | 58 | 7,600 |
| 63⅞ | 56 | Erie R. R. 2d pf. (4) | 58 | 58 | 57½ | 57½ | −3½ | 55 | 58 | 2,100 |
| 54 | [illegible] | Eureka Vac. Clnr. (4) | 40 | 41 | 39½ | 41 | −2 | 41 | 42 | 2,800 |
| 27½ | [illegible] | Exchange Buffet (1½)* | 25¾ | 25¾ | 25¾ | 25¾ | .. | 25¾ | 26 | 10 |
| 10 | 4 | Fairbanks Co. | 8¼ | 8¼ | 8¼ | 8¼ | .. | 5 | 9 | 100 |
| 35 | 11 | Fairbanks Co. pf.* | 22 | 22 | 15 | 15 | −7 | 15 | 22 | 50 |
| 54⅞ | 29¾ | Fairbanks-Morse (3) | 39¾ | 39¾ | 29¾ | 29¾ | −11 | .. | 30 | 5,000 |
| 110⅞ | 106 | Fbks.-Morse pf. (7)* | 107 | 107 | 107 | 107 | −1 | 107 | 108 | 30 |
| 72⅝ | 41⅛ | Fash. Pk. Assoc. (k2½) | 41⅛ | 41⅛ | 41⅛ | 41⅛ | −5⅞ | 41 | 45 | 700 |
| 104 | 97½ | Fed. Lt. & Tr. pf. (6)* | 99⅞ | 99⅞ | 99⅞ | 99⅞ | −⅛ | 99⅞ | 106 | 100 |
| 315 | 205 | Fed. Min. & Smelting | 205 | 205 | 205 | 205 | −10 | 175 | 200 | 300 |
| 102 | 95 | Fed. M. & S. pf. (7) | 95 | 95 | 95 | 95 | −1 | 94½ | 96 | 300 |
| 22⅝ | 5 | Fed. Motor Truck (80c) | 5 | 8 | 5 | 8 | −1½ | 6½ | 9 | 6,300 |
| 123 | 63 | Fid. Ph. Fire Ins. (2) | 76[illegible] | 77 | 63 | 63 | −14 | 50 | 70 | 6,900 |
| 13¾ | 6 | Fifth Av. Bus (64c)* | [illegible] | 6¼ | 6¼ | 6¼ | −2¾ | 6¼ | 7 | 80 |
| 98½ | 51 | Filene's Sons | 5[illegible] | 51 | 51 | 51 | −8 | 51 | 59 | 700 |
| 90 | 60 | First Nat. Stores (1½) | [illegible] | 67 | 60 | 60 | 7¾ | 60 | 64 | 12,600 |
| 20⅛ | 4 | Fisk Rubber | 5⅛ | 5⅛ | 4 | 4½ | 1⅛ | 4¼ | 4½ | 21,100 |
| 72½ | 25 | Fisk Rubber 1st pf.* | 27 | 27 | 25 | 25 | −3 | .. | 26 | 300 |
| 82½ | 25⅛ | Fisk Rub. 1st pf. cv.* | 25⅛ | 25⅛ | 25⅛ | 25⅛ | .. | 25 | 30 | 210 |
| 54 | 42 | Florsheim Shoe, A | 42 | 42 | 42 | 42 | −3¼ | 42 | 50 | 700 |
| 102½ | 90⅛ | Florsheim Shoe pf. (6) | 90⅛ | 90⅛ | 90½ | 90⅛ | −⅞ | 90 | 95 | 100 |
| 82¾ | 35¼ | Follansbee Bros. (†3) | 40 | 40 | 35¼ | 35¼ | −17¾ | 35¼ | 37 | 3,500 |
| 69⅝ | 25 | Foundation Co. | 25 | 25 | 25 | 25 | −3 | .. | 25 | 300 |
| 105⅝ | 40 | Fox Film, Class A (4) | 50 | 65 | 40 | 48 | −20 | 46 | 50 | 54,500 |
| 110 | 98½ | Franklin Simon pf. (7)* | 100 | 100 | 100 | 100 | .. | 100 | 102 | 90 |
| 33⅞ | 5 | Gabriel Snubber, A | 5¼ | 5½ | 5 | 5 | −3 | 5 | 6 | 4,800 |
| 83½ | 68 | Gamewell Co. (5) | 68¼ | 68¼ | 68¼ | 68¼ | +¼ | 65 | 70 | 500 |
| 25 | 3¾ | Gardner Motor | 5 | 5¼ | 3¾ | 4¼ | −⅝ | 4 | 5 | 7,400 |
| 123½ | 81 | Gen. Am. T. Car (‡4) | 90¼ | 93 | 85 | 87¾ | −12⅝ | 88 | 90 | 27,200 |
| 94¾ | 48¼ | Gen. Asphalt | 51½ | 51½ | 48¼ | 48¼ | −5¼ | 48 | 50 | 11,400 |
| 140 | 130 | Gen. Baking pf. (8)* | 130½ | 130½ | 130 | 130 | −⅜ | 120 | 130 | 100 |
| 69¾ | 26 | Gen. Bronze (2) | 27 | 33 | 26 | 30 | −5½ | 30 | 34 | 3,400 |
| 61 | 32 | Gen. Cable | 40 | 40 | 32¼ | 32¼ | −7¾ | 31 | 36 | 14,900 |
| 120½ | 70 | Gen. Cable, A (4) | 80 | 82 | 70 | 74¾ | −11¾ | 74 | 75 | 9,900 |
| 107½ | 104 | Gen. Cable pf. (7) | 106¼ | 106¼ | 106¼ | 106¼ | −½ | 103¼ | 106⅛ | 200 |
| 122 | 112¼ | Gen. Cigar pf. (7)* | 116½ | 117½ | 116½ | 117½ | +1 | 117½ | 118 | 200 |
| 403 | 210 | Gen. Electric (†6) | 245 | 245 | 210 | 222 | −28 | 219 | 223 | 136,300 |
| 11¾ | 11 | Gen. Elec. special (60c) | 11⅛ | 11⅛ | 11⅛ | 11⅛ | −⅛ | 11 | 11¼ | 13,100 |
| 91¾ | 35 | Gen. Foods Corp. (3) | 42¼ | 46½ | 35 | 40 | −8¾ | 39¾ | 40 | 97,500 |
| 112 | 70 | Gen. Gas & El., A (e1½) | 73 | 73 | 73 | 73 | −4¾ | .. | .. | 5,000 |
| 116½ | 100 | Gen. G. & E. pf., A (7)* | 102 | 102 | 100 | 100 | −2 | .. | 102 | 100 |
| 89⅛ | 50 | Gen. Mills (†3½) | 58 | 59 | 50 | 50 | −11¼ | .. | 55 | 7,800 |
| 100 | 89 | Gen. Mills pf. (6) | 91¾ | 92¼ | 91¾ | 92¼ | +¼ | 91½ | 93¼ | 300 |
| 91¾ | 33½ | Gen. Motors (†3.30) | 45¾ | 45½ | 33½ | 40 | −7½ | 40 | 40¼ | 971,300 |
| 126½ | 119½ | Gen. Motors pf. (7) | 120 | 120 | 119½ | 119½ | −1½ | .. | 120 | 1,400 |
| 52 | 35 | Gen. Out. Adv., A (4) | 40¾ | 40¾ | 35 | 35 | −10 | 30 | 40 | 1,300 |
| 41 | 21½ | Gen. Out. Adv. v.t.c. (2) | 24 | 24 | 21½ | 21½ | −3½ | 21 | 23 | 4,300 |
| 98 | 25 | Gen. Pub. Service (b6) | 25¼ | 28¼ | 25 | 25 | −10 | 25 | 28 | 11,500 |
| 126½ | 70 | Gen. Ry. Signal (5) | 80½ | 90 | 70 | 77 | −17½ | 77 | 80 | 16,000 |
| 88½ | 54⅛ | Gen. Refractories (†4¼) | 60 | 63½ | 54⅛ | 57 | −11 | .. | .. | 4,700 |
| 143 | 100 | Gillette Saf. Raz. (c5) | 104¼ | 104¾ | 100 | 101⅞ | −3¾ | 95 | 102 | 15,900 |
| 48⅛ | 17⅝ | Gimbel Bros. | 18⅝ | 24½ | 17⅝ | 24½ | +3 | 23 | 25 | 8,000 |
| 94 | 76½ | Gimbel Bros. pf. (7) | 77 | 77 | 77 | 77 | −4 | 76 | 81¾ | 500 |
| 64¼ | 26 | Glidden Co. (m2) | 30¼ | 32 | 26 | 27 | −9 | 25 | 30 | 19,500 |
| 106⅛ | 100¾ | Glidden Co. pr. pf. (7)* | 102 | 102 | 100¾ | 100¾ | −3¼ | 100¾ | 103 | 60 |
| 66 | 10 | Gobel (Adolf) | 10 | 11 | 10 | 11 | −5¼ | 11 | 12 | 10,800 |
| 82 | 31½ | Gold Dust (2½) | 35 | 39½ | 31½ | 32⅞ | −7½ | .. | .. | 107,000 |
| 105¾ | 42 | Goodrich (B. F.) (4) | 43 | 55 | 42 | 55 | +5 | 55 | 56 | 21,300 |

| 1929 High. | Low. |
|---|---|
| 106 | 81¼ |
| 106⅛ | 81⅛ |
| 113⅞ | 40 |
| 84½ | 40 |
| 110¾ | 80 |
| 95 | 87 |
| 11½ | 4½ |
| 32½ | 13 |
| 88⅝ | 45⅛ |
| 31½ | 14¼ |
| 18 | 7 |
| 100¼ | 88⅞ |
| 72⅝ | 28 |
| 154¾ | 110 |
| 106⅞ | 40 |
| 118 | 96 |
| 46 | 30¼ |
| 108 | 71¼ |
| 113⅜ | 94⅛ |
| 115½ | 90 |
| 48 | 30 |
| 59 | 21⅛ |
| 63 | 40 |
| 114¾ | 60 |
| 255½ | 120½ |
| 24 | 13⅜ |
| 82½ | 50 |
| 105½ | 80 |
| 26 | 11½ |
| 38⅝ | 15 |
| 37¾ | 22½ |
| 87 | 60⅛ |
| 57½ | 24 |
| 35⅝ | 21 |
| 39½ | 20 |
| 7½ | 5 |
| 89⅞ | 30 |
| 104 | 28 |
| 18 | 4⅛ |
| 72⅜ | 29 |
| 125 | 120 |
| 108½ | 59⅛ |
| 29½ | 15⅜ |
| 49⅛ | 35 |
| 34⅞ | 9 |
| 27 | 21½ |
| 105 | 102 |
| 69⅝ | 9¼ |
| 54½ | 20 |
| 122⅞ | 59 |
| 39⅞ | 23¾ |
| 5⅛ | 1 |
| 3⅝ | 1 |
| 321 | 145 |
| 28⅞ | 7 |
| 43⅝ | 10 |
| 3⅞ | 2 |
| 87 | 68¼ |
| 65¾ | 30 |
| 107½ | 99 |
| 101⅝ | 55 |
| 149 | 120 |
| 156⅞ | 49½ |
| 81⅜ | 42 |
| 6½ | 1½ |
| 31⅜ | 3¼ |
| 55⅛ | 27 |
| 81⅞ | 10 |
| 61¾ | 40½ |
| 100⅞ | 20 |
| 67½ | 30 |
| 118⅞ | 40 |
| 240 | 186 |
| 41⅞ | 15⅛ |
| 48¼ | 13 |
| 71 | 12¾ |
| 236¾ | 142 |
| 146 | 140 |
| 145¾ | 64 |
| 86½ | 36 |
| 37¾ | 26¾ |
| 96 | 91 |
| 58 | 15 |
| 210 | 132 |
| 141½ | 138⅛ |
| 122 | 116 |
| 71¾ | 25¼ |
| 17 | 2 |
| 41 | 6⅝ |
| 3⅝ | 1 |
| 144 | 108¼ |
| 91¾ | 35 |
| 98½ | 65 |
| 62⅞ | 25 |
| 156 | 120¼ |
| 113 | 50 |
| 49¾ | 38¼ |
| 256½ | 175 |
| 109¼ | 100 |
| 58⅝ | 38 |
| 90 | 82¾ |
| 379 | 155 |
| 132½ | 80½ |
| 134¾ | 114⅝ |
| 14⅛ | 1 |
| 115 | 108¼ |
| 103 | 96 |
| 290 | 191 |
| 186¾ | 70 |
| 54½ | 51¼ |
| 103⅝ | 99 |
| 64½ | 47½ |
| 118⅞ | 85 |
| 114⅝ | 82 |
| 6⅛ | ⅜ |
| 45 | 19 |
| 64½ | 8 |
| 69⅝ | 17 |
| 99¼ | 82 |
| 10⅞ | 2½ |
| 90 | 75 |
| 95¾ | 50½ |
| 450 | 276 |
| 55 | 31½ |
| 108 | 96⅞ |
| 96½ | 70½ |
| 89½ | 50 |
| 40 | 20½ |
| 98¾ | 51 |
| 37 | 22 |
| [illegible] | [illegible] |
| [illegible] | 59 |
| [illegible] | 116⅞ |

Alas for President Herbert Hoover, whose cheerful plans for a statesmanlike term of office were wrecked by the onrushing economic storm. He called conferences, issued many reassuring statements, but they were all to no avail.

The panic—which did not end with the sixteen-million-share day, but went on smashing prices until November 13, 1929—was no mere matter of a bunch of speculators losing their shirts, while other investors simply saw the paper value of their securities diminish. It was much worse than that.

For in the first place, great numbers of people who had bought stock on margin—paying only a part of the purchase price—had to sell everything they owned in the vain attempt to protect their holdings, and were stripped clean of their lifetime savings. In the second place, so many billions of dollars had been loaned to brokers to carry margin accounts that when prices collapsed the whole credit structure was shaken. And in the third place, all sorts of business undertakings, such as the great systems of holding companies, had been predicated on high security prices and now were badly undermined.

What was politely called a "recession" in business began, and after a brief recovery in the spring of 1930, and a preposterous "Little Bull Market," continued its discouraging course. The Great Depression was under way. Lucky Calvin Coolidge, who no longer had to sit in the seat of authority while a catastrophe quite outside his experience overtook the country! He had retired to Northampton, where he and Mrs. Coolidge in due course moved from their duplex apartment on Massasoit Street to a fine house, The Beeches, scene of the photograph below. He was writing magazine articles and—until he ran out of ideas—a syndicated newspaper column. The turn of economic events depressed him deeply, but at least he did not have to cope with it.

As the depression deepened, businesses thre
off employees in a grim attempt to make bo
ends meet; factories laid off hands, cut wag
Each reduction in the working populatic
each wage cut, diminished the purchasi
power for goods. And so unemployment gre
and grew—with no means of relief open
those whose funds were exhausted but
appeal (if and when they could conquer the
shame) to private charity. For state reli
funds were inadequate, and there was
federal relief. At the left you may see wh
happened in Cleveland at the end of 19
when the George H. Bowman Co. store
Euclid Avenue advertised that it would ta
on 150 people for Christmas holiday jo
applicants surged about the building. (No
how many of these people were well dresse
You can be very hungry a long time befo
your good clothes give out.) Below, jobl
New Yorkers, at the end of 1930, are engag
in selling apples on the sidewalk.

# ESTIMATED UNEMPLOYMENT

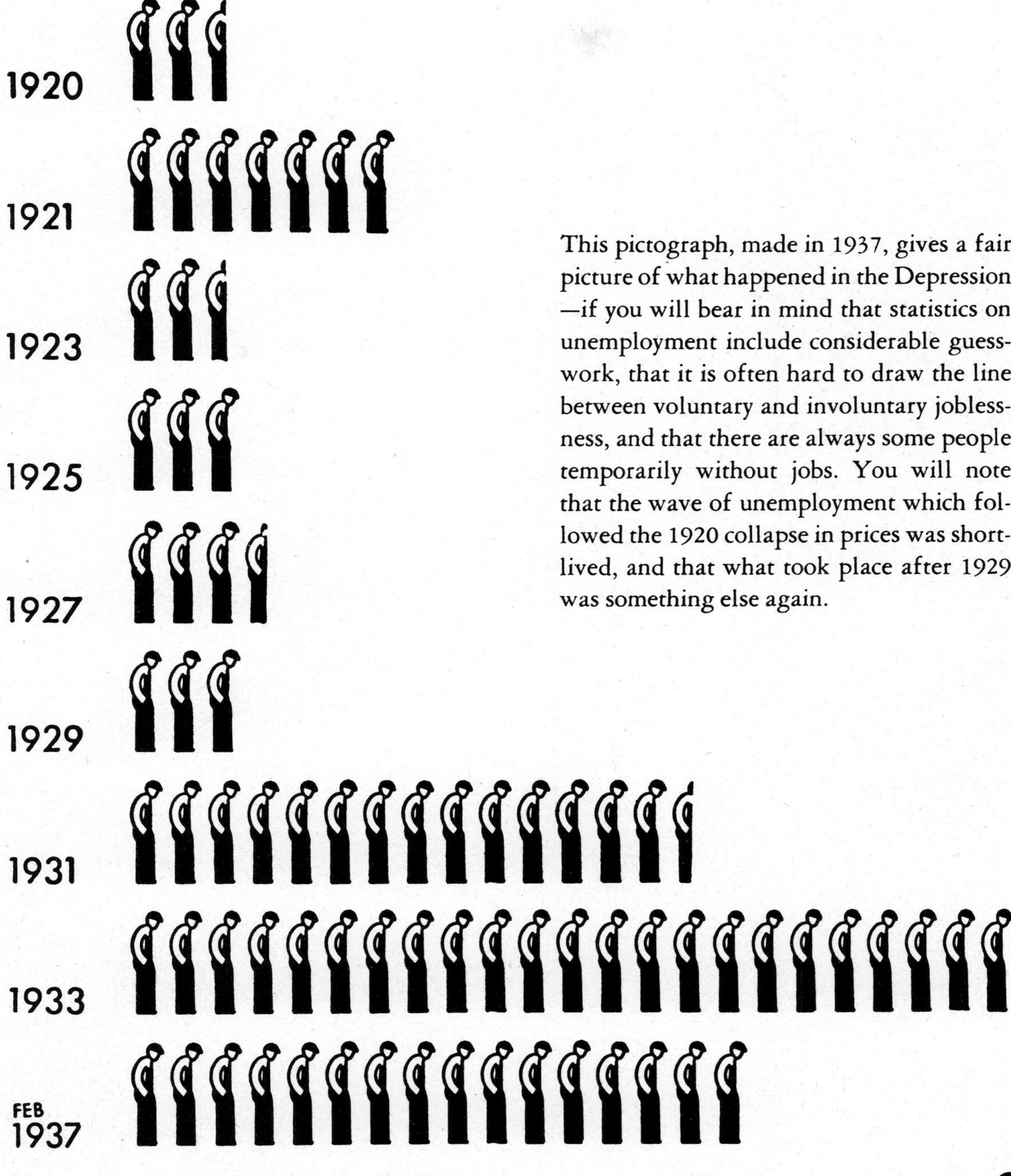


Each figure represents 600,000 unemployed

©

This pictograph, made in 1937, gives a fair picture of what happened in the Depression —if you will bear in mind that statistics on unemployment include considerable guess-work, that it is often hard to draw the line between voluntary and involuntary jobless-ness, and that there are always some people temporarily without jobs. You will note that the wave of unemployment which followed the 1920 collapse in prices was short-lived, and that what took place after 1929 was something else again.

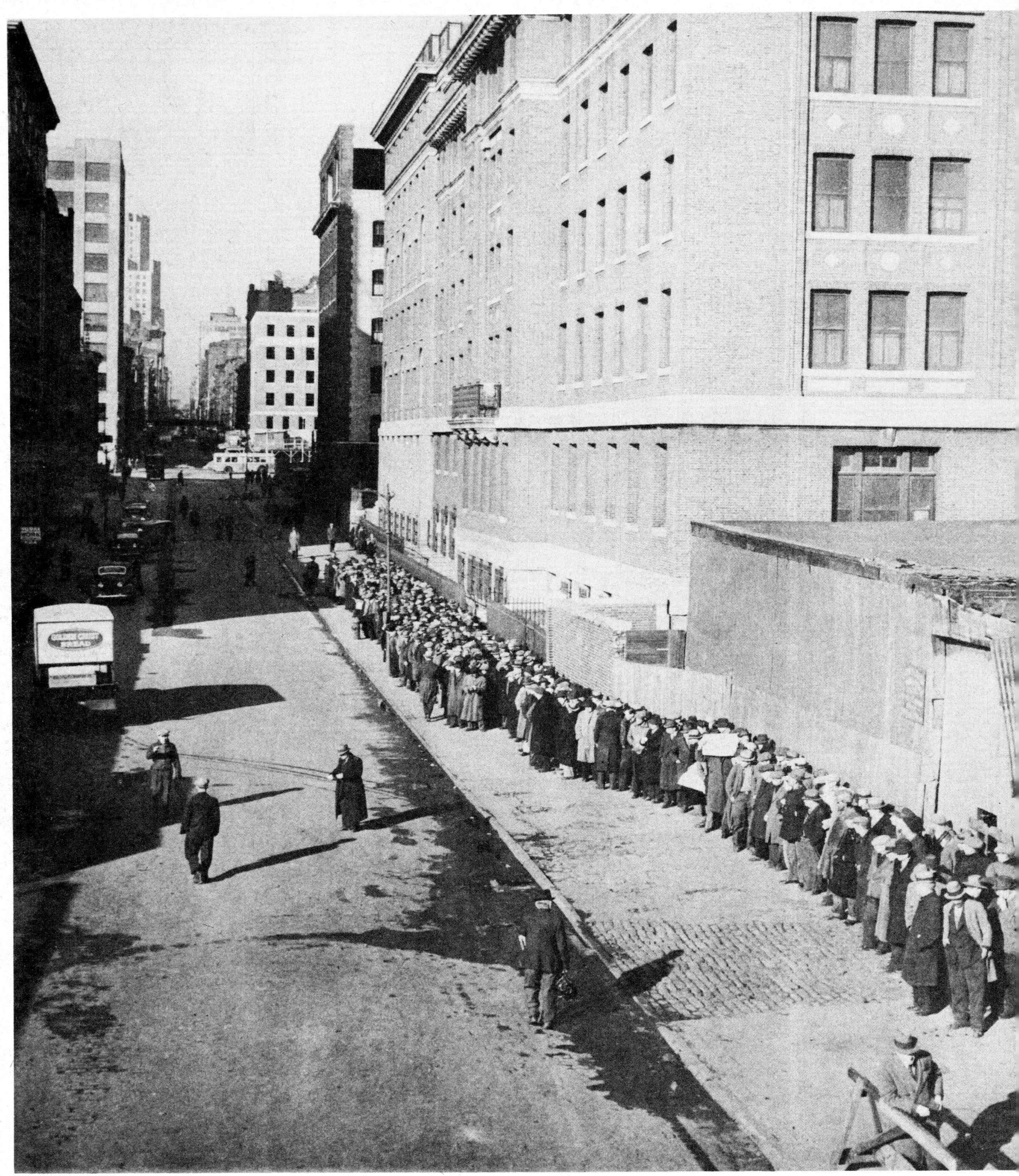

One of the strangest things about the Depression was that it was so nearly invisible to the casual eye (and to the camera, for that matter). To be sure, the streets were less crowded with trucks than they had been, many shops stood vacant, there were many beggars and panhandlers pleading for money, the railroads ran shorter trains (with pullmans sometimes almost empty), and chimneys which should have been smoking were not doing so. But these were all negative phenomena. There just didn't seem to be many people about. (In the mid-forties, by contrast, there seemed to be more people than ever before. Poverty stays at home, prosperity is out and about.) One of the few visible signs of trouble was the breadline.

ther sign of trouble: the
n collections of shacks on va-
t lots, cruelly called "hoover-
es." The upper view is of a
verville on the Seattle water-
nt in March 1933. At the
t is a shack, made of barrels
tar paper, on the river shore
t. Louis; one of a mile-long
of such makeshift huts. The
ure was taken in 1931.

In the terrible summer of 1932 a "Bonus Army" of unemployed veterans gathered in Washington, demonstrated (above) on the Capitol steps, settled themselves (below) in Anacostia Park, and were dispersed in Washington's streets by federal troops.

Under the circumstances, the patience of the American people was extraordinary. They shared the bewilderment of Charles M. Schwab, the great steel executive ("I'm afraid, every man is afraid. I don't know, we don't know, whether the values we have are going to be real next month or not"), and of Andrew W. Mellon, Ambassador to Great Britain and former Secretary of the Treasury ("None of us has any means of knowing when and how we shall emerge from the valley of depression in which the world is traveling"), and of ex-President Coolidge ("We all hope it will end, but we don't see it yet"). If a Morgan partner was alleged to have said, "As for the cause of the Depression, or the way out, you know as much as I do," how could ordinary men and women tell what had hit them? They tried, here and there, unorthodox schemes such as barter and the use of scrip currency; they were fascinated by such cure-all notions as Social Credit and Howard Scott's Technocracy; sometimes they were goaded by desperation into lawlessness—as when farmers simply refused to let foreclosure sales take place; but the vast majority took their adversity with astonishing calmness. Above, we show a group of radical "hunger marchers" gathering in New York for a "march on Washington" in November 1932, with Red banners and the chanting of the Internationale. But in the election held that month, the Communists had polled only 102,991 votes, the Socialists only 884,781—out of a total of 39,816,522!

Gentlemen like the subject of the cartoon at the right (by Perry Barlow in *The New Yorker* for February 27, 1932) tended to think at first that the depression was caused by "lack of confidence," and to repeat the slogan, "Prosperity is just around the corner," but after a while those words seemed to lose their savor. Of course, one could discharge most of one's servants and make out bravely without them, but it was awful just the same: Insull going broke, Kreuger killing himself (and proving to have been a crook), bond prices diving, many banks in trouble; Steel common (which had been over 260 in 1929) at the miserable price of 21¼; Radio at 2½; General Motors at 7⅝; the federal budget unbalanced. And was a revolution coming?

*"Imperial Can dropped eight points, sir. The temperature in New York today is fifty degrees. Sorry, sir."*

• •

*"Mr. St. Pierre called. He wants to know if you can squeeze in some handball this afternoon."*

And even those who most wanted to work h and get things done often found that even if t had jobs, there was very little to do except sit watch the business on which they had built b their income and their pride slowly crumble aw For such people it was a relief to be remin that the situation had humorous aspects—as in Steig drawing, in *The New Yorker,* of an auto bile salesman dozing, and another man shaking h and shouting, "Hey, wake up! I'm a prospect! or as in the Perry Barlow drawing at the left, fr *The New Yorker.* March 12, 1932.

If Americans didn't go in for revolution when hard times came, they went in for gambling. The stock market having proved a bad bet, they not only patronized slot machines, succumbed to the numbers racket, and played the horses to an extent which belied their poverty, but went in for various new gambles. There was bingo, a game so respectable that it became an institution even at church suppers. (It is pictured on page 191.) There was pinball, which originated in 1932—and in its simpler forms could be played simply for fun, as a game of skill, at a nickel a throw. There was that bright solace of the movie-house proprietors, bank night, which was introduced in Colorado in 1932-33, and swept the country. There was the chain-letter epidemic, rampant in the mid-thirties ("Scratch out the top name and send a dime"). And among the first of the novelties in gambling was the institution illustrated above.

Our picture is not of a scene from a musical show, but of the "Fairyland" setting for the draw in the Irish Hospitals Derby Sweepstakes, held in the Mansion House, Dublin, Eire—a lottery for which tickets were sold all over the world. It has been estimated that in 1933, at the bottom of the Depression, something like 400,000 American tickets got into the draw—and heaven only knows how many more were bought and never reached Ireland. Presently word would come that some humble housewife or jobless janitor had won $150,000, and the rest of us would wonder what it was like to be suddenly rich, and interviewed, and put on the sucker lists.

The heyday of the gangsters went right on. The law at las caught up with Capone and he went to Alcatraz—but the fac that he went on income-tax charges only advertised the helpless ness of the ordinary forces of the law. By now small boys all ove the country were playing gangster in the streets, with ver pretty imitations of the rat-tat-tat of a sub-machine gun. No could New Yorkers claim that racketeering was a Chicago in stitution. For Arnold Rothstein, murdered in 1928, had been big financier of underworld business; Arthur Flegenheime ("Dutch Schultz"), taking control of the "numbers" racket i Harlem, was said to run it to the tune of a million dollars a year and as for splendor, the funerals of Frankie Uale and "Joe th Baker" were said to have cost $40,000 or more apiece—large sums than had been spent on the obsequies of Dion O'Banion i Chicago. At the left is a New York hoodlum, Jack ("Legs") Diamond, temporarily in the hands of the law in Troy, New York, in July 1931, a few months before he came to an en ironically suggestive of the status of the gangster in society; h was shot to death while lying drunk after celebrating his acquit tal! Below are Edward G. Robinson (right) and Sidney Blackme in a scene from a gangster movie, "Little Caesar."

In the year 1930—the year when millions of people were discovering the nightly delight of listening to Amos 'n' Andy over the radio, and Bobby Jones won his quadruple crown, and women's dresses began to exhibit ruffles and flounces, and their evening gowns actually touched the ground, and business men and public officials were tirelessly repeating that "business was fundamentally sound" though very clearly it wasn't, and the Little Bull Market pushed stock prices up and then faded out in a long, new liquidation—in that year a new fad arrived: miniature golf. Garnet Carter of Lookout Mountain, Tennessee, had built a little "Tom Thumb Golf Course," and late in the summer of 1929 he had gone to Miami to install one there, and the thing had caught on, and by the summer of 1930 miniature golf courses were springing up everywhere by the roadside—putters and balls provided by the management, greenswards made of cottonseed hulls, and pipes through which your ball must roll. (Driving ranges became popular the next year.) It was great fun, for a time, to stop your car by a miniature course and have a game; but it was perhaps a sign of the state to which economic thinking had descended that some people seriously claimed that this industry might lift the country out of Depression.

High, during those years of the downswing, rose the vogue of contract bridge. It was in the toboggan-slide year 1931 that Mr. and Mrs. Ely Culbertson played a contract match with Sidney Lenz and Oswald Jacoby which was flashed over the news wires, play by play, from the Hotel Chatham in New York to an eager public. Sales of playing cards did not slip that year, when almost everything else did; they actually gained. Above are Mr. and Mrs. Culbertson in 1931. That was long before he proposed a plan for world security.

At the beginning of the nineteen-thirties Hollywood was still struggling with the new problems of the talking picture—importing dramatists and actors from Broadway, limiting the power of the director to tinker with the script, and improving the quality of sound production. Below is a scene from the movie made from Remarque's *All Quiet on the Western Front,* produced by Universal in 1930.

Remember Marie Dressler, a veteran imported from Broadway (she had sung "Heaven will protect the working girl" in "Tillie's Nightmare" way back in 1910), who became one of the largest—in two senses—moneymakers among Hollywood actresses? At the left, she is acting with Wallace Beery in "Min and Bill" (1930).

Below: Boris Karloff and Dwight Frye, in "Frankenstein" (1931), set a fashion in pictures which was to cause a good many shrieks in movie theatres.

The foremost actress in the Hollywood of the early nineteen-thirties was unquestionably the lovely and elusive Greta Garbo, shown here as she appeared in "Romance" in 1930.

October 1931 saw the production by the Theatre Guild of Eugene O'Neill's trilogy, "Mourning Becomes Electra," which as Rosamond Gilder said "turned to the Greeks for its theme, to Freud for its psychology, to New England for its setting." It was acclaimed by many as a work even greater than his "Strange Interlude" (1928). Alla Nazimova, Alice Brady, and Earle Larimore played the leads before Robert Edmond Jones's set of the Mannons' pillared portico.

O'Neill was not the only dramatist to give distinction to the American theatre in the years of the onrushing Depression. There were many fine plays, and at least one musical comedy which broke new ground, incorporating mature political satire into a very funny show. This was "Of Thee I Sing," by Kaufman and Ryskind, with music by the Gershwins, Victor Moore as the gentle Vice President Throttlebottom, and the slogan, "Posterity is just around the corner." But perhaps the most memorable play of the period was "The Green Pastures," by Marc Connelly, produced in February 1930. At the left is a scene from this play, with Richard B. Harrison taking, in a frock coat, the part of "de Lawd."

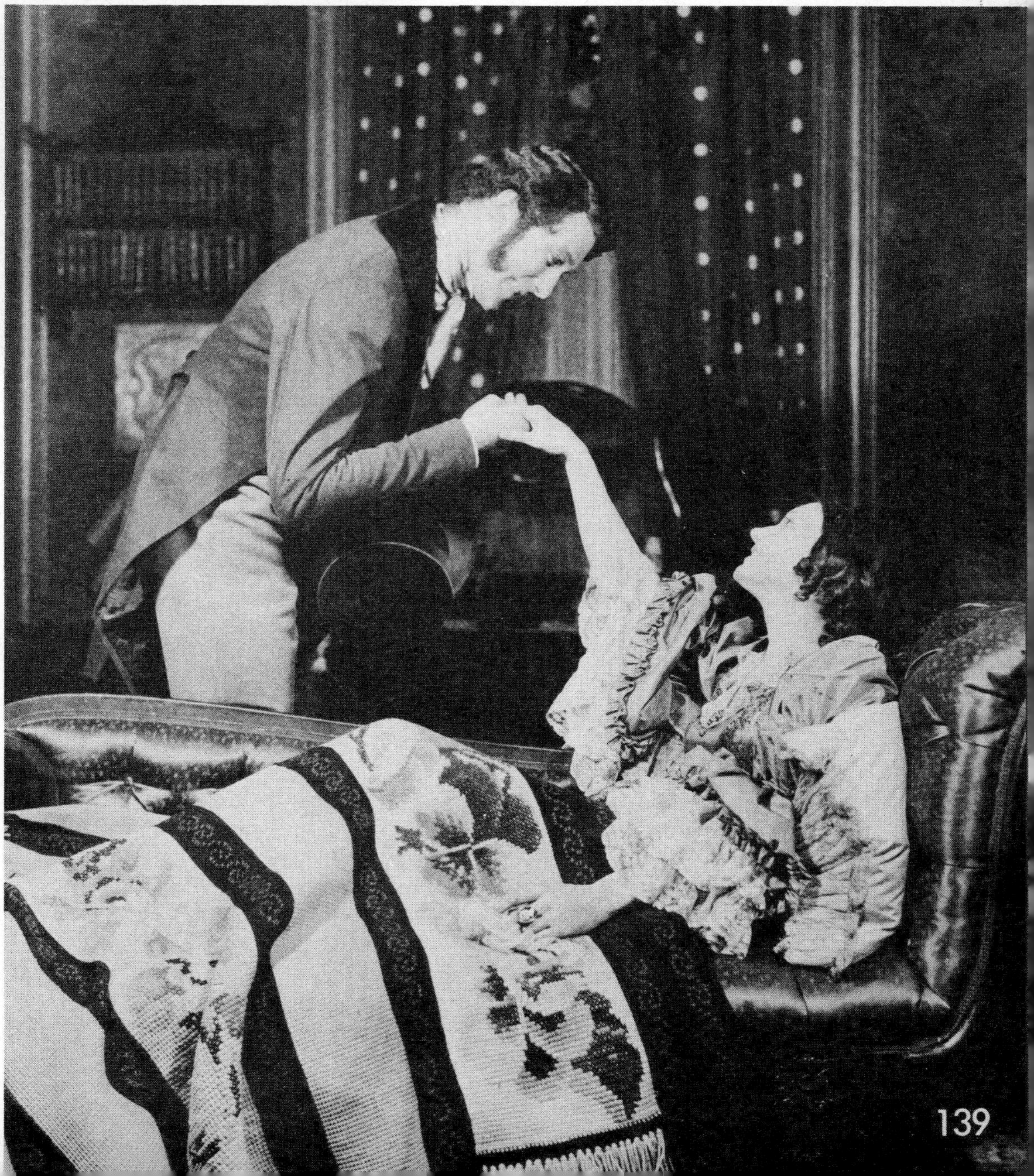

Katharine Cornell made a great popular success in 1931 in "The Barretts of Wimpole Street"—in which we see her at the right, playing the part of the invalid poetess, Elizabeth Barrett, receiving the attentions of Robert Browning (Brian Aherne).

THE STORY
OF
SAN
MICHELE

AXEL
MUNTHE

*The Illustrated Edition*
*With a New Preface by the Author*

Here are the jackets of three books which held the attent of American readers during the downhill years. *The Story San Michele,* after a slow start, became the non-fiction b seller of 1930 (while Edna Ferber's *Cimarron* led the novel *The Good Earth,* published in 1931, received both critical a popular acclaim and headed the fiction best-seller list for t successive years, 1931 and 1932. It was followed the n year by Hervey Allen's *Anthony Adverse,* a long histori novel whose sensational popularity set in motion a wave oversized historical romances which rolled on and on duri the rest of the decade. Were Americans, in their addiction such books, trying to escape the ugly present? Perhaps; note too that the non-fiction best seller of the climactic y 1933 was Walter B. Pitkin's *Life Begins at Forty,* wh offered solace to men and women whose early ambitions h been wrecked by the Depression.

If you don't recognize the men at the left, or even their names, Freeman F. Gosden and Charles J. Correll, don't be ashamed. But you probably know their voices, and you certainly did if you listened to the radio in 1930, when they introduced millions of people to "Amos 'n' Andy." At the left below is the late Floyd Gibbons, the former war correspondent (he had lost the sight of one eye at Château-Thierry in 1918) who became a fast-talking radio reporter; at the right, below, is Ted Husing, as he gave a play-by-play account of a World Series base ball game in 1932.

Here is a sound-effects man of 1930, with a few of the devices then used to convey noises to radio audiences. They have now been largely supplanted by records.

Prices and personal fortunes were not the only things that crumbled during the Depression; another thing that went down was America's pride in her great rigid airships. The German *Graf Zeppelin* made hundreds of long flights without misadventure; the *Los Angeles,* American-operated but German-built, survived a long career in the air before she was decommissioned for economy's sake in 1932. But the American-built *Shenandoah* broke up in a line squall over Ohio in 1925, with a loss of 14 lives; and an even more complete tragedy awaited the *Akron,* which went into commission in the autumn of 1931.

On the page at the left is the vast *Akron*—as big as an ocean liner—as she lay in her hangar in the summer of 1931, with her already assembled crew. After seventeen months of operation she was lost early in 1933 in a storm off Barnegat Light on the New Jersey coast, and 73 out of 76 men aboard her were lost. Below, you will see the largest piece of her to be salvaged; the port fin, as it rested on the deck of a salvage ship after having been hauled up from the ocean bottom.

There was still one more rigid dirigible to come, the *Macon,* which went into service that same year (1933). She broke up and was sunk off Point Sur, California, in 1935, bringing a chapter of American aeronautical history to a close. (The flaming end of the *Hindenburg* is shown on page 178.)

THE BANK OF UNITED STATES
THE BANK OF UNITED STATES
UNITED CIGARS

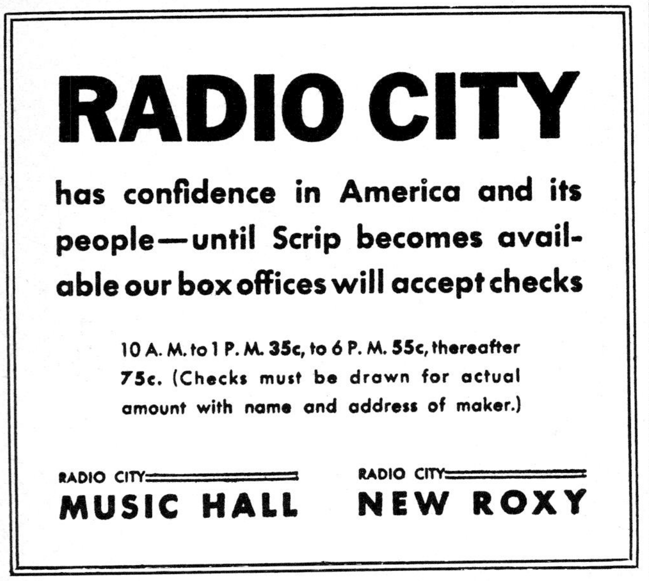

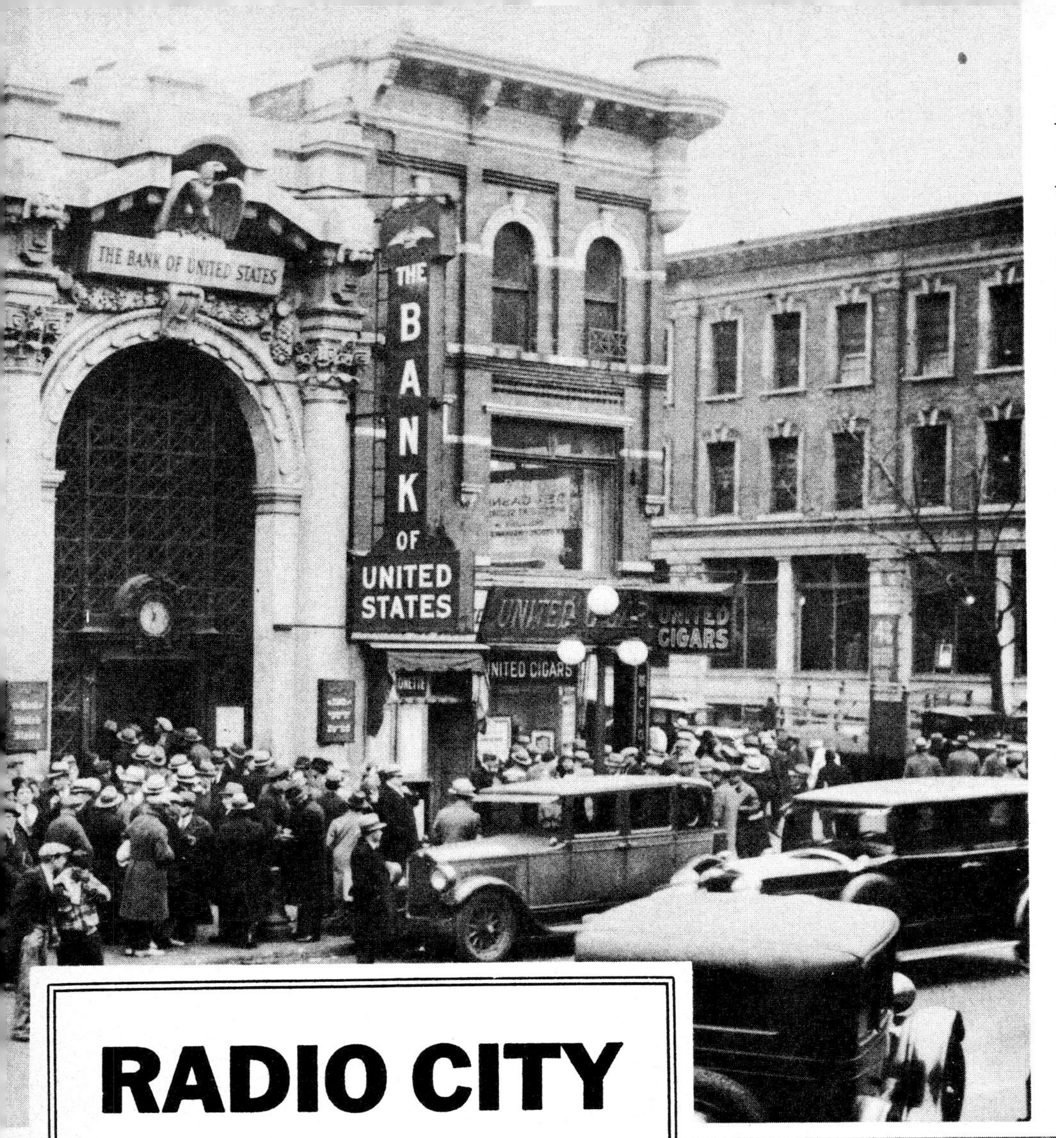

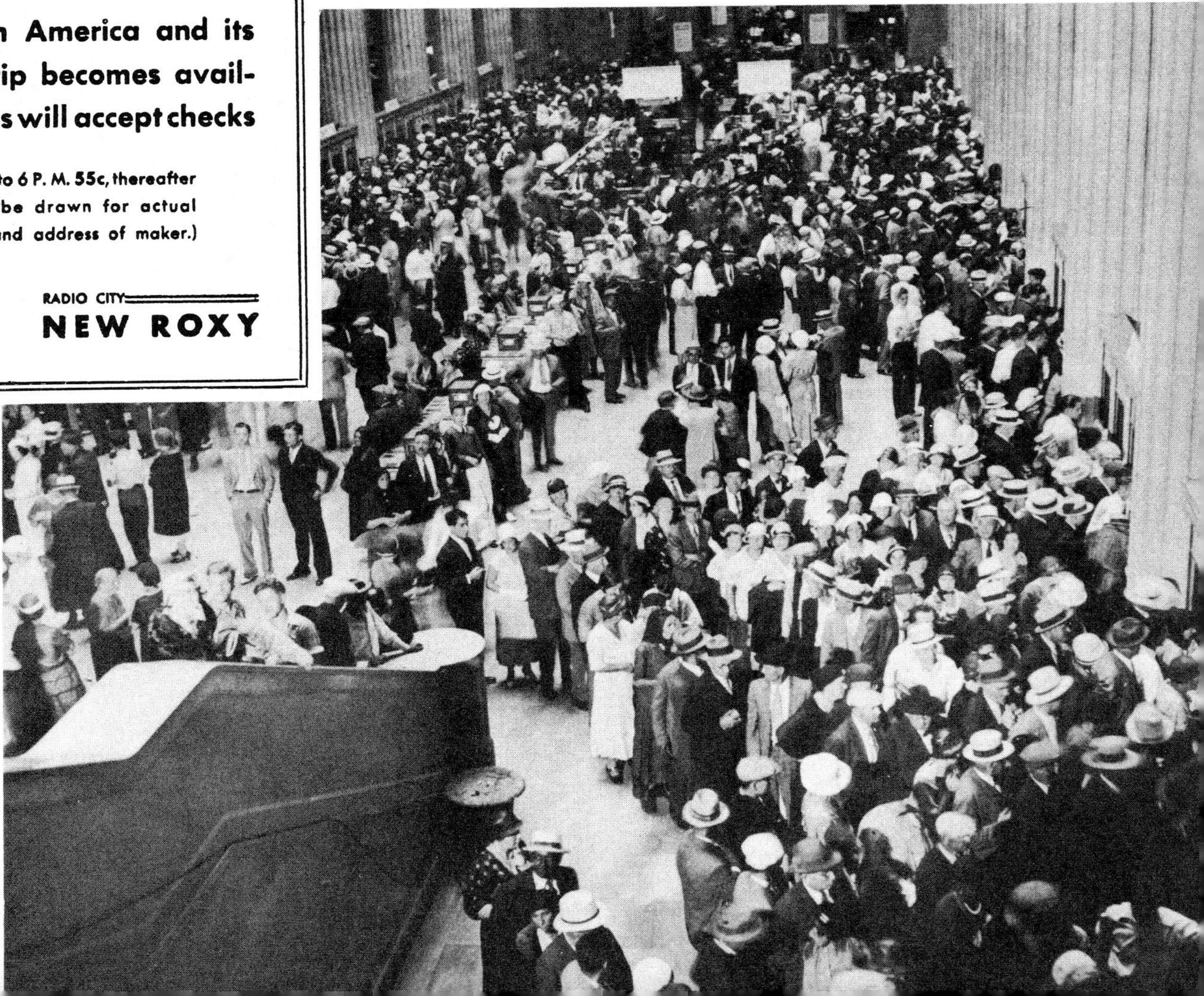

RADIO CITY
has confidence in America and its people—until Scrip becomes available our box offices will accept checks
10 A. M. to 1 P. M. 35c, to 6 P. M. 55c, thereafter 75c. (Checks must be drawn for actual amount with name and address of maker.)
RADIO CITY
MUSIC HALL
RADIO CITY
NEW ROXY

A disturbing feature of the collapse of 1929-33 was the way in which the drop in security values and the fall of business empires undermined the banks. One of the earliest to go was the flagrantly mismanaged Bank of United States, in New York; at the left you see the crowds waiting unhappily about the doors of a branch in the Bronx after the bank was closed in December 1930. The panic grew widespread and intense early in 1933, culminating in the closing of every bank in the country on March 4, 1933—the day Hoover left office and Roosevelt came in.

The Radio City advertisement appeared in New York papers on March 7, 1933, and was typical of the "bank holiday" period, when the government was expected to issue temporary scrip. Other advertisements urged customers to use their charge accounts now.

Below is one of the scenes of the aftermath: depositors of the Union Trust Company in Cleveland, which failed, are filing up to the windows months afterwards, in July 1933, to draw out what is left of their deposits.

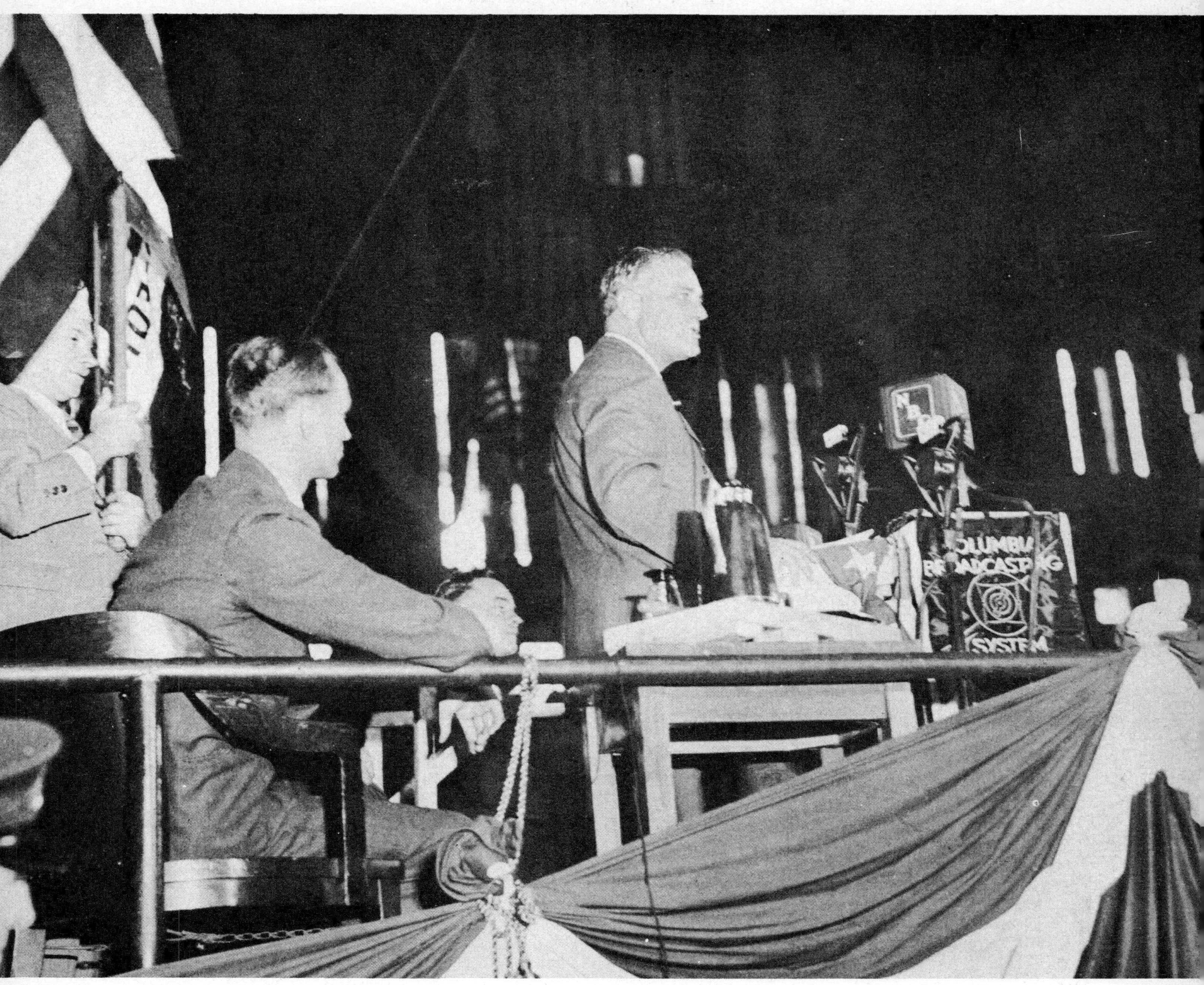


Hoover tried to stop the Depression, and failed. He stood stubbornly for a principle—that the federal government must not give money to individual Americans, lest it undermine local responsibility and individual character—and was a martyr to this principle. For to people in desperate trouble it looked stingy and cruel. As the crisis worsened in 1932, Hoover's chances for re-election dwindled.

The Democrats, taking hope, held a hot and stormy national convention at Chicago and nominated the man you see above. (He is making the acceptance speech that he flew from Albany to Chicago to deliver; his son, James Roosevelt, sits at his elbow.) Roosevelt was by no means a radical. When he had run for the vice presidency in 1920—the year before infantile paralysis struck him down—the *Commercial & Financial Chronicle,* hardly a hot-headed publication, had described him as "an experienced and energetic public man, with conservative opinions on public questions"; and though his character had deepened since his illness, and he had acquired solid executive experience as governor of New York, he had certainly not gained a reputation as a firebrand, and to many he seemed to have more political ambition than political courage. But he liked innovation—witness his flying to Chicago—and he knew that great crises require bold measures; and so he gathered about him a group of intelligent young "brain trusters," and plenty of political advisers, and from these varied sources he drew a mixed program, part progressive, part conservative, that at least promised manifold action—and also was well calculated to win votes. He campaigned vigorously, radiated charm, and won in a landslide.

But not until March 4, 1933—the day when he took office—did Roosevelt's stature become really impressive.

"All the News That's Fit to Print."

# The New York Times.

LATE CITY EDITION
WEATHER—Fair and slightly warmer today and tomorrow.

Copyright, 1933, by The New York Times Company.

VOL. LXXXII....No. 27,401. Entered as Second-Class Matter, Postoffice, New York, N. Y. NEW YORK, TUESDAY, JANUARY 31, 1933. TWO CENTS In New York City | THREE CENTS Within 200 Miles | FOUR CENTS Elsewhere Except in 7th and 8th Postal Zones

## HITLER MADE CHANCELLOR OF GERMANY BUT COALITION CABINET LIMITS POWER; CENTRISTS HOLD BALANCE IN REICHSTAG

### GROUP FORMED BY PAPEN

Nationalists to Dominate in Government Led by National Socialist.

DR. HUGENBERG GETS POST

Frick in Interior Ministry to Control Police, but Army Has Non-Partisan Chief.

REDS URGE STRIKE TODAY

Cabinet Stresses That It Will Not Attempt Monetary or Economic Experiments.

By GUIDO ENDERIS.
Special Cable to THE NEW YORK TIMES.

BERLIN, Jan. 30.—Adolf Hitler, leader of the National Socialist party, today was appointed Chancellor of Germany after being twice rejected last year for that office.

### Hitler Pledges Fight in Cabinet

By the Associated Press.

BERLIN, Jan. 30.—A proclamation emphasizing that the present Cabinet is not truly representative of Hitlerism and the nation was issued today by the new Chancellor, Adolf Hitler. In it the Nazi leader announced a determination to "carry on the fight within the government as tenaciously as we fought outside."

"After a thirteen-year struggle the National Socialist movement has succeeded in breaking through to the government; the struggle to win the German nation, however, is only beginning," the proclamation said.

"The National Socialist party knows that the new government is no National Socialist Government, but it is conscious that it bears the name of its leader, Adolf Hitler. He has advanced with his shock troops and has placed himself at the head of the government to lead the German people to liberty.

"Not only is the entire authority of State ready to be wielded, but in the background, prepared for action, is the National Socialist movement of millions of followers united unto death with its leaders. Our historic mission is now in the field of political economy."

Calling Herr Hitler's appointment "historic," the document lauded President von Hindenburg with these words:

"In this hour we wish to thank President von Hindenburg, whose immortal fame as a Field Marshal in the battlefields of the World War binds his name perpetually to that of young Germany, which is striving with burning heart to gain its liberty."

### MODERATE CABINET PLANNED IN FRANCE

### HOOVER SKEPTICAL OF SUCCESS ON DEBT

## NEW BRITISH RATES AFFECT U. S. GOODS FINISHED IN CANADA

After April 1, 50 Per Cent 'Empire Content' Is Required for Preferential Duty.

1,000 PLANTS INVOLVED

Many Expected to Be Moved to England or Withdrawn to United States.

HUGE CAPITAL AT STAKE

$1,500,000,000 Invested in Factories in Dominion—Political Struggle There Foreseen.

Special Cable to THE NEW YORK TIMES.

LONDON, Jan. 30.—United States manufacturers who apply minor finishing touches on their goods in Canada and then send them to Great Britain under imperial tariff preferences as "empire goods" will lose that privilege under an order issued by the Board of Trade tonight.

"Certain classes of empire goods imported into Britain," the order says, "in order to qualify for the imperial preferences agreed upon at Ottawa, must contain in the future a minimum of 50 per cent of empire material and labor instead of 25 per cent as at present."

The regulation will go into effect April 1. The list of goods affected

## MORTGAGEES STAY $200,000,000 DEBT OF IOWA'S FARMERS

Insurance Companies Here Act to Suspend Foreclosures Pending Legal Relief.

GOVERNOR'S PLEA HEEDED

Policy Announced by New York Life Followed by Other Eastern Organizations.

NEBRASKA NAMES BOARD

Bryan Appoints Seven Conciliators as Debtors' Resistance Drive Spreads Through West.

In the most extensive private effort to cooperate with the owners of mortgaged farms ever made, a number of the leading Eastern life insurance companies, with nearly $200,000,000 invested in Iowa farms, have decided to suspend foreclosure activities throughout that State until the Legislature can enact its program to improve the position of the debtors.

This decision became known yesterday after the publication of an announcement of such a policy in behalf of his own company only, by Thomas A. Buckner, president of the New York Life Insurance Company. This company has been the object of stormy criticism in

## LEHMAN ASKS $84,000,000 IN NEW TAXES, 1% ON '33 GROSS INCOMES, ¾% ON SALES; STATE BUDGET CUT 23% TO $234,998,531

### Gov. Lehman's Revenue Proposals

Special to THE NEW YORK TIMES.

*ALBANY, Jan. 30.—Governor Lehman's chief proposals on the budget included the following:*

INCOME TAXES—Lowering of exemptions for a single person from $2,500 to $1,000 and a married person from $4,000 to $2,500, the $400 exemption for dependents to remain unchanged. Emergency rate to be continued. Establishment of a 1 per cent gross income tax, no personal exemption allowed, on every single person whose income is $1,000 or more and every married person whose income is $2,500 or more. Capital gains and losses excluded, and interest, bad debts, contributions and other actual losses subtracted. This tax, an emergency levy for one year, to be in addition to the regular State income tax. Both the lowered exemption and the emergency tax to be applicable on 1933 incomes, payable in April, 1934.

SALES TAX—Enactment of a three-quarter of 1 per cent levy on retail sales of all tangible personal property, exclusive of food products and motor fuel, effective from April 1, 1933, to June 30, 1934.

MOTOR FUEL TAX— emergency levy ef making the tax p

SALARIES—Reductio $2,000 a year of per cent on that

FEES FOR PAMPHL partments to be preparation and p

PUBLIC SERVICE charge against a such inquiry.

MACHADO SAYS

### CENT ADDED ON GASOLINE

Sales Impost Proposed on All Retail Items Except Food.

FOR LOWER EXEMPTIONS

Governor Suggests Drop of $1,500—Pay Cut for State Employes Urged.

The Depression was worldwide, and brought grim changes elsewhere. Above is part of the front page of the *New York Times* for January 31, 1933; below, a demonstration against Hitler held in front of City Hall, Philadelphia, after he had begun his persecution of the Jews in Germany.

# IV. ALL ABOARD FOR WASHINGTON

It was a smiling, courageous, and contagiously optimistic Roosevelt who took office on March 4, 1933, successfully re-opened the banks, and within a hundred days drove through an overwhelmingly Democratic and happily dazed Congress an extraordinary jumble of legislation. The New Deal program, thus launched, was full of improvisations and inconsistencies, but at least it gave the country a wonderful sense of action and hope. The picture above was taken a year later, on April 13, 1934, when the President, returning to Miami, Florida, after a fishing trip, was greeted by General Hugh Johnson (Mayor Sewall of Miami stands between them, facing the camera, and James Roosevelt is at the right); but it suggests better than any other photograph, perhaps, how the Roosevelt who said in his Inaugural Address, "The only thing we have to fear is fear itself," radiated energy and confidence.

Roosevelt liked to surround himself with a group of unofficial advisers, speech-writers, and confidants—but they were a changing group. The leading figure of his pre-election Brain Trust (or Brains Trust, as he himself called it) was Professor Raymond Moley (above, left); he became disillusioned by the President's capriciousness by the summer of 1933, lingered on the fringes till 1936, and thereafter, on *Newsweek,* was an outspoken opponent. Another early Brain Truster, along with Adolf A. Berle, Jr., was Professor Rexford G. Tugwell (above, right); he was placed in the Agriculture Department, became a chief target of conservative invective, and moved out in 1937. Henry A. Wallace (at the right), not an original Brain Truster but Roosevelt's first Secretary of Agriculture and a trusted friend, stayed with the ship and in 1940 became Vice President; scholar, idealist, able administrator, and combative politician, he remained a center of recurring and violent storms.

At the left, laughingly accompanying Judge Ferdinand Pecora to a Congressional hearing, is a leading figure of what might be called the second Brain Trust, of 1934-36: Tom Corcoran, the effervescent young accordion-playing drafter of bills to regulate business. Below are two more recently familiar faces: those of Harold L. Ickes, the honest curmudgeon who became and remained Secretary of the Interior, and was at intervals a close adviser to Roosevelt; and (standing) Senator James F. Byrnes, who was chosen by Roosevelt for the Supreme Court, then became a leading war administrator, and later was President Truman's able and energetic Secretary of State.

There is no space in these two pages for a complete gallery of presidential intimates and consultants: for Louis Howe, the loyal invalid who was Roosevelt's personal political mentor until he died at the White House in April 1936; for Adolf A. Berle, Jr. of the original Brain Trust or Benjamin Cohen of the second one; for Samuel N. Rosenman, the most durable of the inner group; or for others such as, for example, Henry Morgenthau, Jr., who was Secretary of the Treasury and a devoted follower of the President's shifting financial policies from the day when he took over the Treasury from the dying William H. Woodin. But room there must be for Harry Hopkins, the social worker who was brought to Washington to head up the government's vast relief enterprise (which in 1935 took shape in the WPA), who was later Secretary of Commerce, and who during Roosevelt's last years was closest to him of all, living at the White House and serving as confidant and troubleshooter on all manner of things, both domestic and foreign. Hopkins is shown at the left as he looked in 1938, at the Washington Senators' opening baseball game of the season.

The NRA, with the Blue Eagle as its symbol and the rambunctious General Hugh Johnson as its leader, was the most spectacular — if short-lived—of the early New Deal organizations. It is hard to believe, now, with what fanfare it was launched. Here is New York's NRA parade, 250,000 strong, going up Fifth Avenue (past 42nd Street) on September 13, 1933.

From the pinnacle of prestige, the bankers and brokers descended step by step to the doghouse. When the Panic first broke, a mere report that the leading bankers were meeting at "the Corner"—23 Wall Street, headquarters of J. P. Morgan & Co.—had been enough to rally the market. But as the Depression wore on, the awe decreased; and when congressional investigations disclosed many a shabby boomtime financial practice, all financiers, the incorruptible along with the rapacious, shared in the public disrepute. Above are the three leading men of the leading financial house—Thomas W. Lamont (at the left), George Whitney, and J. P. Morgan, conferring at one of the numerous investigations. At the right is a sample of the gross impertinence which bankers now had to swallow; during a session of the Senate Banking Committee in the late spring of 1933, a man placed a circus midget on J. P. Morgan's knee, to the photographers' joy.

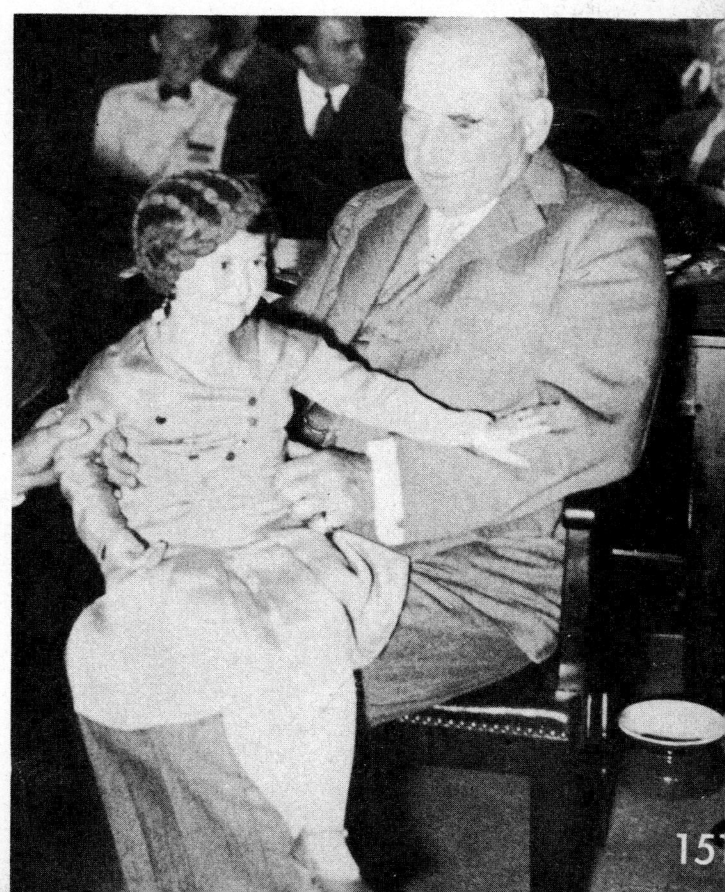

How were the mighty fallen! At the left are O. P. and M. J. Van Sweringen, railroad holding-company promoters, looking sadder and wiser in 1933; above is Ivar Kreuger, the Swedish match king, who fixed his books and then killed himself in 1932; below (with Arnold L. Stuart and Samuel Insull, Jr.) is Samuel Insull, just before his acquittal in 1935, following the catastrophic collapse of his financial empire.

The crowning—or was it anti-climactic?—note of irony was added years later, after Wall Street had been thoroughly chastened and put under regulation. When the Panic first broke on October 24, 1929, it had been Richard Whitney, vice president of the Stock Exchange, who had acted for the big bankers to stem the tide of selling: it was he who had walked out on the Stock Exchange floor to put in an order to buy Steel at 205. Subsequently he had been president of the Exchange. And now in 1938 he was discovered to have been misappropriating trust funds, and went to Sing Sing! Below, he is being sworn in at an open hearing on his tangled affairs.

# WORKS PROGRAM EMPLOYMENT

JULY 1935

DEC. 1935

JULY 1936

DEC. 1936

Each man represents 200,000 people employed

If you find the pictures on this page unexciting, there's little wonder. For they record a dreary chapter in our national experience. When the soaring hopes of the Hundred Days faded, when business expanded, slumped, and then stagnated in 1934 and 1935, the New Deal, committed to the idea of federal responsibility for relief, tried this and that system and in 1935 set up the WPA. The idea was magnificent: no more handouts, but pay for honest work. But what work? It must not compete with private business—and useful projects which did not were hard to find. Hence "boondoggles" — which originally meant weaving belts out of ropes, and came to mean silly or useless projects generally. In the chart at the left you will see how the WPA grew in 1935 and did not shrink much in 1936, though times were better. It remained large, for it was habit-forming; always open to political manipulation; and, despite some fine imaginative projects, an unhappy measure of our failure really to lift ourselves out of Depression.

Above is a typical WPA scene in a city—timbermen laying forms for concrete-pouring in New York in 1937. At the right, WPA men on a useful rural job, building an earth fill and drop inlet to replace a bridge on a road near Blair, Nebraska

Happier in its general effect was the CCC—Civilian Conservation Corps—which put young men, otherwise jobless, into rural camps where they did conservation work in the forests and National Parks. At the right, a CCC boy is planting trees; below, another one is helping to put out a forest fire.

Building the Fort Loudon Dam, one of the units of the TVA.

The most magnificent and widely useful of the New Deal projects authorized during the Hundred Days was the TVA—Tennessee Valley Authority—which not only built dams on the Tennessee River and provided public electric power (over which there was a great battle with the private utilities, led for a time by Wendell L. Willkie) but helped the farmers of the region to rehabilitate their farms. Few recent developments in America have won more worldwide attention than the TVA. Above, visitors at the Watts Bar Dam look from the control building down upon the powerhouse; at the right is the Norris Dam switchyard.

America's men of wealth, and her successful business men generally, watched the New Deal half hopefully —some of them enthusiastically—during the Hundred Days of 1933. They had been badly battered during the Great Nosedive; Roosevelt's first moves had been encouraging and exciting; and anything was better, anyhow, than to see prices sliding downhill. But they lost their equanimity when, later in 1933, the President tried to restore prosperity by raising the price of gold (with no very noticeable effect on the volume of business). They became deeply angry when—as if they hadn't had trouble enough already—he drove ahead with regulatory legislation in 1934 and 1935. And they burned red hot when in the 1936 campaign he threw restraint to the winds, called them "economic royalists," and talked as if he were enlisting the American people in a holy war against them. They looked with acute disfavor upon Tugwell, Corcoran, Cohen, Wallace, and others, and many of them ridiculed the peripatetic Mrs. Roosevelt; but it was "That Man," a "traitor to his class," who really stoked the fires of their wrath. No chronicle of the interwar years would be complete without mention of their prolonged and wonderful incandescence. Since this was not readily recorded by photographers, we reproduce two of the numerous cartoons with which *The New Yorker* deftly held it up to satirical attention.

Richard Decker's cartoon appeared in *The New Yorker* for May 2, 1936, before Roosevelt had coined the "economic royalist" phrase. Those were the days when the Supreme Court had already invalidated the NRA, the AAA, and other New Deal laws, and gentlemen like Stewart spoke very reverently about it—somewhat more so than in subsequent years.

*"Now, Stewart, you know the doctor told you that you shouldn't talk about Roosevelt."*

*". . . the need of an experienced hand at the helm. And so let us fervently hope that the great pilot who has steered us so surely through the perilous currents of the past eight years may be prevailed upon . . ."*

Wallace Morgan's cartoon, on the other hand, appeared on February 17, 1940 — nearly four years later. Mighty fires burn a long time.

Some people thought, not that the New Deal was doing too much, but that it was not doing enough. The Communists sniped at it for "organizing scarcity"; the Townsend Planners, millions strong, were out for $200 a month for all people of sixty or over; Father Coughlin's radio tirades, Upton Sinclair's EPIC ("End poverty in California"), and Floyd Olson's Farmer-Labor Party were all going strong. And there was also Huey Long, the Louisiana Kingfish, who cried "Share Our Wealth" and liked machine-guns, graft, and power. We show him here in one conversational and three oratorical poses. Huey was a potential dictator—with the special American advantage of having a caustic humor. But he came early to a dictator's end: late in 1935 he was assassinated.

During the four years from the Panic (1929) to the New Deal (1933) the whole aspect of the American woman was transformed. It was not simply that since 1930 her evening dress had been touching the ground, or that her daytime dresses had descended (step by step with security prices) until by 1933 they reached a point half way between her knees and the ground, or even lower. It was not simply that she had abandoned the tight helmet hat, had experimented with such frivolities as the Eugenie model of 1931, and had gone in for a variety of small pert hats which sat atop her head. Or that she had taken up using dark nail-polish—and matching it with her lipstick. Or that she was letting her hair grow longer. What was most striking was that her physical shape seemed to have changed. No longer was she flat-breasted, long-waisted, with the perpendicular line unnaturally accented; now her waist was permitted by fashion to be where nature had intended it to be. And she no longer tried to flatten her figure; in some cases she was even disposed—as one anecdote had it—to make mountains out of molehills. It was almost as if a new species had appeared in our streets. Above are some dressmaking designs published in *Vogue* for September 1, 1933.

# Philippine and Imported Lingerie

To point the contrast, we present on these two facing pages some pages from the catalogue of Altman's department store, in New York. On this page, the underwear of 1926, as shown in the Spring and Summer number of that year; with some 1926 street dresses in the lower right-hand corner, to suggest the outer aspect of a woman who wore such underpinnings. On the opposite page, the underwear shown in the December 1935 catalogue, a little less than a decade later. A cynic has said that when times are prosperous, men are a dime a dozen and the smart woman naturally prefers to look unattainable, seeming not to be trying to advertise her specific allurements; but that when times are hard, eligible males are rare and she has to put out in the show window everything she's got. A very pretty theory—but why, then, did skirts get longer when prosperity departed?

The ladies on the left-hand page are wearing the lingerie of 1926, the year when Rudolph Valentino died, Aimee Semple McPherson vanished, Gertrude Ederle swam the Channel, Tunney beat Dempsey at Philadelphia, Queen Marie was welcomed, and the Hall-Mills case went to trial. The ladies on this right-hand page are wearing the lingerie of 1935-36, when the Supreme Court, having already killed the NRA, killed the AAA; when orchestras were playing "The Music Goes 'Round and 'Round," and Mae West reported earnings for the year of $480,833, and Major Bowes's amateur hour was the sensation in radio, and a young special prosecutor named Tom Dewey was going after racketeers, and Bruno Hauptmann was awaiting execution for the Lindbergh murder.

Spring dress event
An Altman early spring dress event! Smart town and countr
dresses, all made of a fine, soft, closely-knitted pin-checke
rayon fabric ... each 4.5
62A Short puffed sleeves, Peter Pan collar, shirred yoke front an back ... 4.5
62B Long sleeves, draw-string neck, Ascot tie, yoke front an back ... 4.5
62C Long sleeves, saddle shoulder, tie at neck, yoke in front ... 4.5
Sizes 14 to 20
Colors: brown and white
royal blue and white
green and white
These dresses will also be available at this price in February
62-B $4.50
62-A $4.50
62-C $4.50


Even the advertising pictures of women, and the shop-window manikins, wore a different aspect now. They had left off their world-weary languor and had become brisk, bright, practical-looking—much better company for hard times. This page is from the Altman catalogue for January 1934. Compare the faces with those in the 1926 catalogue; and don't fail to note the prices!

We now jump you ahead a few years more, to 1940. The lady in the long evening negligée is from an Altman catalogue of 1940; the street dresses are from *Vogue* of August 1 in that year. Times had changed. The war in Europe had begun, France had been beaten, the United States had gone into a huge defense program, and Willkie was the Republican choice to stop Roosevelt.

Women looked somewhat different by then. The open-toed shoe had arrived. The short evening dress (for practicality's sake) had appeared, but had not supplanted the sweeping one. The hair was longer; the page-boy cut had come, and then by 1939 some women had begun to put their hair up, while others rebelled at the idea. Daytime skirts were now much shorter, as you can see. But these were minor modifications, not by any means fundamental changes.

72-5

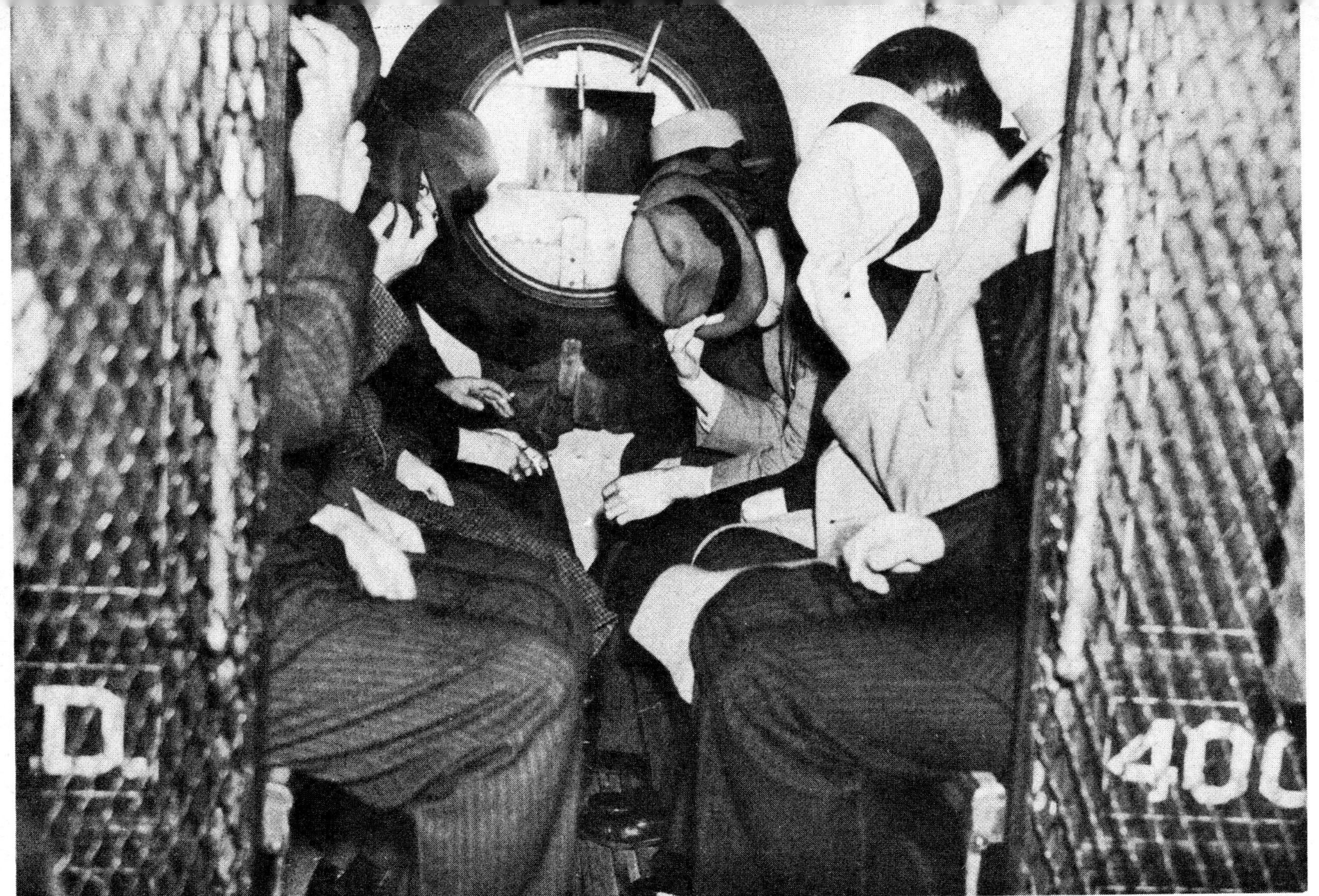

Gangsters in a patrol wagon on their way to Dewey's office

Dutch Schultz, boss of the numbers racket, on trial in 1935

John Dillinger, "Public Enemy No. 1," killed in 1934

Prohibition was repealed in 1933, the cocktail bar opened to a prosperous business, and the forces of organized crime didn't have things quite so easy. And they were out of luck in other ways too. The reform spirit ran high. The Lindbergh horror and other kidnappings, and the rackets which preyed upon business, had aroused general public wrath. The time was ripe for action. The FBI went into high gear, tracking down Dillinger, "Pretty Boy" Floyd, "Baby Face" Nelson, and others; James Cagney popularized the stalwart "G-man" as a movie hero; and in New York a special prosecutor named Thomas E. Dewey began to round up racketeers with ruthless but effective thoroughness. At the right (in a light suit) is J. Edgar Hoover, head man and chief publicizer of the FBI, with the young Melvin Purvis who in 1934 led the group of agents who waited outside a Chicago theatre for the disguised Dillinger, and shot him as he emerged. Below is Dewey, elevated to District Attorney at the end of 1937, with New York's energetic reform mayor, Fiorello H. LaGuardia.

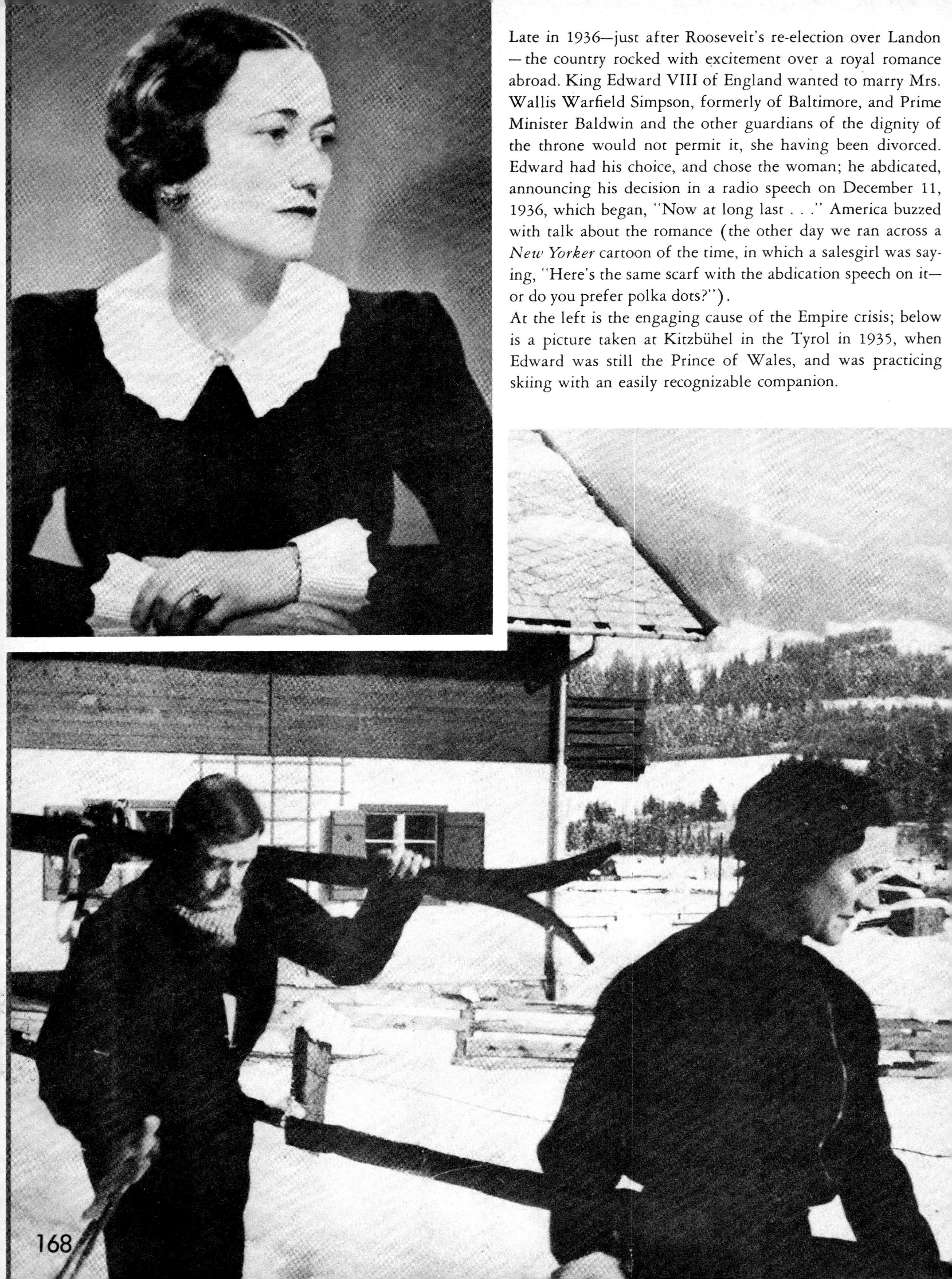

Late in 1936—just after Roosevelt's re-election over Landon —the country rocked with excitement over a royal romance abroad. King Edward VIII of England wanted to marry Mrs. Wallis Warfield Simpson, formerly of Baltimore, and Prime Minister Baldwin and the other guardians of the dignity of the throne would not permit it, she having been divorced. Edward had his choice, and chose the woman; he abdicated, announcing his decision in a radio speech on December 11, 1936, which began, "Now at long last . . ." America buzzed with talk about the romance (the other day we ran across a *New Yorker* cartoon of the time, in which a salesgirl was saying, "Here's the same scarf with the abdication speech on it—or do you prefer polka dots?").

At the left is the engaging cause of the Empire crisis; below is a picture taken at Kitzbühel in the Tyrol in 1935, when Edward was still the Prince of Wales, and was practicing skiing with an easily recognizable companion.

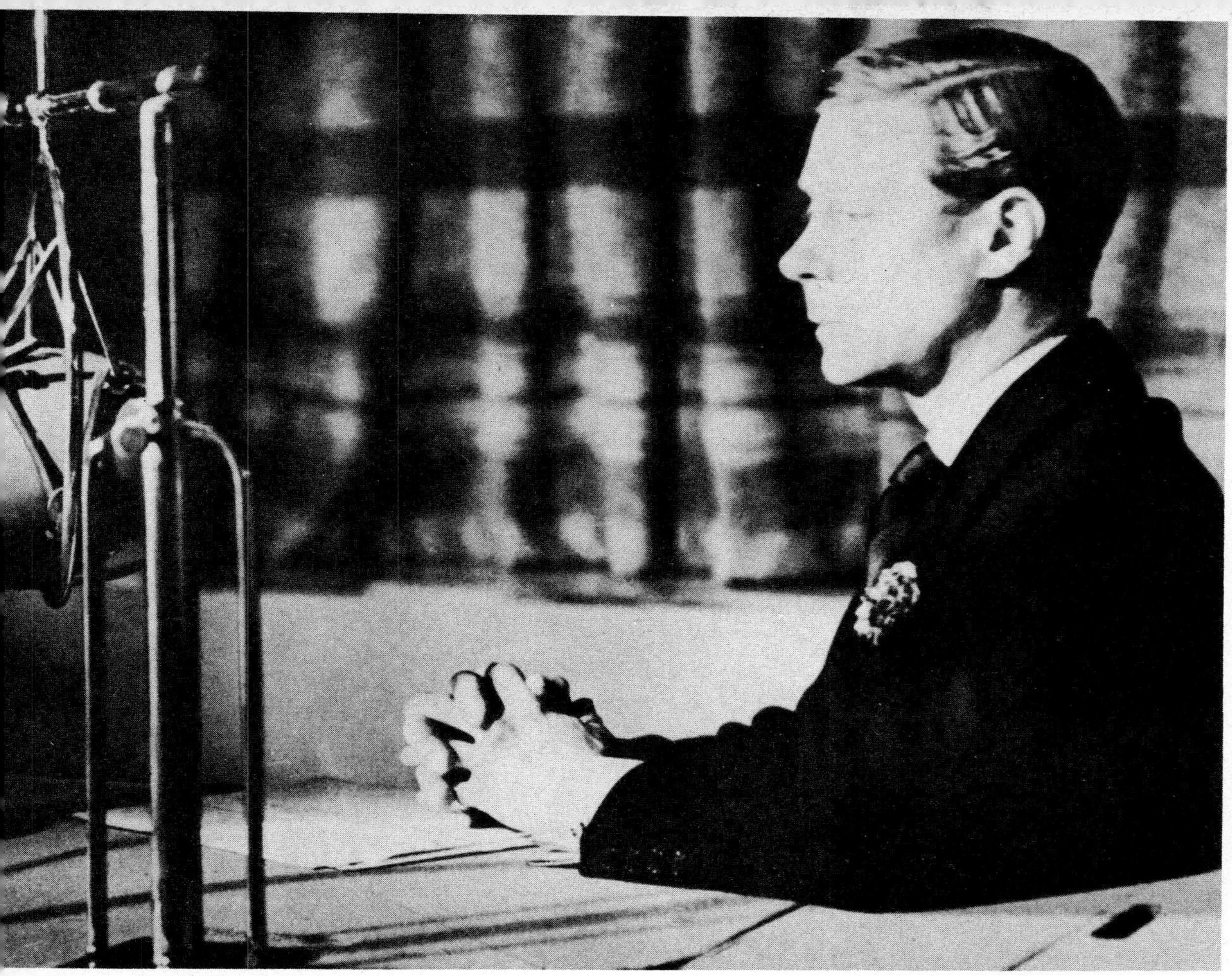

Above, Edward VIII broadcasting. Below: the wedding party at the marriage which took place later in France. At the left, Herman Rogers, the couple's American host; then the Duchess and Duke of Windsor, as they were now to be called; then the best man, Major Metcalfe.

A few pages back we were looking at the changes in the aspect of American women between the days of Coolidge prosperity and the days of the WPA. Let us now glance at some items of men's wear. The boy at the left illustrates a progressive change in the age of consent to long trousers. In the nineteen-twenties this age was likely to be fourteen or so; in the next decade it moved down to twelve or so; since this picture appeared, in the 1940 Altman magazine, it has moved down still further to—well, we haven't had a good look at a baby carriage in the past few minutes, but we wouldn't be at all surprised. And where did knickers go?

The man at the right is from a Jantzen advertisement in *The New Yorker* on June 10, 1933; those big holes under the arms represented a stage in the abandonment of the top; by 1934 the topless suit was on its way in, and soon it was standard.

The shirt advertisement below appeared in the Altman magazine of January 1935; we reproduce it out of pure unkindness. Look at the prices!

## extraordinary sale of men's shirts . . . 1.45

A shirt value that justifies your purchasing a season's supply. Smart, British-type colored stripings woven into quality broadcloth. Fine-fabric whites. All constructed from combed, long-staple yarns, and expertly tailored in the wanted collar styles, sizes and sleeve lengths. Stripings in blue, tan, gray, or green. For your convenience we are enumerating, below, and giving a few details about each shirt sketched . . .

**27-35** White broadcloth, neckband style. Sizes 14 to 18. Sleeve lengths 33 to 35 . . . . . . . . . . . . . . . . . . . 1.45

**27-36** White broadcloth with collar attached. Sizes 14 to 18. Sleeve lengths 33 to 35 . . . . . . . . . . . . . 1.45

**27-37** Striped broadcloth with two matching stiff collars. Sizes 14 to 18. Sleeve lengths 33 to 35 . . . . . . 1.45

**27-38** Striped broadcloth with regular soft collar. Sizes 14 to 18. Sleeve lengths 33 to 35 . . . . . . . . . . . 1.45

**27-39** Striped broadcloth with tab collar. Sizes 14 to 17. Sleeve lengths 33 to 35 . . . . . . . . . . . . . . . . . . 1.45

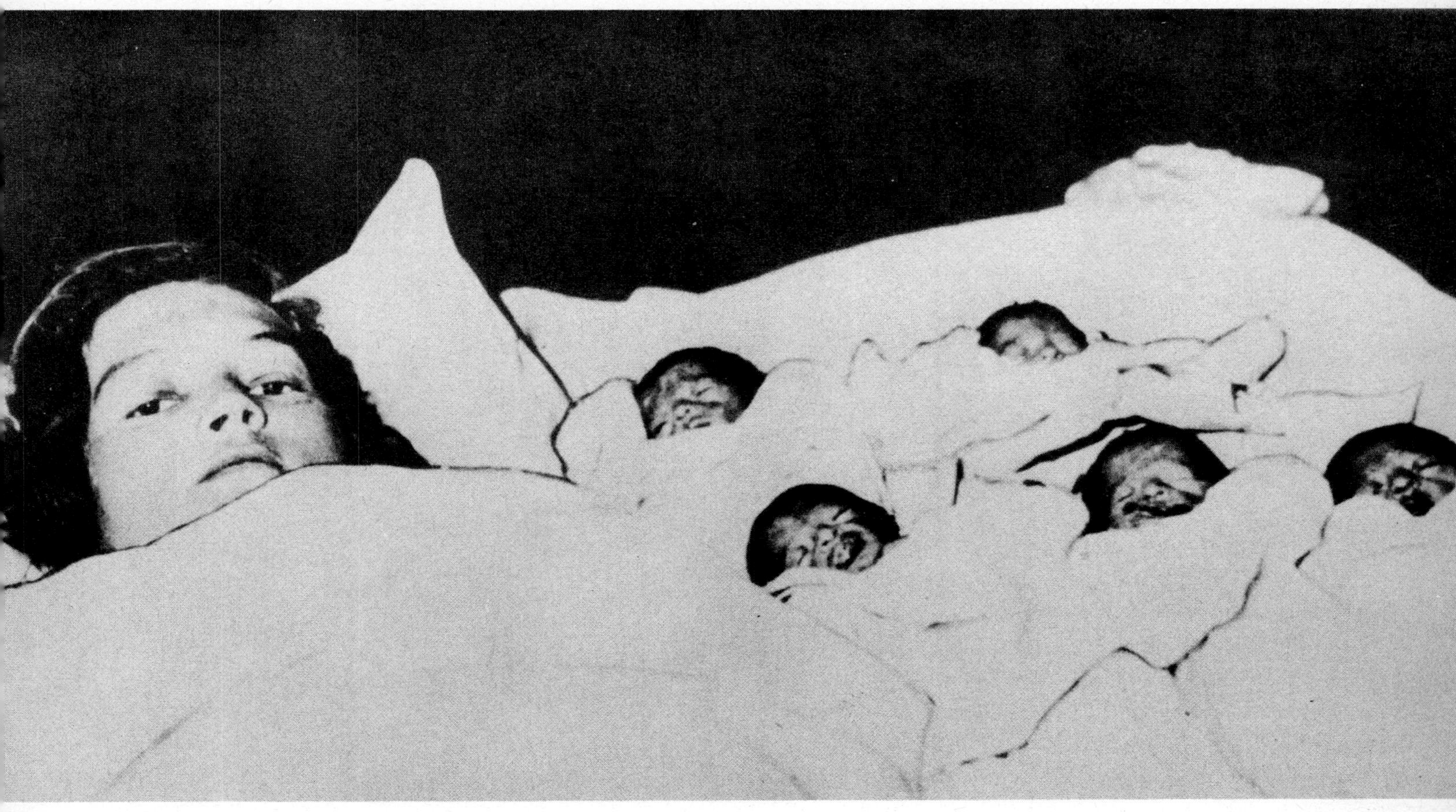

The public passion for personal drama—for the event or the situation which is readily intelligible in human terms—is confined to no one decade. If Americans got excited, in 1925, over a Kentucky boy trapped in a cave, they also got excited, in 1934, over the arrival of quintuplets in Callander, Ontario.

In that remote town in the Canadian backwoods, on May 28, 1934, Mrs. Ovila Dionne, twenty-five years old and already the mother of six children (one of whom had died), gave birth to five little girls, identical twins whose combined weight at birth was less than ten pounds. Dr. Allan Roy Dafoe, the country doctor who had brought them into the world, saw to it that they all survived. Then—as newspapermen, movie men, advertising men, and tourists converged upon the scene—began an extraordinary story which, if it did not win headlines quite as steadily as that of Floyd Collins, was of longer duration and more sensational magnitude.

By 1938 the town of Callander, which had been a half-abandoned lumber town with a box car for a railroad station, was booming. Over a wide, paved highway, 3,000 visitors a day (8,000 on week-end days) converged in summer upon what Merrill Denison called "the most spectacular, if refined, sideshow on earth." To protect the Quintuplets against exploitation, they had been made wards of the King. They had fourteen people on their payroll. Already, at the age of four, they owned $600,000 in government bonds, earned through movie contracts and other fees. And despite the fact that Dr. Dafoe and the Board of Guardians took every precaution not to commercialize them unduly and that no admission was charged for the privilege of seeing them in the Dafoe Nursery—where they were on delightful exhibition somewhat as in a very demure zoo—they were estimated to be worth at least twenty million dollars a year to the Canadian tourist business!

In the picture above we cannot give you left-to-right identifications, front row and rear; but the names of the Quints, in case you have forgotten, are Yvonne, Annette, Cecile, Emilie, and Marie.

Among the strange happenings which caught the popular imagination because they involved the predicament of a single person, few were stranger than the last hours of John Warde, the young man who on a summer morning in 1938 climbed out on a ledge on the seventeenth floor of the Hotel Gotham, New York, threatening to leap—and after attracting a huge crowd and tying up metropolitan traffic for eleven hours, finally did leap, to his death. In the picture at the right his sister, a rope around her waist, is trying to coax him in.

On a bigger scale was the tragedy of the liner *Morro Castle,* which burned mysteriously off the New Jersey coast in the late summer of 1934, with a loss of 137 lives. The fire had first been detected in a locker off the portside writing room, and had spread with curious rapidity. Later the smoking hulk of the *Morro Castle* went ashore on the beach at Asbury Park, where crowds of curiosity-seekers stared at her—while fishermen fished calmly on.

The short-lived NRA, which gave business managements permission to organize as never before—remember the "codes"?—also gave labor the right to organize. The explicit permission was put into Clause 7a of the NRA's enabling act. Thereupon John L. Lewis, toughest and most aggressive of American labor leaders, saw his opportunity. The law was now on his side! He undertook a swift organizing campaign to sign up the workmen in hitherto unorganized mass-production industries. In 1935 he and Hillman and Dubinsky and other leaders set up an aggressive organization inside the slow-moving American Federation of Labor, and called it the CIO (Committee for Industrial Organization); the next year it was read out of the AF of L but remained the CIO (Congress of Industrial Organizations). It grew fast. When the Supreme Court killed the NRA, and Clause 7a died with it, Lewis was not long handicapped; for Congress quickly passed the Wagner Labor Relations Act to fill the breach. Thereupon began an era of labor militancy, and of red-hot strikes, unparalleled since 1919-20. Below is Lewis, pictured in 1939.

The strikes were at their fiercest in 1937, when the CIO's United Automobile Workers staged a "sit-down" against General Motors, and then—after the U. S. Steel Corporation had signed with Lewis — the CIO's Steel Workers' Organizing Committee led a strike against the "little steel" companies. The bitterest battles were waged between the workers of Republic Steel and its unreconstructed management, led by the hard-boiled Tom Girdler; in May 1937 a crowd of pickets at South Chicago were pursued and shot down by police—four killed, six fatally injured. Below, a Republic Steel striker is being restrained by friends after a battle with the police.

Above, a Republic Steel striker is led away, teargassed, after a battle with "vigilante" police at Monroe, Michigan, in June 1937.

In a time of rebellion and hot tempers, even a student strike can cause lively disorder. At the left is a scene in a fight between striking and non-striking students of Columbia University in April 1932, after President Butler refused to reinstate Reed Harris as editor of the Columbia *Spectator*.

Sit down strikes became epidemic. The picture above shows girl employees of Woolworth's five and ten cent store on West Fourteenth Street, New York, sleeping on the floor of the store during their strike in March 1937. (Sympathizers outside the building passed food and bedding in to them.) What they were striking for reads a little strangely today: they wanted union recognition, a forty-hour week, and a minimum wage of $20 a week. The strike wave lasted until late in 1937, when times suddenly became worse, and unemployment—which remained high all through the nineteen-thirties—increased sharply. The country was headed into that relapse into depression which became known by the polite name of "Recession."

The panic of 1929 ended the skyscraper-building mania, but it didn't quite end skyscraper-building—for some people had gone too far to stop. Take New York, for example. When the Panic came, the old Waldorf-Astoria Hotel was just being torn down to make room for the Empire State Building (which was designed—because of the success of the *Graf Zeppelin*—with a mooring mast for dirigibles). The project had to go on. And at the moment of the Panic John D. Rockefeller, Jr., was deep in plans for a huge civic center west of Fifth Avenue; it was to be clustered about a new Opera House. At the right is the residential region he was planning to transform. The picture was taken in 1930, before the demolition of 229 houses began.

After the Panic, the Opera House decided not to move. But Rockefeller had to go ahead somehow—and only skyscrapers would pay their way on such expensive property. So the brownstones were torn down and Rockefeller Center—at first called Radio City—went up, building by building, at a moment when the noise of the riveter was little heard elsewhere. At the left is the excavation for the International Building, opposite St. Patrick's Cathedral, as it looked after a late 1933 snowfall.

The pinnacles of Rockefeller Center, Manhattan, completed in the nineteen-thirties.

Toward evening on May 6, 1937—when the sit-down strikes were raging, and Roosevelt was trying to reorganize the Supreme Court, and the Duke of Windsor was in Austria awaiting his wedding to Mrs. Simpson, and Charlie McCarthy was just beginning his rise to popularity on the air waves—an NBC radio reporter was at Lakehurst, New Jersey, describing the approach of the German airship *Hindenburg* to the mooring mast there. He was reading his script quietly —telling all about this successor to the famous *Graf Zeppelin,* and her successful transatlantic flights with passengers in 1936, and the completion of her first trip to America of the 1937 season—when suddenly he gasped, "It's burst into flame!" and then began a strange, hysterical, sobbing outburst of clichés and awkward phrases like "Oh, the humanity!"—the sort of things that come to one under awful stress. What had happened was that the after part of the hydrogen-filled *Hindenburg* had exploded; she went down in a roaring mass of wreckage, killing 36 people. The photograph above was taken almost at the instant of the explosion. Note the two men standing on the mooring mast at the right.

A characteristic American triumph in applied science during the interwar years: a million-volt x-ray unit radiographing a big casting in search of flaws.

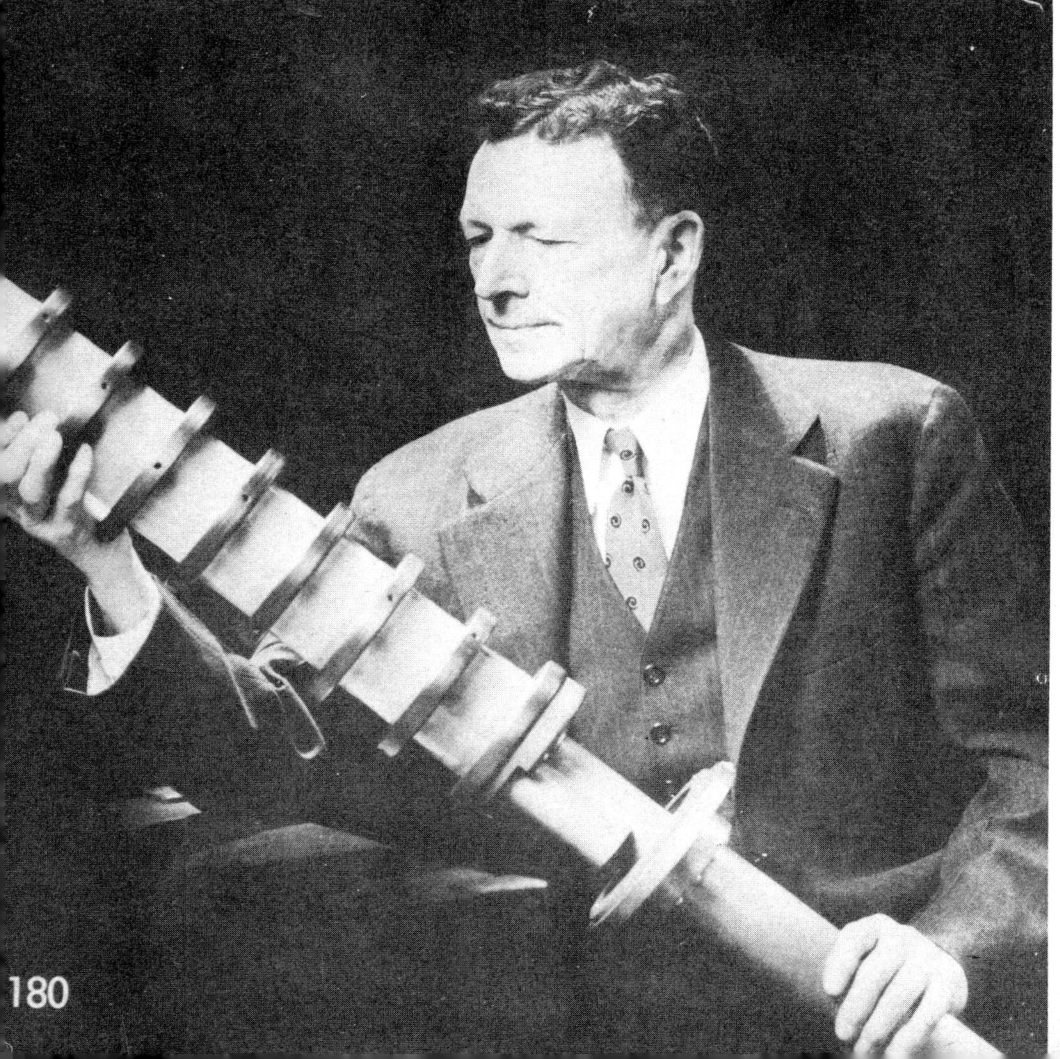

Which were more important, the strikes which were headline news day after day in 1937, or the advances in applied science and industrial engineering which won few headlines, but represented an application of the American genius for which we were to be profoundly thankful after 1941? We show here, as symbolic of that advance, a photograph (above) of some huge gears for turbines, machined at General Electric to an accuracy of 1/10,000th of an inch; and one (left) of Dr. W. D. Coolidge of the same company holding a million-volt x-ray tube in whose development he led.

We have made no attempt, in this book, to picture the fundamental scientific discoveries of the years between the wars. The most significant work in pure science lends itself ill to the camera. But at least we can give a hint of one phase of it by showing a piece of apparatus—of pretty considerable size—used in carrying out researches on the behavior of atoms. The pictures on this page are of an atom-smasher at the Westinghouse Laboratories at East Pittsburgh, Pennsylvania, built in 1937—many years before the word "atomic" came to connote, in the minds of most people, terrific destruction.

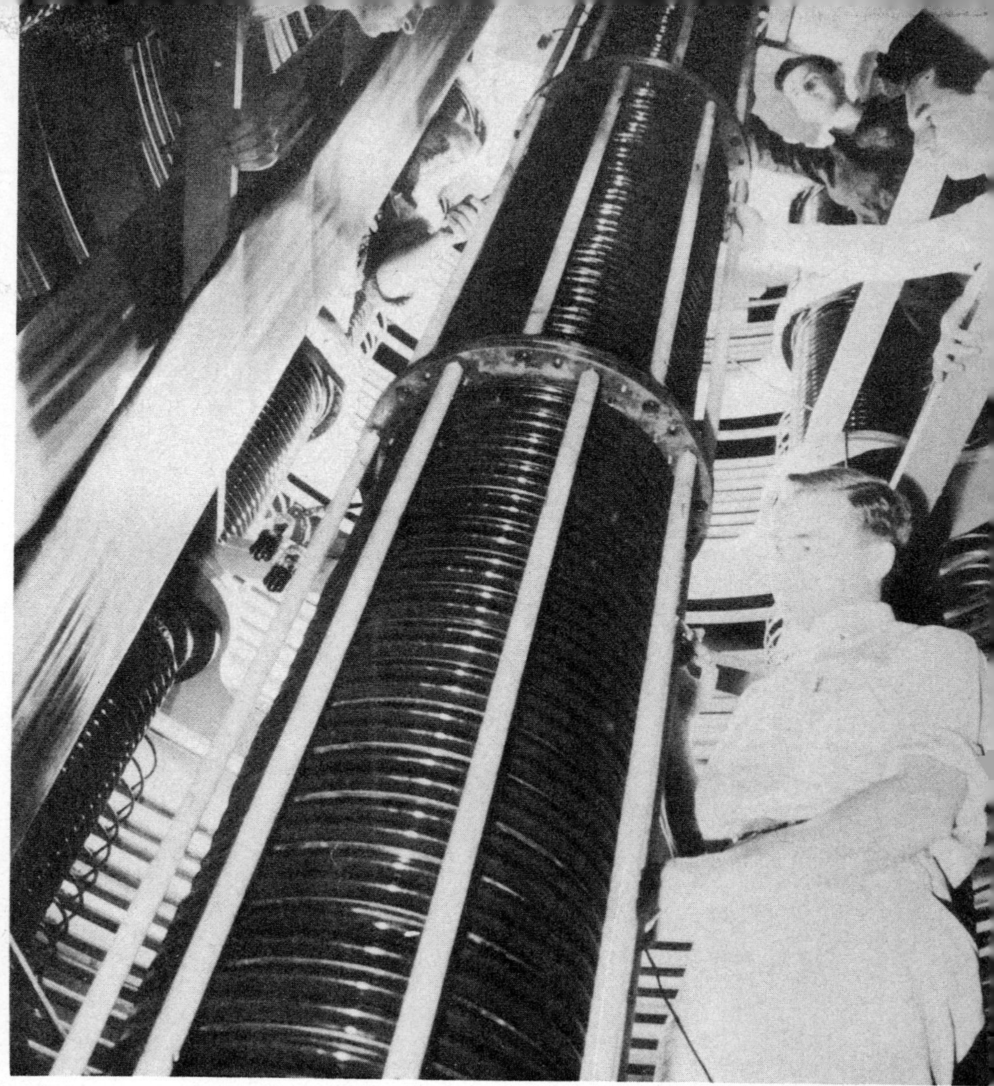

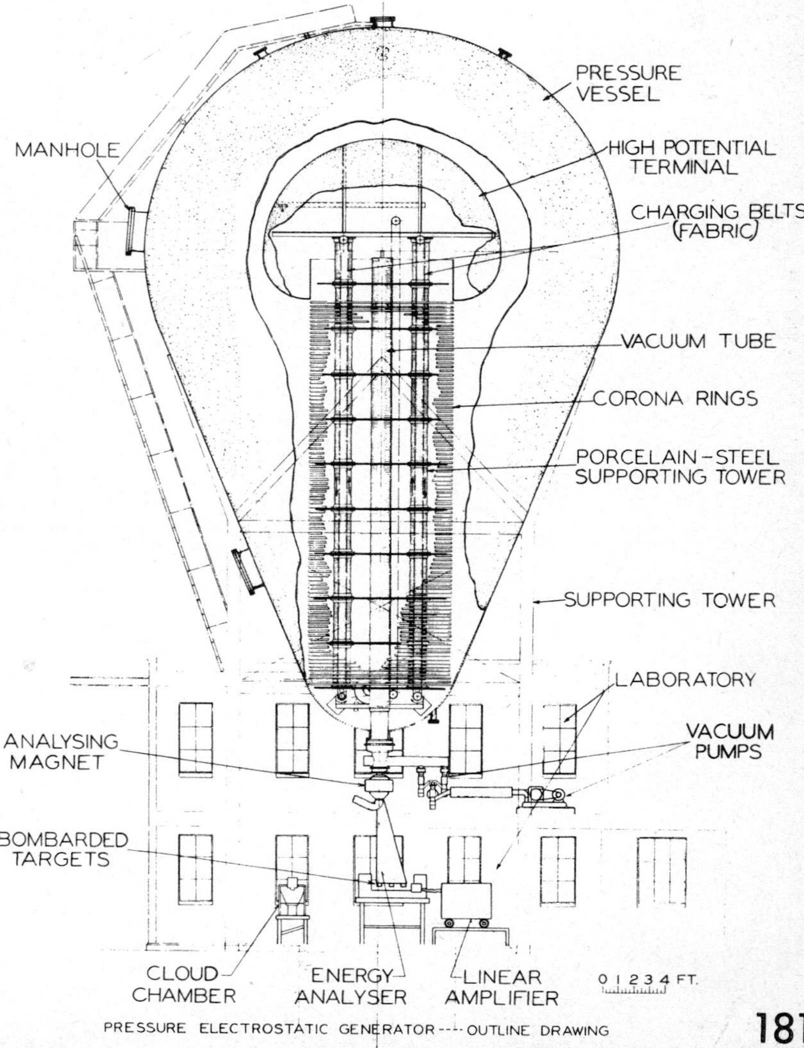

PRESSURE ELECTROSTATIC GENERATOR---- OUTLINE DRAWING

At the top of the page, right, men are looking at the 40-foot vacuum tube atom "gun" in the center of the atom-smasher. Above, you have an outside view of the 90-ton pear-shaped structure in which the "gun" is housed, atop the laboratory building; and at the right is a diagram of the apparatus, which shows the vacuum tube serving as the central spine of this odd tower. The "gun" could mobilize 4,000,000 volts to shoot sub-atomic particles at the target on the ground floor.

At the left is a picture of a result of research in applied science which it doesn't take a doctor's degree to grasp: the first experimental sale of nylon stockings, held in Wilmington, Delaware, under the auspices of the Nylon Division of the duPont Company, on October 25, 1939. These stockings came from a single pilot plant; production on a big scale followed later.

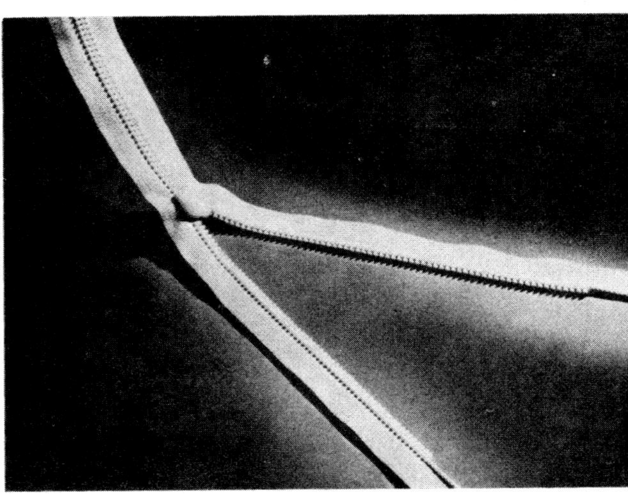

Here are some other synthetics to which we were introduced during the interwar years. At the left, the upper picture shows contact lenses made of "lucite," or, if it will make you easier in your mind, methyl methacrylate resin; the middle picture a slide fastener—zipper to you—molded of FM-1 nylon to make it immune to dry-cleaning solvents and unharmed by ironing temperatures; the lower picture, some plastic razor cases. Above are various types of boxes made of ethocel sheeting with drawn tops and cardboard bottoms.

There was a change, between the wars, in household interiors. Any such evolution is hard to picture accurately, because at any moment one can find houses whose equipment and decoration date, essentially, from a much earlier time. But housewives may catch a reminder, from the pictures on this page, of what happened when modern design, color, and—for that matter—servantless housewives invaded the kitchen. The room at the right is unashamedly pre-modern.

At the left is a dream kitchen of about 1930: the sort of room that was built to demonstrate the very latest thing in equipment, and that aroused fierce yearnings in housewives' hearts. The aesthetic eye has been at work, as you can see, but the stove and icebox have not yet been quite assimilated into the decorative scheme of the room.

At the right is a dream kitchen of the nineteen-forties, with three "work-centers": a refrigeration and preparation center, a sink and dishwasher center, and a range and serving center. The whole design hangs together, the lighting is fluorescent and provides "adequate shadowless illumination," and altogether we seem to have made considerable progress.

At the left is an unregenerate pre-nineteen-twenties living room, in which the lighting fixtures, the furniture, and the picture-hanging show no trace of the influx of modern ideas in household decoration. (Privately, we think the pillows a little unfortunate even for 1918.)

At the right is a model living room of the latter nineteen-twenties, with less obtrusive lighting, a general lightness of effect, and less clutter. (No pillows at all, you will note.) The improvement is so great that we dare say a good many readers would be willing to settle for this room today.

Our nineteen-forties exhibit, showing the effect of the modern influence, is not a living room at all, but a bedroom. Pretty antiseptic-looking, it seems to us, and are pictures supposed to keep one awake? But the lighting is admirable and the design is wholly (if severely) harmonious. During the twenties and thirties, the "modern" was only one decorative style among several; there was a strong Victorian revival as well, and many women still clung to the ruffles and roses of the "Colonial" period.

Not only women, but automobiles too, went in for curves in the nineteen-thirties. The two pictures above are both of Chryslers. On the left, a 1930 straight eight sedan; on the right, a 1934 Chrysler Airflow, in which for the first time the "streamlining" idea was wholeheartedly adopted. Subsequently Chrysler modified its streamlining; but no manufacturer returned to anything like the angularity of the designs of the nineteen-twenties. Below is a sample of the road-building of the thirties: a parkway connection above the Harlem River in New York City. It reminds us that our super-parkways with their clover-leaf intersections and other traffic-dispersion intricacies are almost all products of the years since 1929.

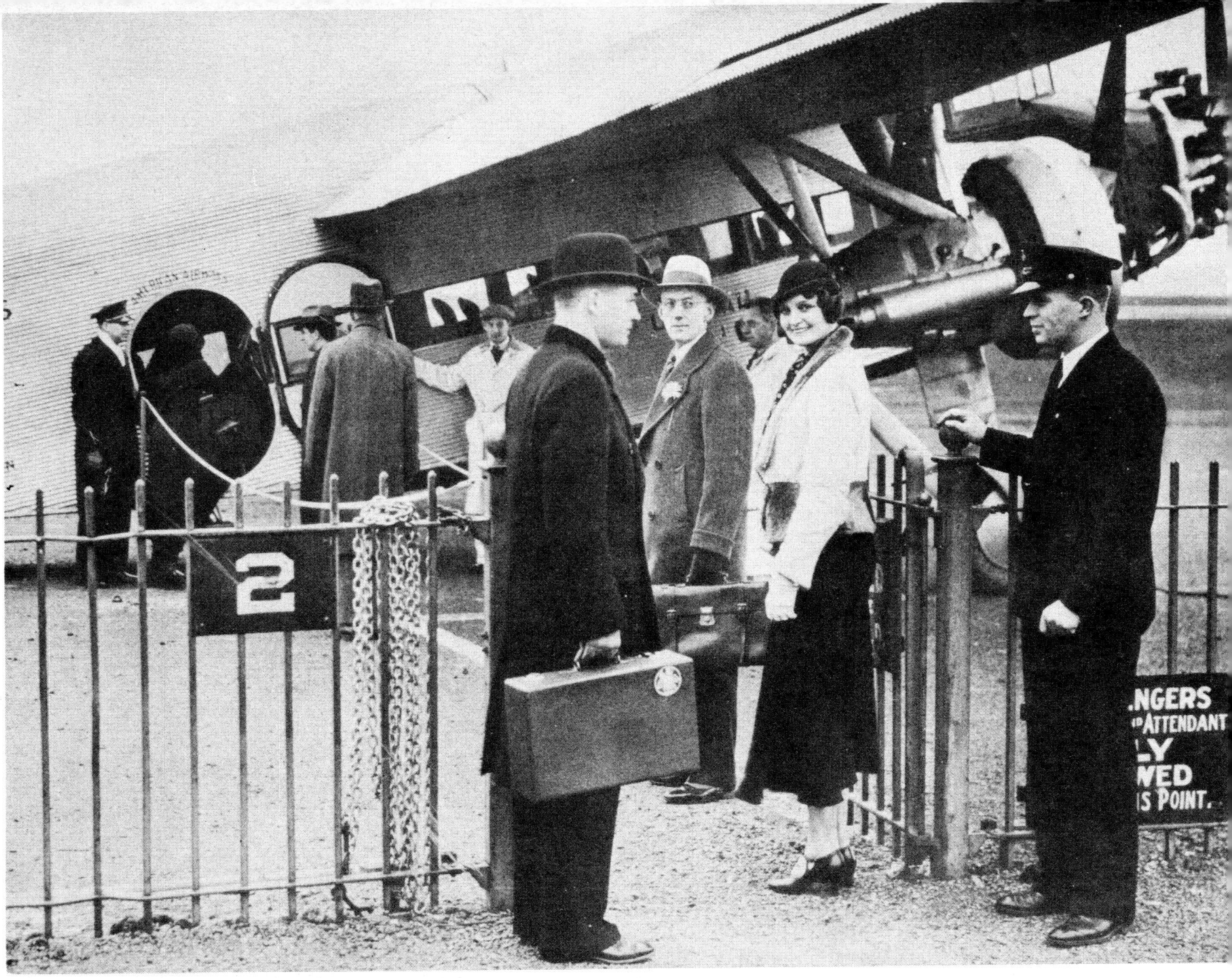

The development of our airlines was prodigious during the nineteen-thirties. Above is a plane departure in about 1932, with a Ford tri-motor plane about to leave; it carried only twelve passengers and cruised at 125 miles an hour. At the left are some air stewardesses of 1935, when small girls were preferred and they all had to be nurses.

ring the latter part of the dec-
the Douglas DC-3 (C-47
military purposes) was the
ndard plane of the airlines.

vas followed by the DC-4 (in
itary use, the C-54), with a
ising speed of 211 miles an
ır at 10,000 feet.

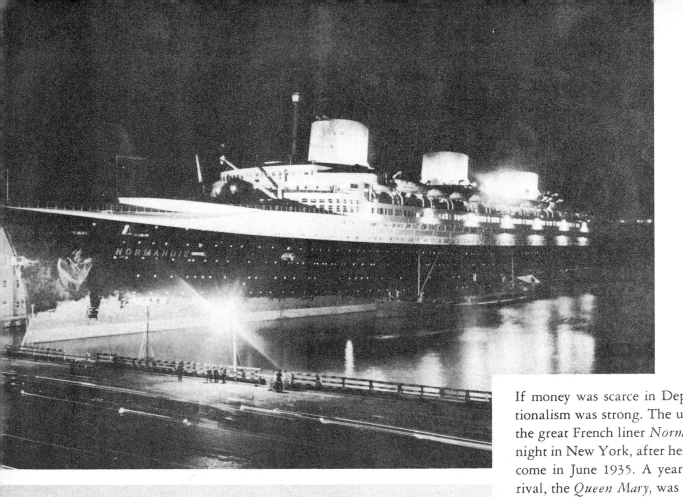

If money was scarce in Depression days, nationalism was strong. The upper picture is of the great French liner *Normandie* on her first night in New York, after her tumultuous welcome in June 1935. A year later her British rival, the *Queen Mary,* was likewise applauded as she completed her first crossing; the lower picture shows her leaving New York.

At the beginning of the nineteen-thirties skiing was the sport of only a few people—but its popularity leaped until by 1937 snow trains or snow busses operated out of New York, Chicago, Pittsburgh, Portland, San Francisco, and other cities on favorable week-ends. At some of the popular centers, ski-tows were built to eliminate (as illustrated at the right) the uphill anguish of a downhill sport. In the lower picture, busses are meeting a New Haven Railroad train to take urban devotees to a spot where the law of gravity can put on a really convincing demonstration.

Chicago, which had hit a depression year for its World's Fair of 1893, managed to repeat the feat in 1933. Its "Century of Progress" show was noted for bold modern architecture, rickshaw boys, and the rise to fame of Helen Gould Beck, otherwise Sally Rand, who did a very much appreciated fan dance wearing openwork sandals and nothing—well, al most nothing—else. Sally Rand used to disapprove of organized nudist camps according to Stanley Walker she said that all the nudists she had ever seen "had scratches all over their rear end where they had been sitting down on thorns." Nevertheless this page seem the appropriate place for Whitney Dar row's *New Yorker* cartoon of June 24 1933, celebrating a cult that during th early nineteen-thirties attracted a few very earnest disciples and a great deal c merciless public ribaldry.

*"Last night I saw him in a blue serge suit. Zowie!"*

Among the publicized oddments of the time was goldfish swallowing. It began at Harvard in 1935, when Lothrop Withington, Jr. (right), a freshman, gulped one down on a bet. Three days later, at Franklin and Marshall College, a young man ate three. According to our possibly incomplete researches, the record was set in 1938 by Albert E. Hays of M.I.T., who put away 42 goldfish in succession.

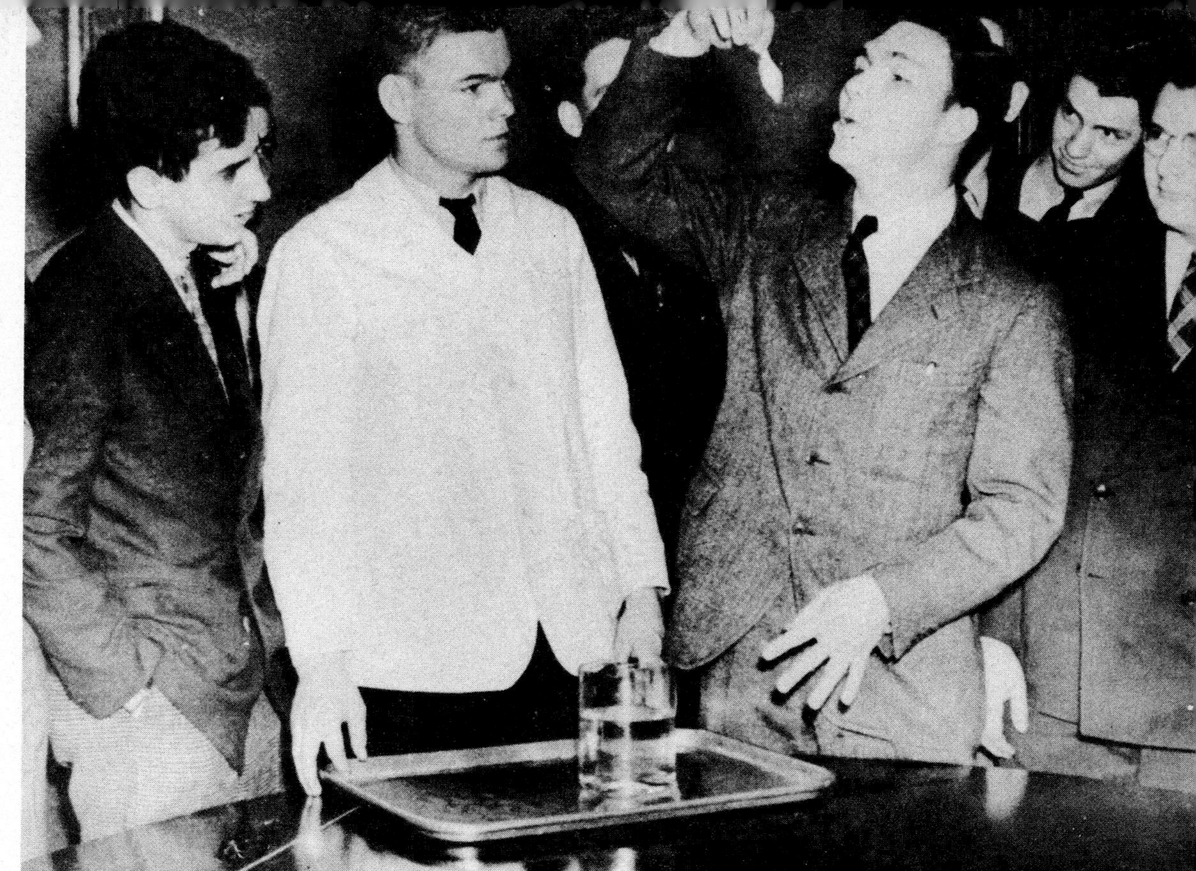

By 1938 bingo was considered by many people the most popular money game in the country. The churches generally smiled upon it, but it was also organized commercially. In the picture below, automobile workers are playing it at a carnival at Dearborn, Michigan.

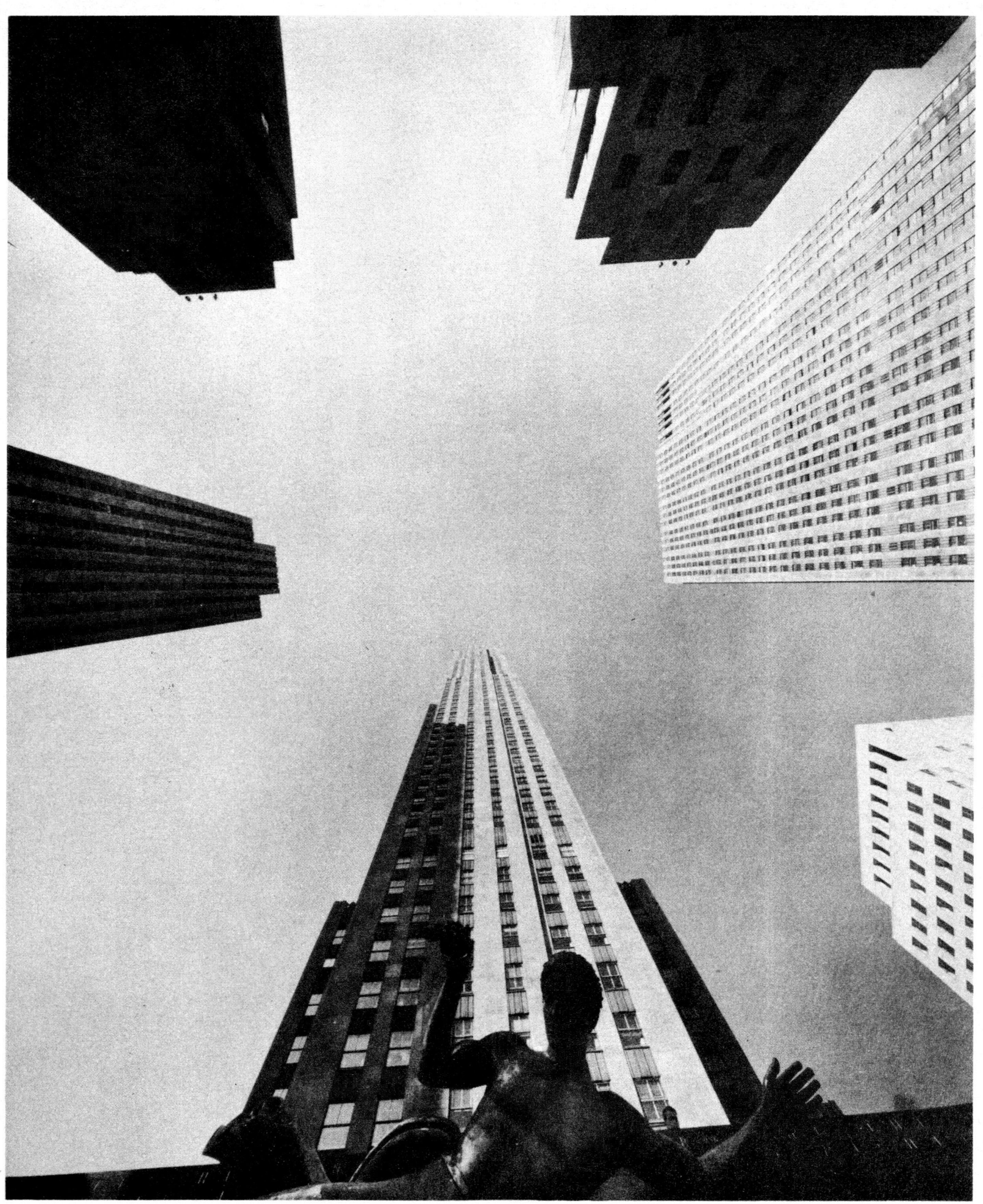

In the mid-nineteen-thirties a camera craze swept the country. It grew out of the growing popularity of Leicas and other imported German cameras; it set people of both sexes and all ages to rushing about taking "candid" shots and buying complex apparatus; it hastened the birth of *Life, Look,* and other popular picture magazines; and it immensely improved photography technically and in artistic value. We illustrate it here only with a trick shot of Rockefeller Center, New York, taken with a wide-angle lens by Wendell MacRae; but many other pictures in this book—notably the sociological studies beginning on page 195, which were stimulated by the expert interest and contagious enthusiasm of Roy Stryker of the Farm Security Administration—benefited by it.

Few sporting heroes of the nineteen-thirties rivaled Dempsey, Ruth, and Jones in popular acclaim, but some rode high. After Tunney's retirement in 1928, boxing fell into comparative doldrums, and even Max Baer, whom we show (above) knocking out Primo Carnera in the 11th round on June 14, 1934, failed to capture the public as the men of the previous decade had. On September 24, 1935, Baer was knocked out in the fourth round by young Joe Louis, whom you see at the right standing over his fallen opponent, and things began to look up. In 1937 Louis eliminated James J. Braddock, the heavyweight titleholder, and for the rest of the decade, and longer, we had a champion of undeniably major stature.

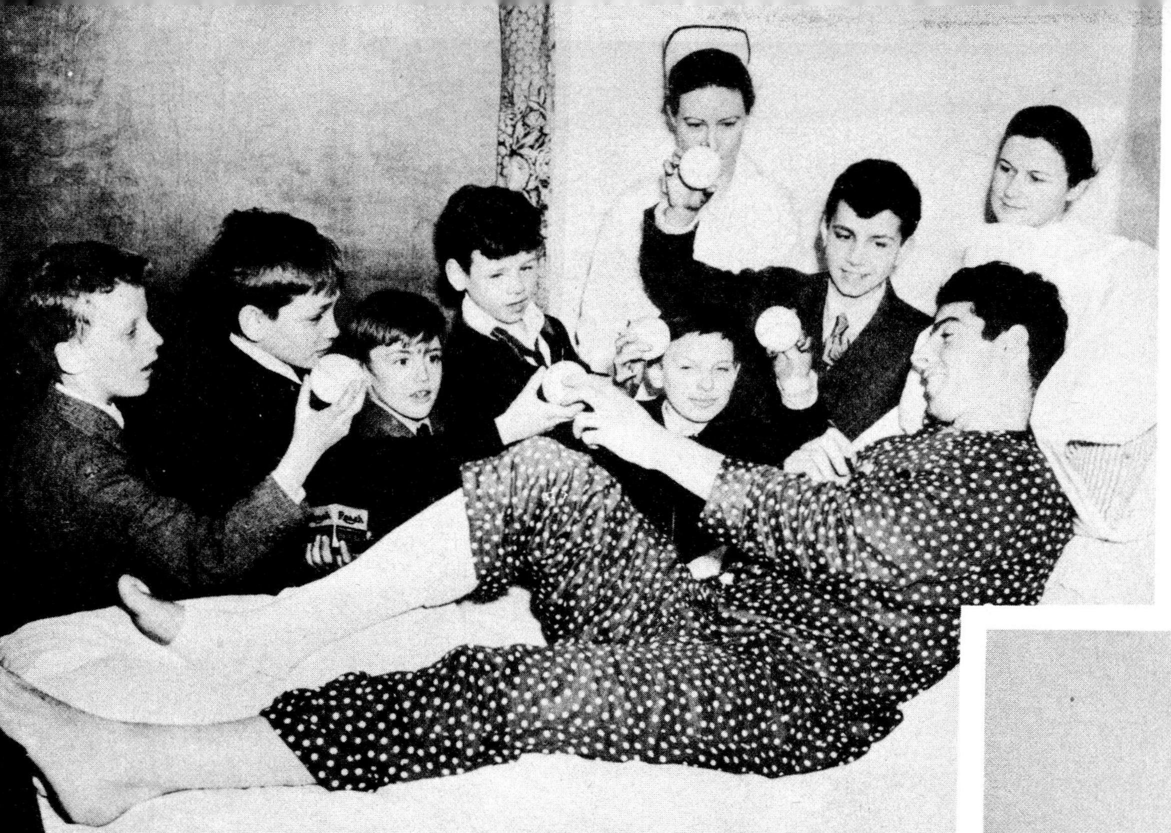

In baseball there was, among other DiMaggio, pictured here with som mirers as he was recovering from jury in 1939, the first year in whi led the American League in ba (He did it again in 1940.)

In track there was Jesse Owens, the Negro sprinter who won at the 1936 Olympics in Germany, to the embarrassment of Nazis who proclaimed the supremacy of Nordic blonds; but the man who did most to give a new popularity to indoor track events was Glenn Cunningham (shown at right), greatest of the American milers who drove the record down close to four minutes.

With gambling more widely legali racing became hugely popular as decade wore on. No single horse co rival Man o' War, but we might as name here the three biggest money- ners of the years between the Panic Pearl Harbor: Gallant Fox (1930), Flight (1931), Whirlaway (1941).

Beginning in 1933, a series of hot, dry seasons afflicted the Great Plains. Farming had never made a real recovery after the collapse of farm prices in 1920-21; the Depression, which drove prices down to the cellar, had come as an additionally grievous shock; and no sooner did things seem to be improving than droughts and dust storms came as the worst shock of all to the Dakotas, Kansas, Nebraska, Oklahoma, the Texas Panhandle, and parts of other states. Below, you see an Oklahoma farm as it looked in 1937, after the topsoil of the Great Plains had been blowing away for years.

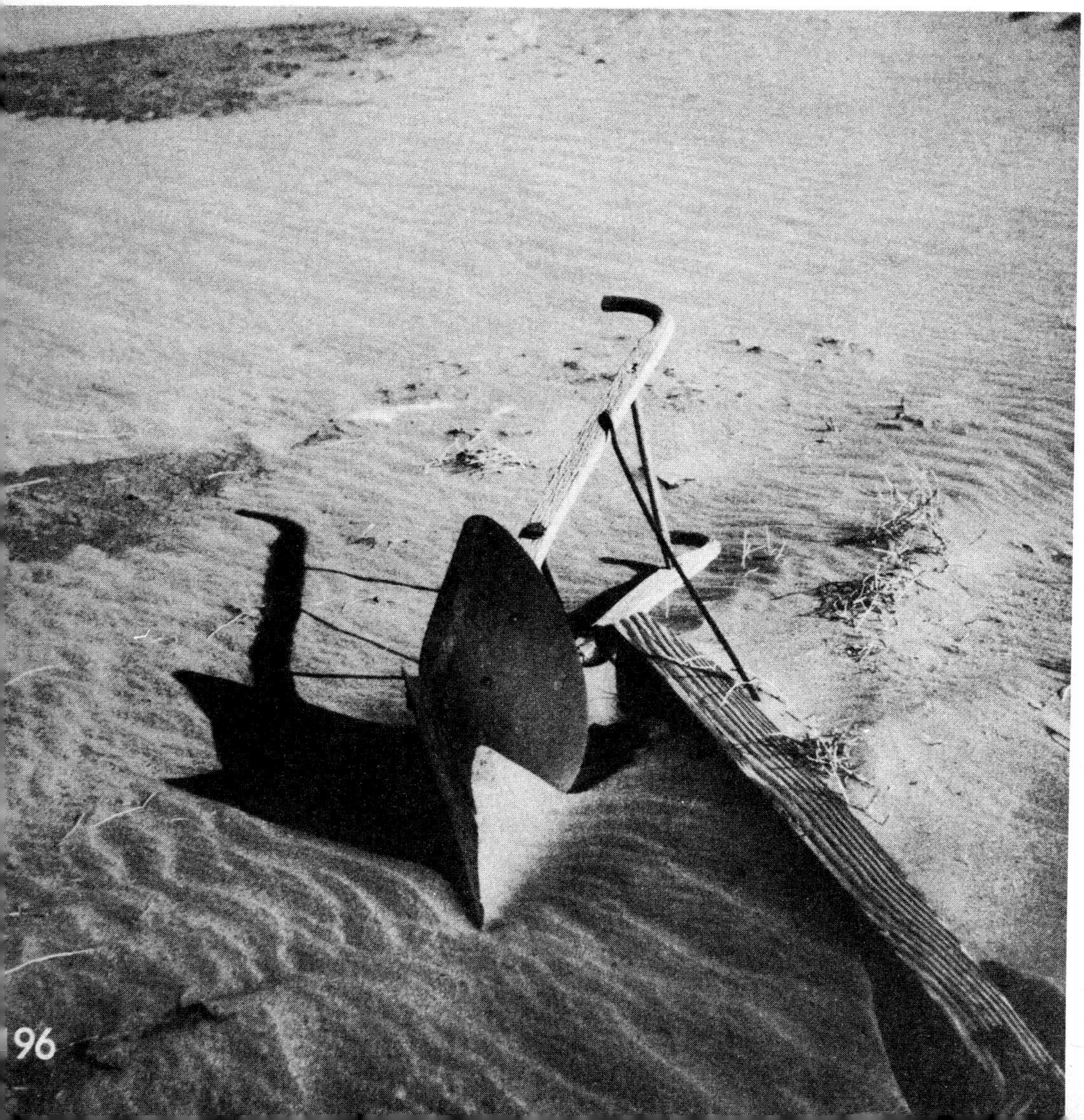

When the dust storms struck, it grew black as night, and when the sun came out again, dust was drifted everywhere like snow. Both the pictures on this page were taken in Cimarron County, Oklahoma, in April 1936.

Great numbers of people had to abandon their farms because of the dust storms; others had to because their inability to make both ends meet forced them to sell their land to people who could farm big acreages with tractors. The owners of the abandoned farm in the upper view on the opposite page — taken in the Texas Panhandle in 1938—had been "tractored" off.

No wonder the disaster which hit the Great Plains called national attention to the evils of soil erosion, as graphically shown in the lower picture on the page opposite, taken in Alabama.

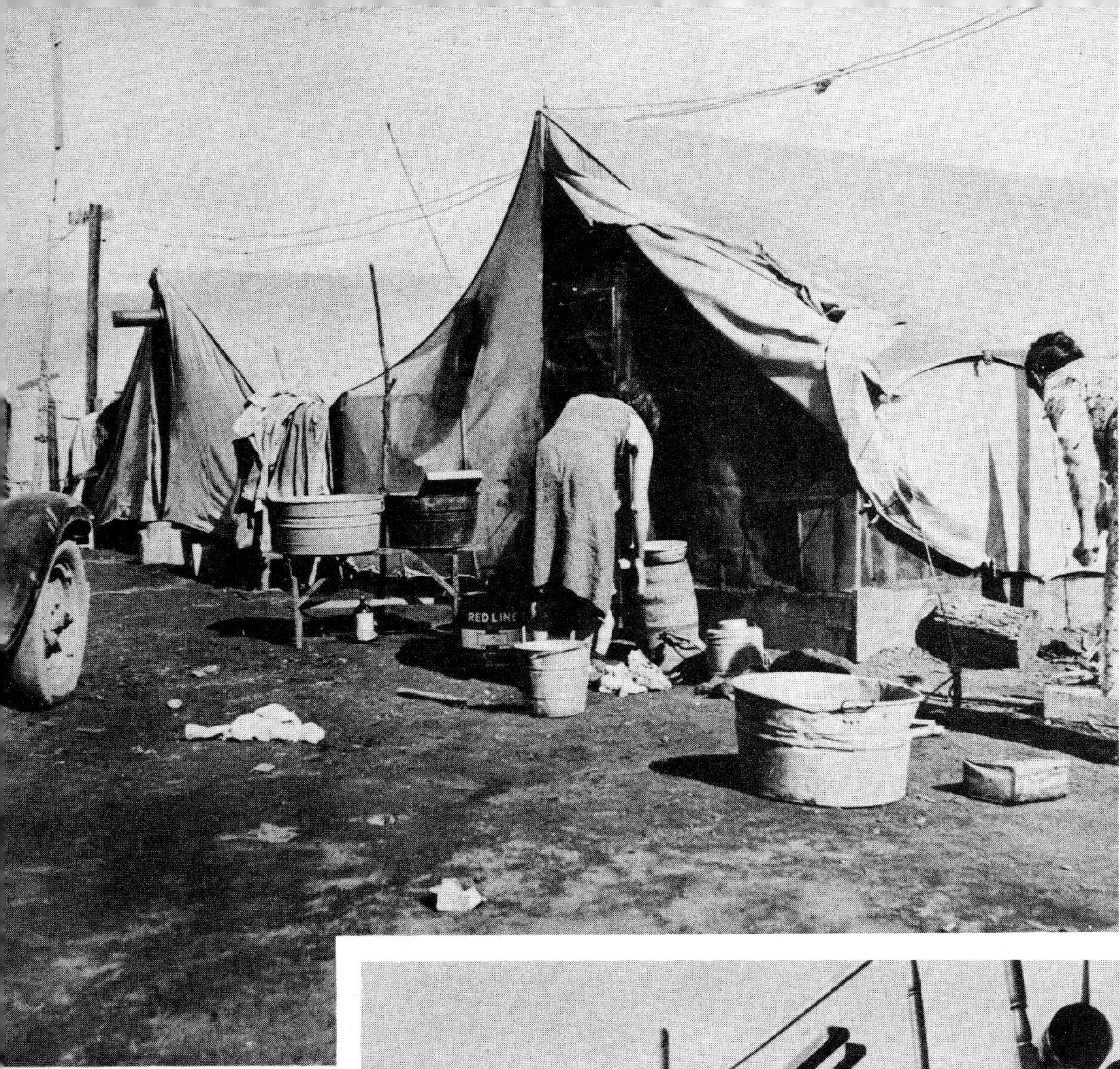

Where could they go, these refugees from dust? Year after year, most of them converged upon Route 66 to California, where they were not wanted in any such numbers and were ill-housed and ill-paid. At the left is an orange pickers' camp in Tulare County, California, in 1938; below, a sample of the way the "Okies" traveled west. This family (from Missouri) reported, "Broke—baby sick—car trouble." That was in 1937.

The flight from the Dust Bowl to California, and the tragedy of the displaced Okies, constituted together an important development in American history; yet few Americans grasped its scope and emotional impact until John Steinbeck (above) wrote *The Grapes of Wrath,* which became the runaway best seller of 1939.

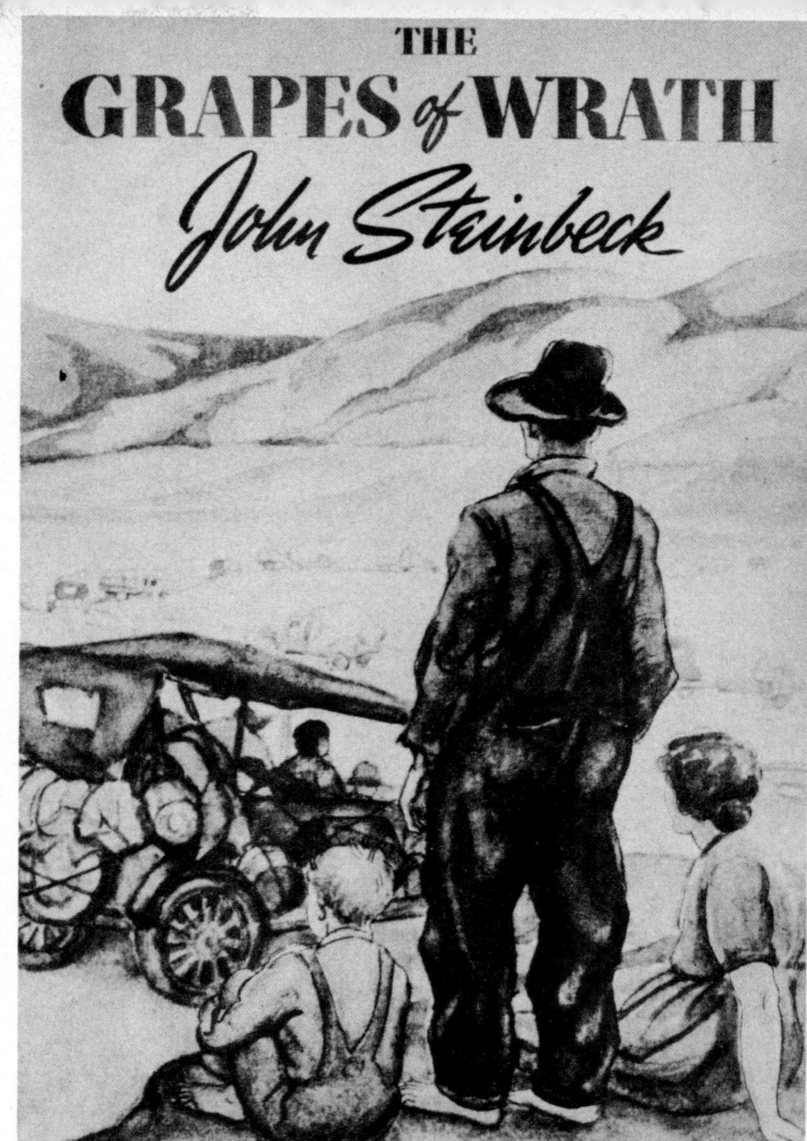

More extensively publicized was the sad state of the share-croppers of the South; and one of the most effective advertisers of it was Jack Kirkland's play, "Tobacco Road," made from Erskine Caldwell's novel of the same name. Opening in New York on December 4, 1933, it combined a reputation for impropriety with a sociological lesson so effectively that it ran on and on until it had broken the record set in the preceding decade by "Abie's Irish Rose." At the left is Henry Hull as Jeeter Lester, the role in which he preceded James Barton.

The troubles of the American farmers during the years of Depression and drought had at least one favorable result. They so dramatized the need for better defenses against erosion that, with the aid of the effective educational work of the government's Soil Conservation Service, a great change took place in many regions in methods of planting. By the end of the decade travelers by air could see how many farmers had taken up contour plowing; and the government's photographers now could find such lovely subjects as this farm in Brown County, Texas, a model of the use of terraced land for wheat, millet, and barley.

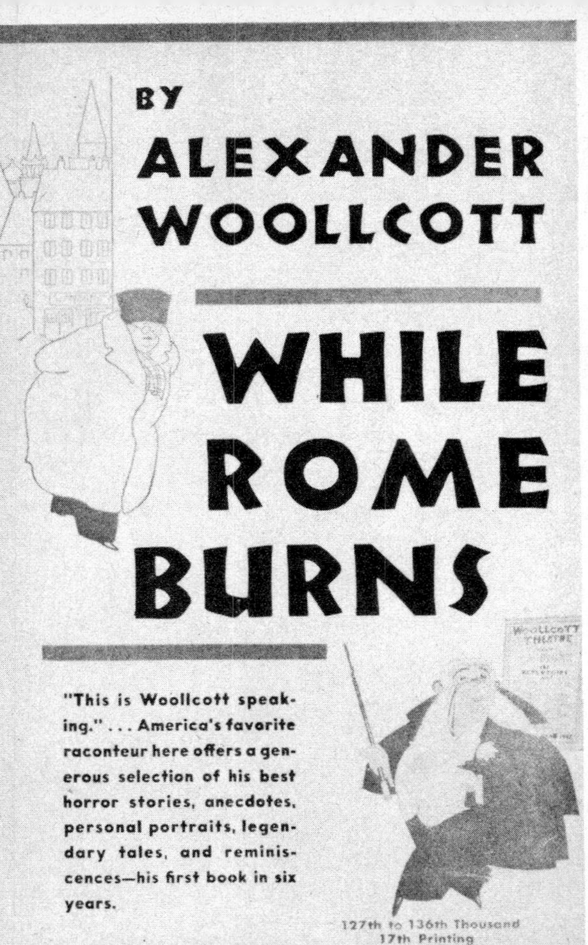

BY
ALEXANDER
WOOLLCOTT
WHILE
ROME
BURNS
"This is Woollcott speaking." . . . America's favorite raconteur here offers a generous selection of his best horror stories, anecdotes, personal portraits, legendary tales, and reminiscences—his first book in six years.
127th to 136th Thousand
17th Printing


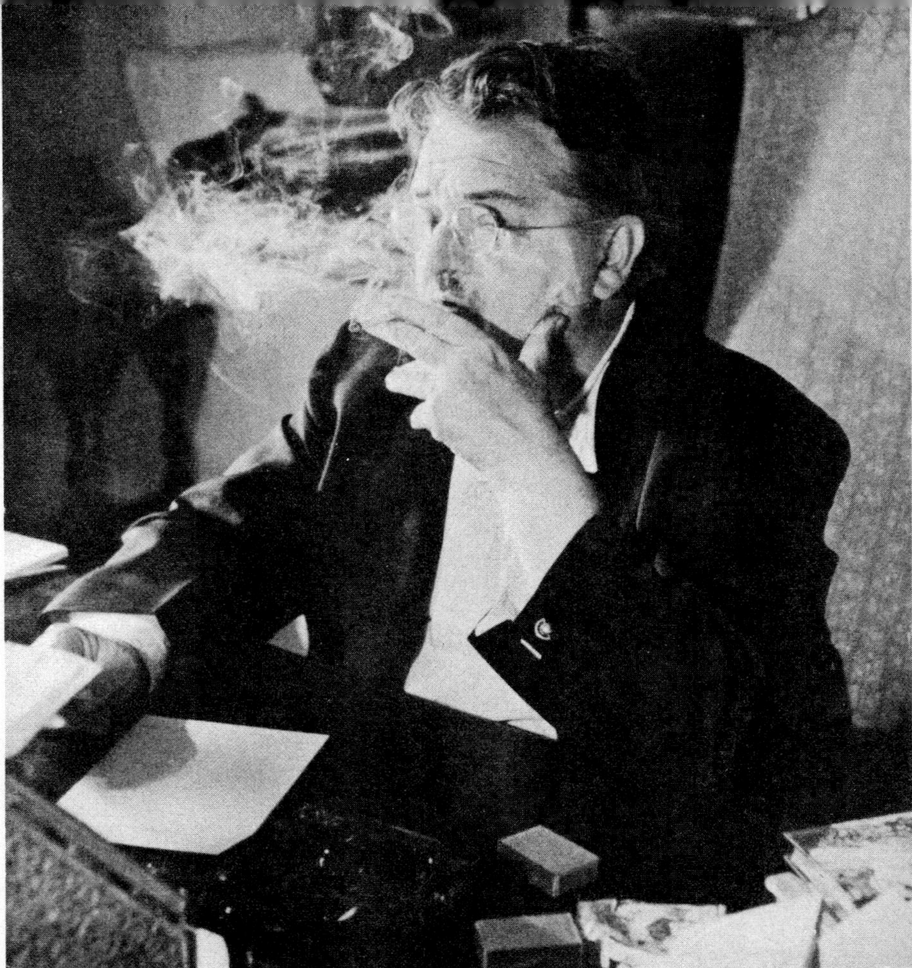

Alexander Woollcott, the critic, raconteur, and eccentric who appears above, came into his own in the nineteen-thirties as "The Town Crier" on the radio. He discoursed so takingly about books and his friends that his own book, *While Rome Burns*, became a best seller of 1934.

Iore important to American literature was the work of James '. Farrell, the Chicago novelist whose *Studs Lonigan* books were mong the solidest and honestest novels of the whole Depresion decade. The jacket that we reproduce is of the trilogy; the hree books came out in 1932, 1934, and 1935.

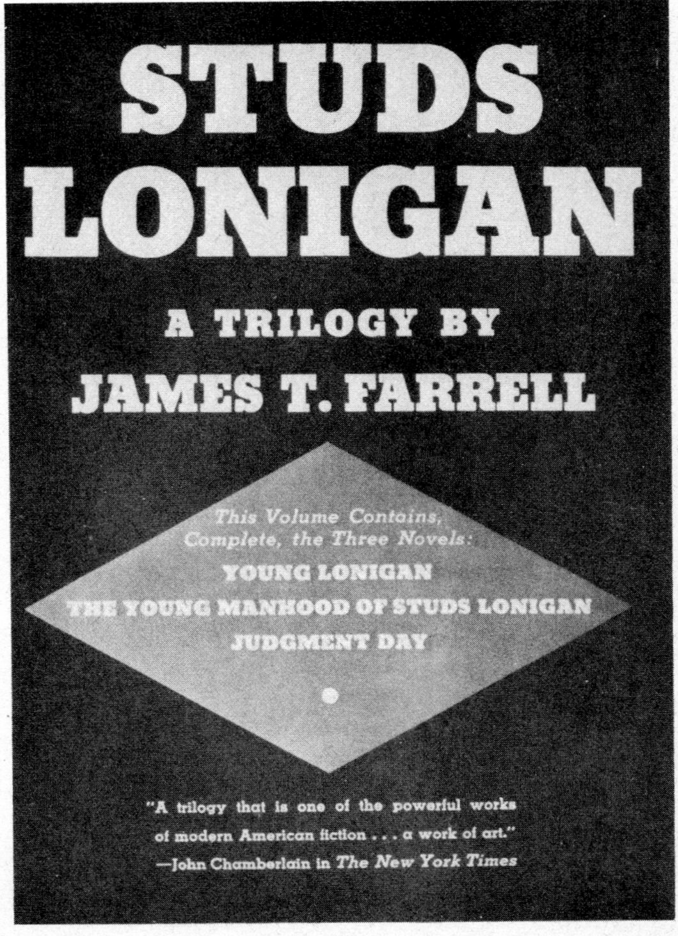

STUDS
LONIGAN
A TRILOGY BY
JAMES T. FARRELL
This Volume Contains, Complete, the Three Novels:
YOUNG LONIGAN
THE YOUNG MANHOOD OF STUDS LONIGAN
JUDGMENT DAY
"A trilogy that is one of the powerful works of modern American fiction . . . a work of art."
—John Chamberlain in The New York Times

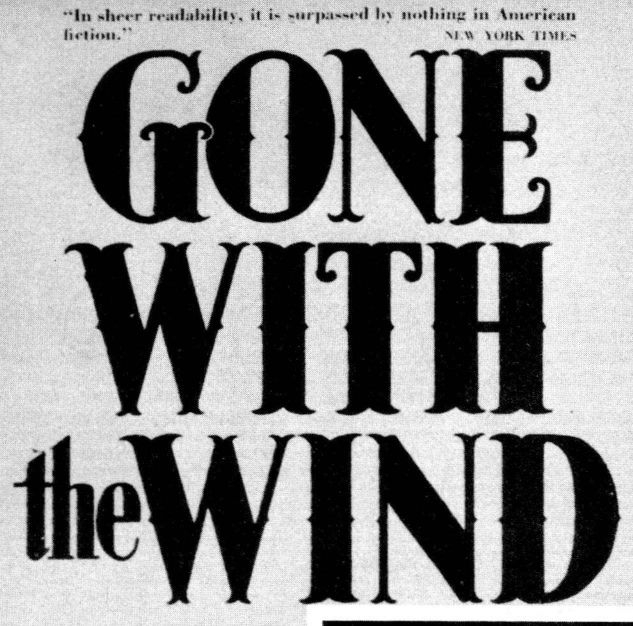

THE LATE
GEORGE APLEY
A Novel in the Form of a Memoir
by
John P. Marquand

'EL 1938

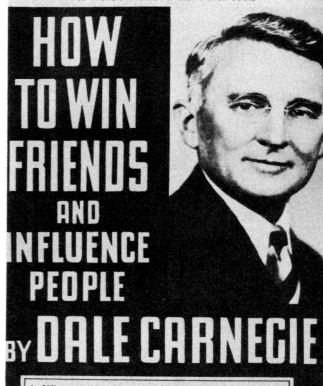

OVER 3,140,000 COPIES SOLD—
A World's Record for Non-Fiction Books

HOW
TO WIN
FRIENDS
AND
INFLUENCE
PEOPLE
BY DALE CARNEGIE

1. What are the six ways of making people like you? See pages 75-133.
2. What are the twelve ways of winning people to your way of thinking? See pages 137-217.
3. Whatarethenineways to change people without giving offense or arousing resentment? See pages 221-253.

The fiction hit of hits during the decade was Margaret Mitchell's *Gone With the Wind,* which first appeared in 1936. Its success was so colossal as to dwarf that of *Anthony Adverse.* This huge 1037-page novel sold a million copies in its first six months and 3½ million (in English) by the end of 1945, by which time it had been issued in 19 foreign countries and serialized in 5 others! The question who would play Scarlett O'Hara and Rhett Butler in the movies agitated Hollywood—and the reading public—for years; for the answer, see page 208. Above is the author, Margaret Mitchell of Atlanta, Georgia.

Another book which launched its author into popularity was *The Late George Apley,* the satire on Bostonian ways which appeared early in 1937 and the following year won the Pulitzer Prize for John P. Marquand (above, right).

In that year 1937 while GWTW (as people abbreviated it) still led all comers in fiction, the non-fiction best seller was *How to Win Friends and Influence People,* by Dale Carnegie (right), a successful manual of the immemorial American art of self-salesmanship.

To people who considered themselves knowing and up-to-date in the nineteen-twenties, there was no more ridiculous character than Queen Victoria, the very embodiment of objectionable conventionalism. It was perhaps a sign of change in the climate that Helen Hayes made the most popular success of her very distinguished career as the star of "Victoria Regina," by Laurence Housman, produced late in 1935.

he picture above shows Helen Hayes s the young Queen with her adored lbert (played by Vincent Price); the ne at the right shows her—in most in-enious make-up—as the aged Widow f Windsor. The play ran in New York or 517 performances, and then went on our; and there was little sign that audi-nces regarded the Queen as deplorable.

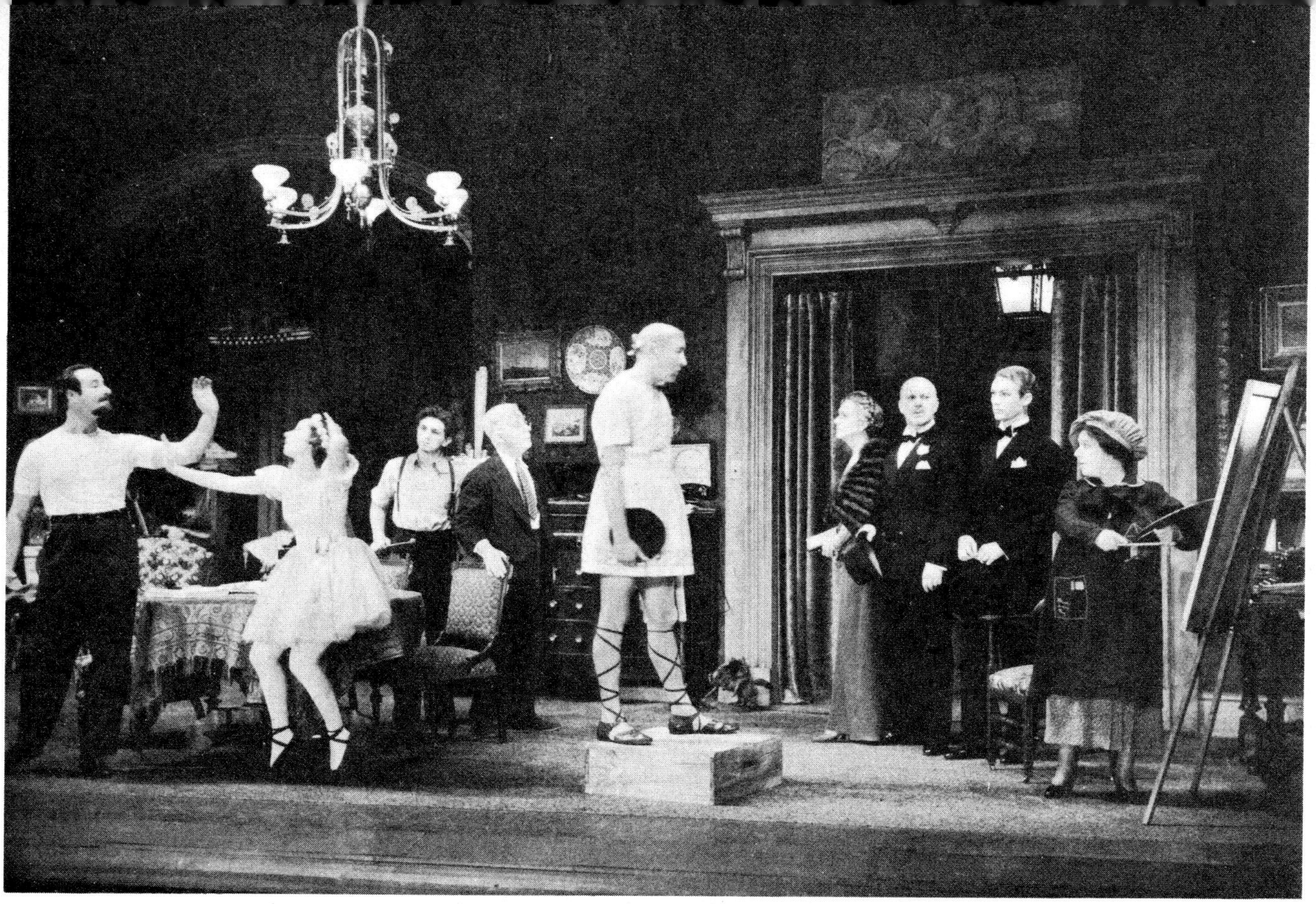

What appears at first glance to be a scene in a happy-go-lucky madhouse, above, is a scene in the family life of the amiable gentleman about whom revolved "You Can't Take It With You," a comedy by George S. Kaufman and Moss Hart which opened in December 1936 and delighted theatre-goers for a long time thereafter. Below are some Ziegfeld Follies girls of the mid-thirties, who make an interesting comparison with the Atlantic City bathing beauties pictured on pages 39 and 40; does it not seem that the feminine figure, while franker about its curves, has become somehow elongated?

We move on to the movies, and remind you of the charm of Myrna Loy as she appeared in "The Thin Man," in 1934, with William Powell (left). The picture in the center is of Johnny Weissmuller—the man who proved that there could be a future in the movies for a man whose 51-second record for swimming 100 yards was to stand from 1927 to World War II—with Maureen O'Sullivan in "Tarzan's Mate," in 1934.

We wouldn't venture to say which of the Marx Brothers' films was the funniest, but anyhow "Duck Soup," produced in 1933, was a wonderful cheer-bringer, showing as it did the adventures of one Mr. Firefly who found himself prime minister of a Ruritanian country, and reaching a climax in the battle scene at the left, in which the brothers appeared in a variety of uniforms.

The only really noted resident of the United State during the nineteen-thirties who was less than a yea old at the time of the Panic was Shirley Templ shown at the left with Lionel Barrymore and Bi Robinson in "The Little Colonel," produced in 193

Below is the tourist-camp scene from one of the mo engaging films of the decade, "It Happened Or Night," with Claudette Colbert and Clark Gable. is said that the fact that Gable, undressing in th camp and disclosing that he wore no undershirt, ha such a catastrophic effect on masculine underwe sales that knitwear manufacturers and garment wor ers' unions protested. Produced in 1934, the pictu won four "Oscars"—for the best actor, actress, produ tion (Columbia), and direction (Capra).

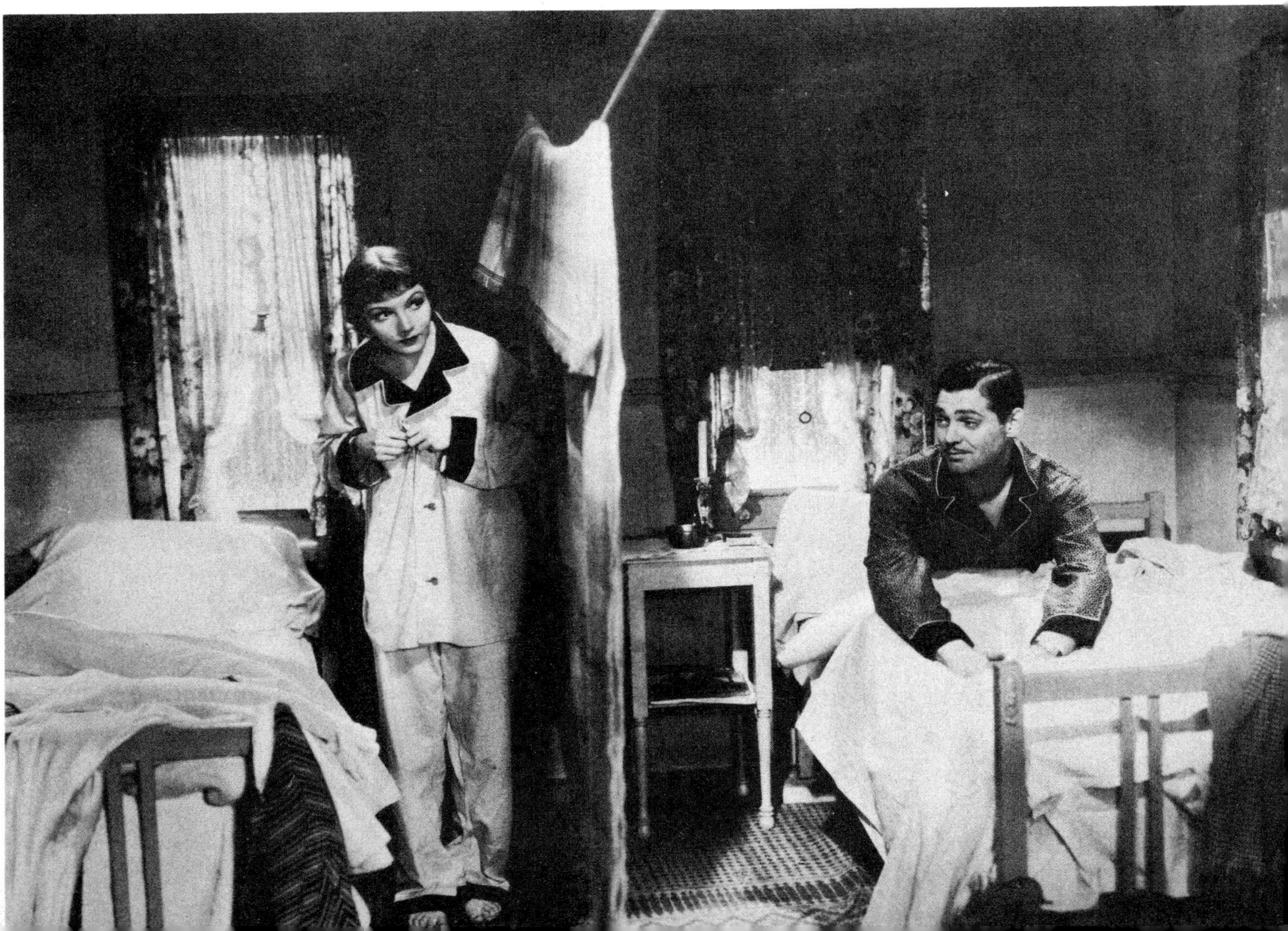

The movies were growing up—and broadening their range. We picture at the right Victor McLaglen in "The Informer," a film of 1935 which well deserved the praise bestowed upon it; but there were many other fine ones to come, including for example "The Life of Emile Zola" (1937), John Ford's version of "The Grapes of Wrath" (1940), "Rebecca" (1940), and of course the Walt Disney fantasies which widely extended the motion-picture field: the enchanting "Snow White" (January 1938), "Pinocchio" (1940), and the more venturesome "Fantasia" (1941).

For sheer pleasure for the audience, one of the best films was "Mr. Deeds Goes to Town" (1936). We show Gary Cooper as Longfellow Deeds, on the rear platform of the train which was to take him away from Mandrake Falls to the city, where he was to find life confusing and sometimes pixillated.

The choice for the part of Scarlett O'Hara in "Gone With the Wind" was the English actress Vivien Leigh, whom we show at the left in her delightful crinoline. Clark Gable took the part of Rhett Butler. Below, Miss Leigh is grouped with Leslie Howard (as Ashley) and Olivia de Havilland (as Melanie) in a scene from the film, which proved to be majestically long, rich in color, and the whopping success of the year 1939.

Radio had immensely broadened its range too, learning during the nineteen-thirties how to produce well-knit variety programs, how to present the best orchestral and opera performances, and how to rival the newspapers in the up-to-the-minute handling of news. And it learned too how to make quiz programs something more than a melange of elementary knowledge, misinformation, and contrived gags; at least two quiz programs made real use of real brains. "Information Please," which first went on the air May 17, 1938, and quickly rose to popularity with a large if literate public, is pictured in operation above, with (from left to right), John Kieran (who had a bad eye when the photograph was taken), Deems Taylor and Mayor F. H. LaGuardia of New York as the two guests, and Franklin P. Adams. At the right is Clifton Fadiman, to whose exceptional skill the success of the program was largely due. Below are "The Quiz Kids," with Joe Kelley as schoolmaster and Jack Lucal, Joan Bishop, Gerard Darrow, Cynthia Cline, and Richard Williams as scholars.

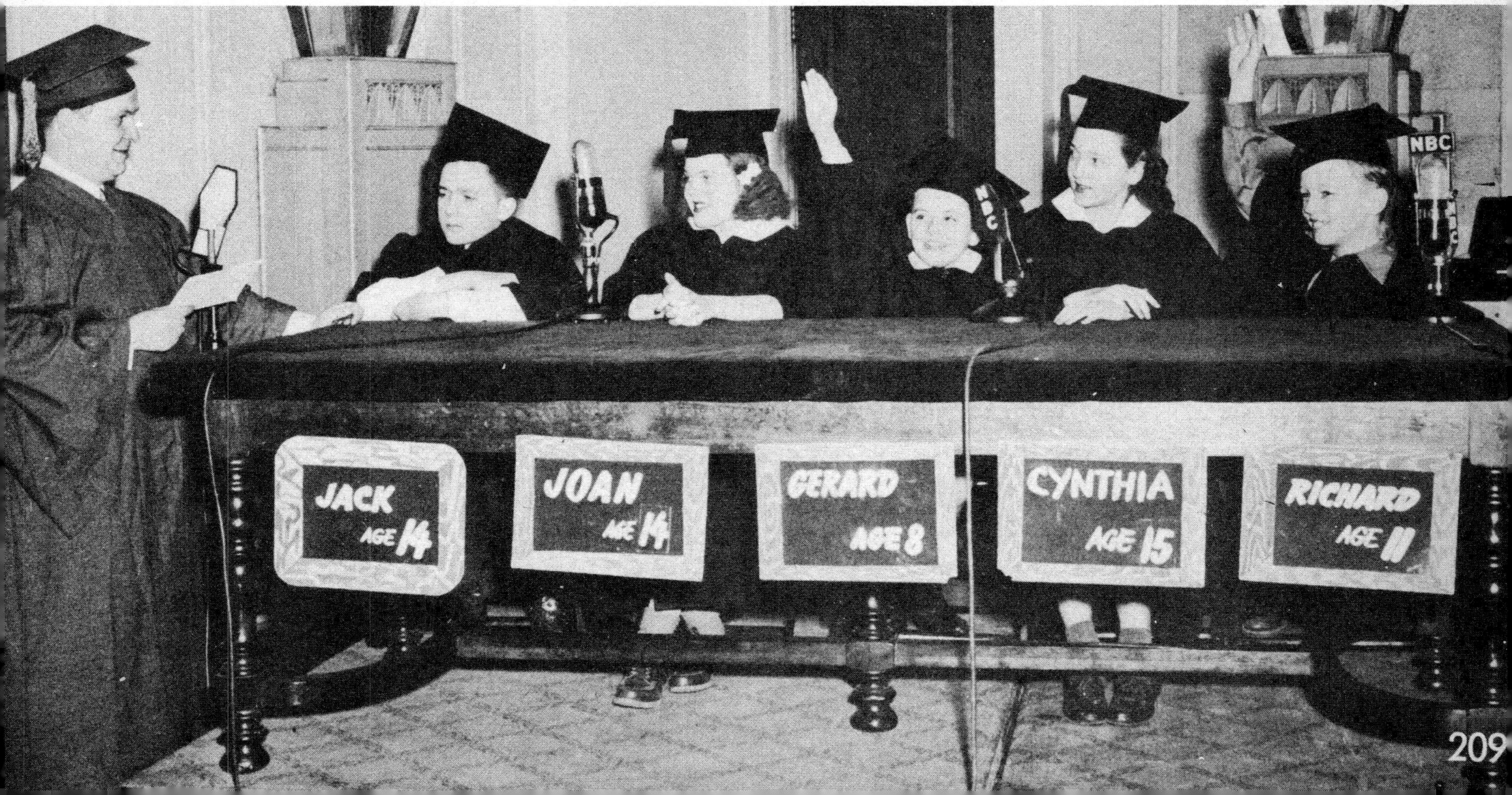

As variety programs improved in technique, they became the consistent favorites of a vast radio public. People might tune in by the millions to a presidential fireside chat or a king's farewell speech or a big fight or a World Series; housewives washed the dishes to the heart-throbs of soap operas, and families enjoyed character comedies of an evening; symphony concerts and grand operas at least won more auditors than had ever before listened to good music anywhere; but the variety shows drew the surest audiences. On these pages we show some of their preferences. At the top of this page is Major Edward Bowes, whose amateur hour was a great success of the mid-thirties. At the left, above, is Kate Smith, a singer widely beloved. And at the right is that master of original wit, Fred Allen.

At the top of this page is the perennial leader in Crossley ratings, Jack Benny, warming up for a program while Van Johnson awaits his turn. Above at the right is, of course, Edgar Bergen with Charlie McCarthy. (Their climb to public favor in 1937 was sensational; prior to that year Bergen had been virtually unknown.) At the left is Bing Crosby, whose high repute as singer, radio performer, and movie actor made him a figure unique in the entertainment world.

With the partial eclipse, after 1929, of the dynasties of inherited wealth and big-business wealth, now beset with taxes and regulations, what had once been called Society became less venerated outside its own ranks; whereas what was nicknamed Café Society—one part wealth, one part fashion, two parts celebrity, two parts night-club press-agentry and gossip-column exploitation—was the envy of millions. Here, at the right, are some glimpses of it at the Stork Club in New York City. At the top, Douglas Fairbanks, Sr., with Lady Ashley, in 1937; in the middle, Douglas Fairbanks, Jr., with the lovely dancer Vera Zorina; and at the bottom, the columnist, Walter Winchell, and the Club's proprietor, Sherman Billingsley. Directly below is the "No. 1 Glamour Girl" of 1938 in New York, Brenda Frazier, as she looked just after her wedding in 1941, with the bridegroom, John S. Kelley.

Irving Berlin, a leading composer of popular music throughout the twenties and thirties, appears above with Mrs. Berlin, the former Ellin Mackay—at the left, on shipboard just after their much-publicized marriage in 1926; at the right, when he received a Hollywood "Oscar" eighteen years later. Below is Eddie Condon, who in the late twenties—when Berlin's name had long been famous—used to play his guitar in basement "jam sessions" in Chicago with Bix Beiderbecke, Teschemacher, MacPartland, Goodman, and Krupa—of whose type of music he later became an influential advocate.

All through the twenties there were a few people who preferred the original jazz, which had started in New Orleans and been developed in Chicago, to the far more popular music which was jazz to ninety-nine Americans out of a hundred—the sort of music of which Paul Whiteman was the high priest. But in the middle and late thirties there was a revolution in taste, with countless jitterbugs as its undisciplined mass army and a few scholars of jazz as its general staff. These scholars reverenced the work of such musicians as "Count" Basie, who at the left is shown at the piano, with the singing Mills Brothers gathered about.

The highest praise of the students of jazz was bestowed upon Edward Kennedy ("Duke") Ellington, composer, arranger, and band-leader, who in the later speakeasy days had had his orchestra at the Cotton Club in Harlem. At the right is Ellington at a concert at Colgate University.

The growing number of jazz devotees took special delight in the work of Louis Armstrong, the trumpeter who appears at the left. Armstrong had begun his career where jazz was born, in New Orleans, had played on river boats, had been a member of King Oliver's band in Chicago, and later led a band of his own. Such men as he, insisted the new school of critics, played jazz; what most people had called jazz for years was nothing but popular ragtime.

While the jazz experts rated most highly such men as Ellington and Basie, the general public were more likely to prefer the music of the Dorseys, who combined the "hot" with much of the "sweet." In the picture at the right, it is Tommy Dorsey who has the cigarette in his mouth. The two brothers, Tommy and Jimmy, had a joint orchestra in 1934-35; subsequently each had his own band.

Whatever might be the relative musical merits of Gershwin, Berlin, Jerome Kern, and Cole Porter on the one hand, and the jazz that originated in the honky-tonks of New Orleans on the other hand, the growing company of radio-listeners and record-buyers always enjoyed the work of instrumentalists who gave what they played an engaging style of their own. During the latter nineteen-thirties the average American, if called to the stage in a quiz program, was less likely to be able to name the president of the Senate than to spot the piano style of Eddy Duchin (left).

Harry James, trumpeter, left Benny Goodman in 1939 to form his own band; and that same year he took on a young and unknown vocalist who created no appreciable stir until much later. Here are James with his trumpet and the obscure youngster, Frank Sinatra, at the microphone.

The one man more responsible than any other for the formation of the vast army of juvenile swing-fanciers, for the rising popularity of such band leaders as Artie Shaw, Gene Krupa, Harry James, Tommy Dorsey, and Glenn Miller, and for the spread of the cult of jazz-record collecting, was Benny Goodman, the clarinetist. For when he formed his own band he was able to combine the discipline and volume of a big group with something of the effect of spontaneity which characterized the best small bands. At the left is Goodman with his clarinet; above is a glimpse of a part of the stampede of excitement which took place when Goodman played at the Paramount Theatre in New York in January 1938, and hordes of young devotees of swing danced in the aisles and even on the stage. Goodman is at the left; the "GK" on the drum stands for Gene Krupa, then with Goodman.

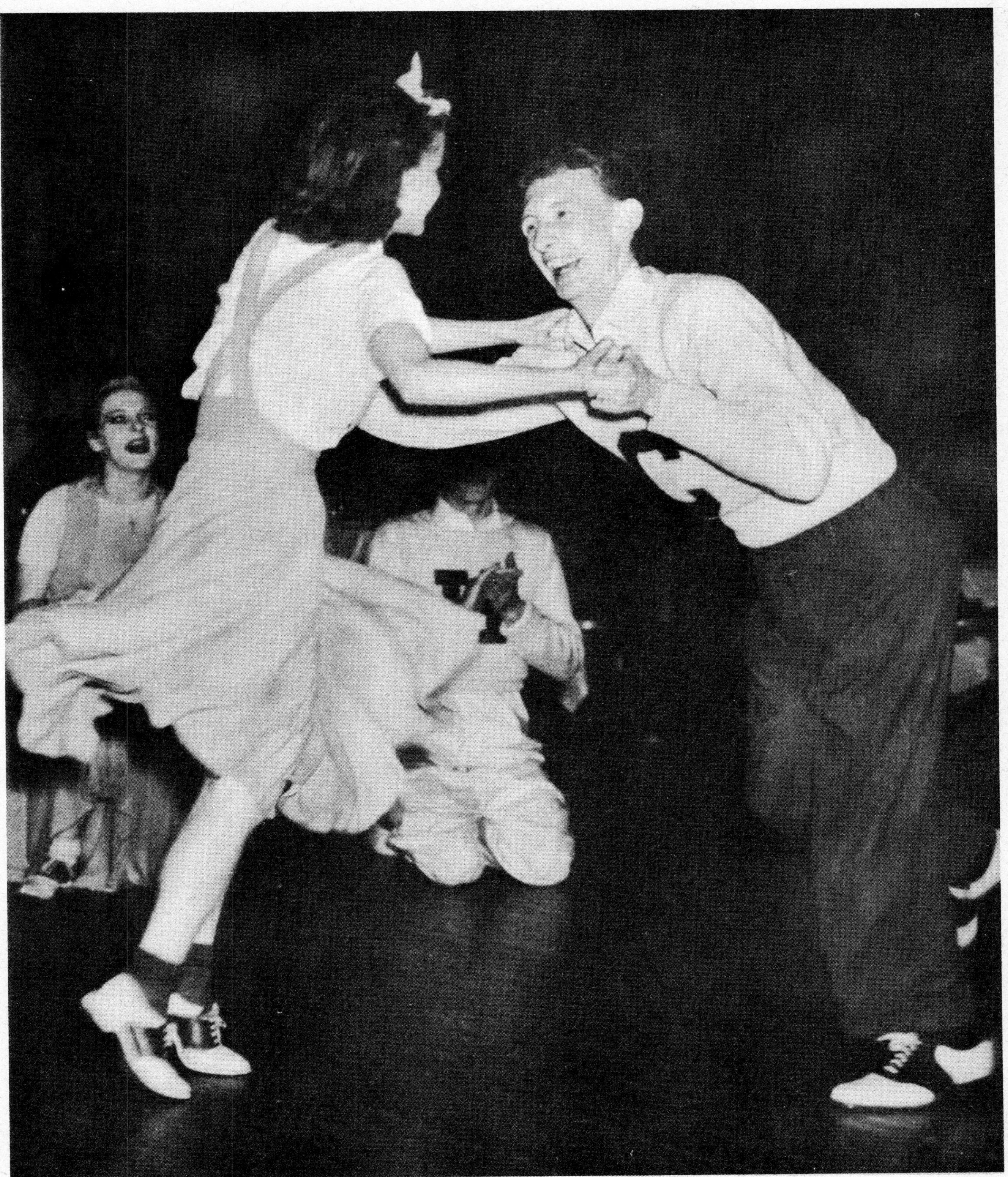

Was it pure chance that "The Big Apple," a modified square dance which was developed by students at the University of North Carolina and became very popular in 1937 and 1938, and the new vogue of square-dancing which accompanied it, represented a less feverish spirit than the Charleston of the previous decade? There was plenty of fever among the jitterbugs and "alligators" of the swing craze; but for organized social dancing there was a return to a tradition that cared less than before about being "advanced" or "sophisticated." By and large, the young people of the nineteen-thirties could take their sex or leave it, without the argument and self-consciousness of the years before 1930. The picture above, showing a young couple dancing "The Big Apple," was taken at the Glen Island Casino, New Rochelle, New York, in 1938.

The years went by but unemployment went right on, the WPA went right on. The years of the New Deal brought their delights and distractions—streamlined cars, "Three Little Pigs," Mae West, "Stormy Weather," the Dionnes, bingo, monopoly, Jack Benny, the royal abdication, ski trains, "Snow White," café society, Charlie McCarthy, "Begin the Beguine," swing, and a host of others—but underneath all of this there remained the uncertainty and misery of joblessness for millions. The photograph below is of unemployed men sitting on the sunny side of the Public Library in San Francisco; and it was taken, not during the time of the Great Nose-dive, but in February 1937—over four years after the New Deal moved into Washington. The NRA, the AAA, regulatory laws, pump-priming, deficit spending, Roosevelt's battle with the Supreme Court—none of them brought a conclusive answer to the overwhelming economic and political problem of our age.

The New York Times.

"All the News That's Fit to Print."

LATE CITY EDITION Generally fair, slowly rising temperatures today. Tomorrow fair, temperatures unchanged. Temperatures Yesterday—Max., 64; Min., 56



VOL. LXXXVIII...No. 29,461. Entered as Second-Class Matter, Postoffice, New York, N. Y. NEW YORK, THURSDAY, SEPTEMBER 22, 1938. THREE CENTS NEW YORK CITY and Vicinity | FOUR CENTS Elsewhere Except in 7th and 8th Postal Zones.

# HURRICANE SWEEPS COAST; 9 ARE KILLED ON LONG ISLAND; 51 DIE IN NEW ENGLAND FLOOD

CITY IS HARD HIT

Storm Batters All New England; Providence Hit by Tidal Wave

# GEN. WESTOVER DIES IN FLAMING PLANE; HEADED AIR CORPS

Officer Burned With Sergeant in Crash as He Attempts to Land in California

EXPLOSION IGNITES HOUSE

# CZECHOSLOVAKIA DECIDES TO GIVE UP; CROWDS PROTEST, CABINET IN PERIL; CHAMBERLAIN TO DEMAND GUARANTEES

PREMIER OFF TODAY

Stalwart Czech Men Sob in Prague; People Tear Up Papers in Disgust

CZECHS ARE BITTER

The New York Times.

"All the News That's Fit to Print."

LATE CITY EDITION Rain and cooler today. Tomorrow generally fair with little change in temperature. Temperatures Yesterday—Max., 72; Min., 58



VOL. LXXXVIII...No. 29,469. Entered as Second-Class Matter, Postoffice, New York, N. Y. NEW YORK, FRIDAY, SEPTEMBER 30, 1938. THREE CENTS NEW YORK CITY and Vicinity | FOUR CENTS Elsewhere Except in 7th and 8th Postal Zones.

# DEWEY NOMINATED BY REPUBLICANS; ATTACKS TAMMANY

HAILED IN OVATION

Rainstorm and Winds Due to Hit City Today

# TORNADOES KILL 26 IN CHARLESTON; HUNDREDS INJURED

Storms Strike City Without Warning, Causing Loss Estimated Up to $5,000,000

OLD LANDMARKS DAMAGED

# FOUR POWERS REACH A PEACEABLE AGREEMENT; GERMANS TO ENTER SUDETEN AREA TOMORROW AND WILL COMPLETE OCCUPATION IN TEN DAYS

Flight to Ireland Goes On Despite New Peace Hope

CZECHS DEPRESSED

Text of 4-Power Accord

NAZI DEMANDS MET

The New York Times.

"All the News That's Fit to Print."

LATE CITY EDITION Generally fair, continued cool today. Tomorrow fair, slowly rising temperature. Temperatures Yesterday—Max., 64; Min., 52



VOL. LXXXVIII...No. 29,470. Entered as Second-Class Matter, Postoffice, New York, N. Y. NEW YORK, SATURDAY, OCTOBER 1, 1938. THREE CENTS NEW YORK CITY and Vicinity | FOUR CENTS Elsewhere Except in 7th and 8th Postal Zones.

# LEHMAN IS DRAFTED FOR FOURTH TERM; HE ATTACKS DEWEY

POLETTI ON TICKET

Democratic Ticket Nominated for State

# NEW DEAL A PERIL, SAYS GEN. MOSELEY; SHARPLY REBUKED

Retiring Atlanta Commander Declares We Face Danger of 'Decay Within'

SEES DICTATORSHIP IN END

# BRITAIN AND GERMANY MAKE ANTI-WAR PACT; HITLER GETS LESS THAN HIS SUDETEN DEMANDS; POLISH ULTIMATUM THREATENS ACTION TODAY

5,000 British Soldiers Will Guard Czech Areas

POLES READY TO ACT

Germans Begin Czech Occupation; Troops Cross Old Austrian Border

PEACE AID PLEDGED

And now the storms that had been gathering abroad—breaking in Manchuria (1931), Ethiopia (1935), the Rhineland (1936), Spain (1936), China (1937), and Austria (spring of 1938) — began more and more ominously to darken the American sky. When in September 1938 Hitler threatened Czechoslovakia, and Neville Chamberlain went to meet him at Berchtesgaden and at Godesburg and at Munich, the sense of menace spread more widely among Americans, and H. V. Kaltenborn's precise analyses of the crisis won breathless radio listeners. As you will note in the headlines above, another storm broke during those days—a hurricane which hit New England on September 21, 1938, and played tricks like the one at the right, photographed in Saybrook, Connecticut.

# V. THE GATHERING STORM

As the war clouds loomed larger, the American public that watched them with growing apprehension wanted none of war. The prevailing feeling was that American participation in World War I had been, if not a mistake, at least a painful disappointment; that while Hitler was an evil force in the world, he would not directly threaten America—nor would the Japanese; that while we might feel deep private sympathy for the victims of aggression, this was none of our business as a nation; that we should be ready to defend ourselves and especially should build up our air force, but should take every precaution to wall ourselves away from war behind our Neutrality Acts. We had our own troubles to attend to—the job of climbing out of the Depression—and for this, we felt, peace was essential. Below is a scene at a World Youth Congress which met at Vassar College in August 1938—when the Czech crisis was approaching—to discuss world peace and how to maintain it.

On Sunday, April 30, 1939, New York opened its World's Fair, with the flags of all nations (or almost all) whipping in the breeze, and with hopeful speeches about international amity resounding over the loud speakers. In the picture above, the round object in the background at the left is the Perisphere; the Trylon is the slender spire to the right of it, under the gay flags. These two structures symbolized the "Theme" of the Fair.

Visit
HEINEKEN'S ON THE ZUIDERZEE
NEW YORK WORLD'S FAIR
1939


It was a wonderful fair, with fantastic modern architecture, waterfalls coming down off buildings, lights shining upward at night upon the bright green of young trees; with fountains, and fireworks, and a General Motors Futurama, and incredible industrial exhibits, and an aquacade where girls swam in patterns to waltz music; with bands playing "Roll Out the Barrel," and a baby panda, and razzle-dazzle sideshows in the Amusement Center, and Holland beer to drink by the Zuiderzee (see the coasters at the left), and busses that piped a merry phrase from "The Sidewalks of New York."

Sixty nations took part; the only conspicuous absentee was Germany. (At that moment Hitler had more pressing business to attend to: it was in the spring of 1939 that he overran Czechoslovakia, in defiance of the Munich agreement.) The Japanese had an exhibit; in the picture below, taken in Tokyo the year before the festivities started at Flushing Meadows, a drawing of it is being shown to Ambassador Joseph C. Grew.

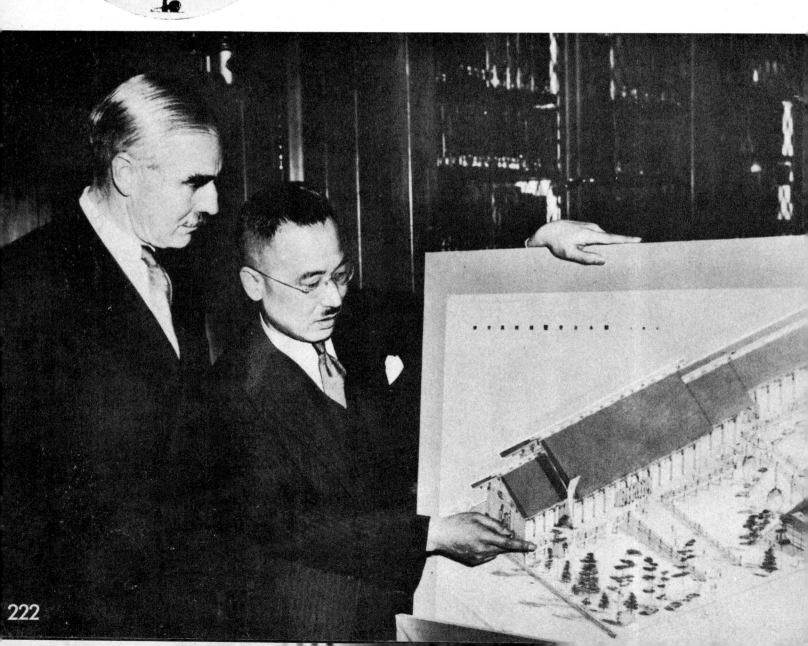

The Russians had a massive building topped with a stainless steel figure of a workman; here, in the Soviet exhibit, was the bas-relief of Stalin which we show at the right. The French had an especially charming big pavilion, with a luxurious terraced restaurant looking out over the "Lagoon of Nations"; below, you see the dedication of this pavilion, with the French Ambassador raising the French flag in a snowstorm on January 13, 1939, surrounded by French officials and Grover Whalen and his aides. Not yet had France been overrun by the Nazis—nor Poland, nor Norway, nor Holland, nor Belgium, all of which were exhibitors. (And there was a majestic Italian building, with a figure of Italia, seated, on its summit and a waterfall coming down its front.) Yet sometimes the hopeful words spoken about peace at Flushing Meadows sounded a little like whistling in the dark. For there was the Czechoslovakia building standing uncompleted, a warning of things to come.

When the late Clarence Day, Jr., ill w arthritis, began in 1931 to write some mc est recollections of his headstrong a conservative father, nothing could ha amazed him more than to be told that *L With Father* would be a big best seller ye. later, that the play made from it by Howa Lindsay and Russel Crouse would run o seven years in New York and have t other companies playing it on the road, a that the movie rights would be one of big prizes of Hollywood competition. T play opened in November 1939; at left are Dorothy Stickney and Howa Lindsay as the elder Days. Below is a sce from another successful comedy of 19 "The Philadelphia Story," with Kathar Hepburn, who was the star not only of stage version but also of the screen one.

Moss Hart and George S. Kaufman "The Man Who Came to Dinner," was produced in October 1939, they its leading character—a noted lecturer t whose manners were deliberately in- —with at least one eye upon Alexander :ott. And though the part was taken at Monty Woolley, Woollcott was happy e a chance to play it later. Here he is, right, as Sheridan Whiteside, the din- est who was compelled by an accident ce a long visit and to occupy a wheel and who was mighty disagreeable about picture below is of a scene from an- comedy that made people laugh while rm clouds were slowly rising: "Arsenic ld Lace." It shows the two nice Brook- ters whose elderberry wine was so very, pecial, with their daft brother who it he was Colonel Theodore Roosevelt.

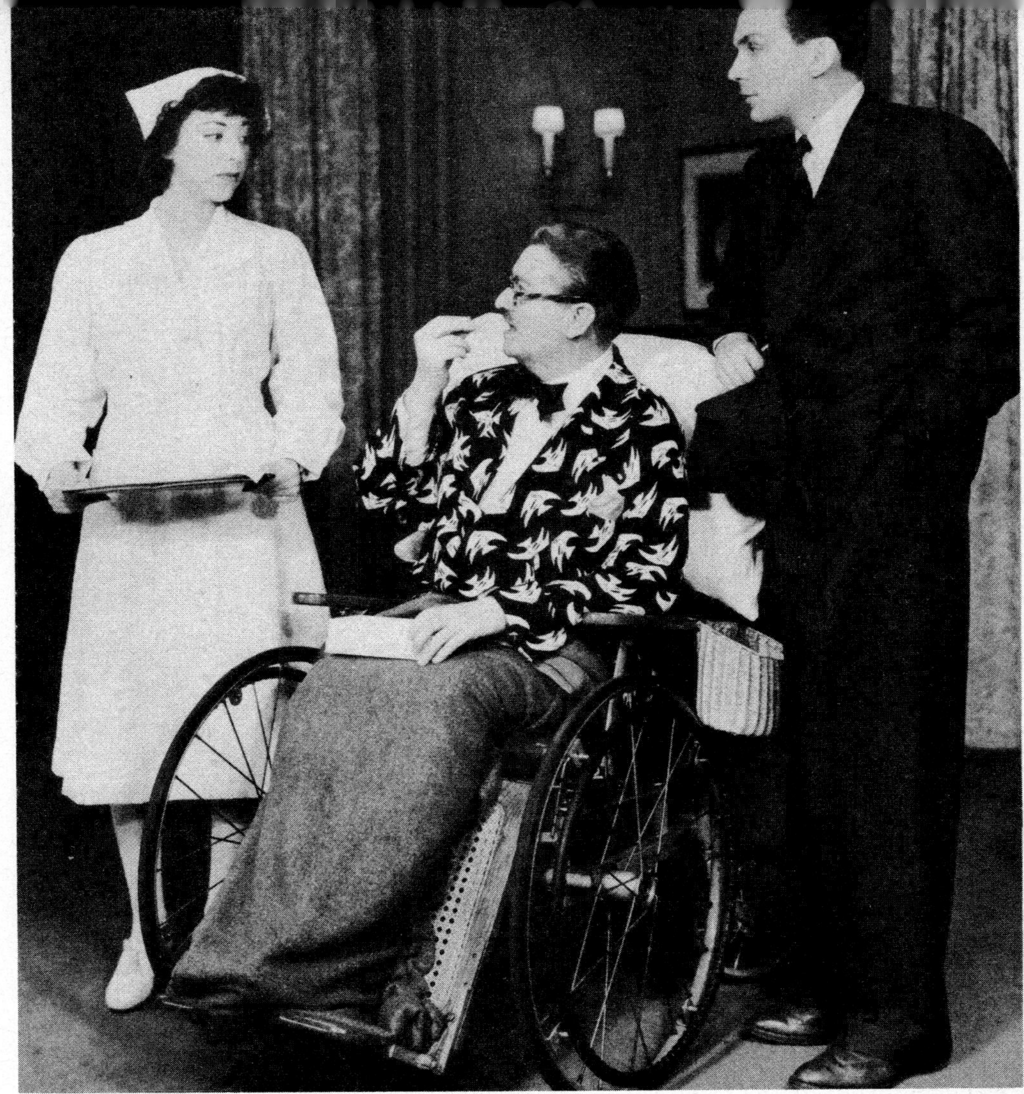

But the theatre was not simply a place of amusement and escape; the storm clouds rolled there too. Robert E. Sherwood had been shocked from the outset by Nazi-Fascist behavior, and as early as March 1936 his play about it, "Idiot's Delight," had appeared. And after the war began in 1939 he became one of the most eloquent American enemies of aggression. It was ironical, in view of subsequent developments, that he should have chosen for the locale of "There Shall Be No Night"—a scene from which, as played by Alfred Lunt and Lynn Fontanne, we show above—not Poland, but Finland, which had been attacked late in 1939 by Russia. But by the time the play was produced in April 1940, the war nearer at hand had ceased to be a "phony war"; Hitler had invaded Denmark and Norway and was about to push across Holland, Belgium, and France, to menace Britain, and to deepen American fears; and those who saw "There Shall Be No Night" could apply its lesson where they willed.

It was a great time for radio commentators, foreign correspondents, and columnists who knew Europe. Above is Walter Lippmann, enlightening columnist; below, Raymond Gram Swing, whose gentle, urgent radio voice became familiar to millions.

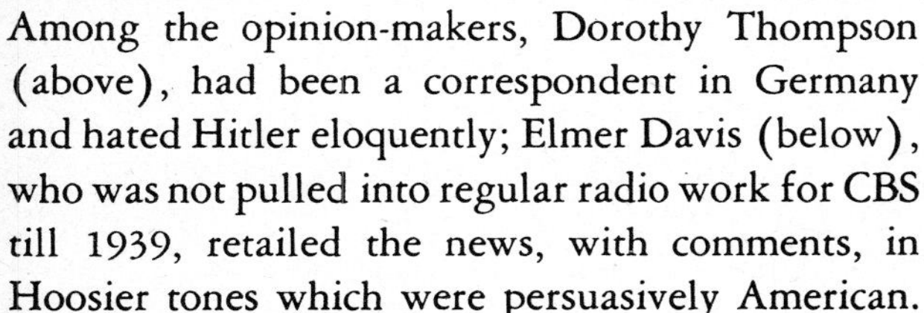

Among the opinion-makers, Dorothy Thompson (above), had been a correspondent in Germany and hated Hitler eloquently; Elmer Davis (below), who was not pulled into regular radio work for CBS till 1939, retailed the news, with comments, in Hoosier tones which were persuasively American.

From 1933 on, refugees came in a steady stream to our shores from Europe. At first they were mostly such Jews as could manage to get out of Germany; then they were other anti-Nazis and lovers of freedom, both from Germany and from other countries; after the spring of 1940 they included many French. These people were of all types and species: sympathy-winning and disarming, hard and greedy; quick to accomodate themselves to our American ways, pathetically out of place here. They included, to our great advantage, some of the ablest men and women of Europe: writers like Thomas Mann and the Zweigs; musicians like Stravinsky and Serkin; architects like Gropius; artists like Grosz, Chagall, and Leger; men of science like Fermi—to say nothing of the man whose influence on scientific thinking the world over had been equaled by no man of his generation—Albert Einstein. We show him above, conferring during the war with Captain Geoffrey E. Sage (seated) and Lieutenant Commander Frederick L. Douthit of the U.S. Naval Training School at Princeton, New Jersey.

Had the news from Europe made people jittery, or was what happened on an October evening of 1938 merely a sign that the radio was a more convincing medium than had been supposed? On October 30, Orson Welles put on the air a dramatization of *The War of the Worlds,* by H. G. Wells, and did it by simulating an actual news broadcast. Bulletins told of Martians landing in New Jersey, laying the land waste with diabolical weapons, planning general destruction. Despite the explanatory introduction and the fact that this was a scheduled broadcast, listeners swamped newspapers with panicky calls, rushed to interrupt church services with the news that the world was coming to an end, ran out of their houses to seek an obscure safety. The *New York Times* received 875 calls, and in Newark 15 people were treated for shock. There were similar reactions the country over. And all without their having seen this picture of Orson Welles (right) that was taken after the broadcast.

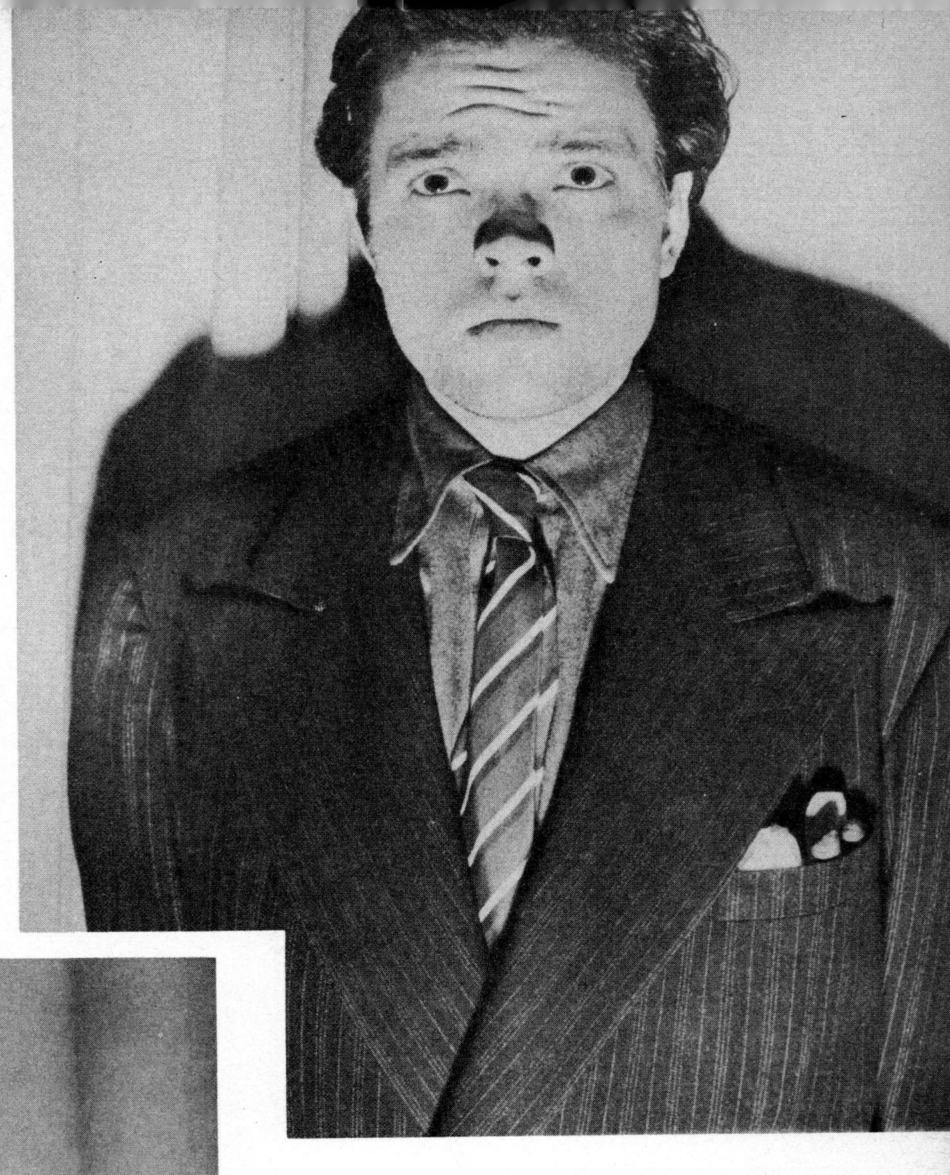

As the news became more disturbing, a curious upsurge of emotional patriotism became noticeable in America. This had nothing to do with party, political credo, isolationism, or interventionism. It was spontaneously evident in the work of many novelists, poets, artists, photographers. Deeply though they might feel that America was wanting in this respect or that, they realized anew that they loved, and wanted to celebrate, its grandeur, its gifts of opportunity, its friendliness—in short, its democracy. A poet had only to string a lot of place names together to make people feel that he was Walt Whitman invoking the American spirit. The new mood caused Irving Berlin's forgotten "God Bless America" to be resurrected into wide popularity; and when Paul Robeson (left), the great Negro actor and singer, sang "Ballad for Americans" on CBS's "Pursuit of Happiness " program on November 5, 1939, the audience shouted applause for full twelve minutes. The ballad was a favorite at party conventions in the summer of 1940.

Charlie Chaplin too felt the anti-Nazi urge; and having always worn as a comedian a small, abrupt mustache similar to the one which Hitler had made famous, he saw his opportunity to portray a comic Hitler. After long preparation, the result was "The Great Dictator," produced in 1940. In the nature of things the film was better in the less ambitious scenes where Chaplin's gift for absurd pantomime could have full sway than in the passages of noble propaganda; but there was some satisfaction in the fact that the movie was banned in Fascist Europe. We show Chaplin as the Dictator, at the end of an office as long as Mussolini's, with the double cross, his symbol, on the wall behind him.

Early in the summer of 1939—that summer when the submarine *Squalus* sank off Portsmouth, New Hampshire, and the New York World's Fair was in full swing, and people were learning about the Okies from *The Grapes of Wrath,* and movie-goers were seeing "Goodbye Mr. Chips," and in Europe Hitler was preparing for his September sweep over Poland—there were royal visitors to America. The President, who was much less concerned with keeping America neutral than with trying to make her weight felt against Hitler, did all he could to make the visit both martial and folksy. When the King and Queen of England arrived in Washington, a procession of sixty baby tanks preceded them; when they went to Hyde Park, there was a picnic at which the King ate hot dogs and drank beer—the consumption of a hot dog being clearly the way to the great heart of America. The picture above was taken at Hyde Park: at the left, Mrs. Roosevelt; then King George VI; then Mrs. James Roosevelt, the President's mother; then Queen Elizabeth; then F.D.R.—all of them apparently enjoying themselves without visible strain.

In September 1939 the war that everybody had been half expecting in Europe, and that so many people had worked and hoped and prayed to avert, at last broke. On the page opposite we show the front page of the extra published by the New York *Herald Tribune* on September 1, the day when the Germans took off into Poland; and of another extra for September 3, when Britain made her reluctant but unavoidable entry into the war. The photograph above is of passengers on the *Conte di Savoia,* an Italian liner which arrived in New York on September 29, crowding to go through immigration inspection—a tiny fraction of the throng of Americans who were driven home before the flames that licked across Europe.

Something to think about over the Labor Day weekend of 1939

New York Herald Tribune

EXTRA

LATE CITY EDITION

FRIDAY, SEPTEMBER 1, 1939

# Hitler Starts Hostilities, Poland Is Invaded; Danzig Annexed; Cities Bombed From Air; Britain, France, U.S. Prepare to Meet Crisis

## 3 Million Begin Exodus From Chief British Cities

Lead Evacuation of London at Dawn, Masks and Food Rations to Trains; Good By and Say Prayers

## Britain Calls Parliament Session Today

Cabinet Meets; Daladier Summons His Ministers and Consults Gamelin

## Roosevelt Notified, Telephones to Hull

Informs Army and Navy of Hostilities on Word From Envoy at Warsaw

## Hitler Takes Danzig, Calls Goering Heir

Tells Reichstag Attack on Poland Is Under Way but Avoids the Word 'War'

## Announces Himself The 'First Soldier'

Nazi Demands 'Modest,' He Says, but Now He'll Meet 'Bomb With Bomb'

## Nazis' Plan Reported Warsaw

THE WEATHER

Today: Generally fair, little change in temperature

Tomorrow: Increasing cloudiness, showers in late afternoon

Detailed Report on Page 9, Sec. III

New York Herald Tribune

Vol. XCIX No. 33,894

SUNDAY, SEPTEMBER 3, 1939

Section One

# Great Britain Declares War on Germ[any]; Mussolini Urges Parley, Hitler Consider[s]; Poland Reports 1,500 Killed in Air Ra[id]

## Nazis Report Polish Planes 'Annihilated'

Air Victory Complete, Says Communique, Corridor Virtually Cut by Armies

## Berlin Crowds Heil Red Army Mission

Reich Hears Enemy Air Raid Was Beaten Off, 27 Polish Planes Shot Down

By Joseph Barnes

## Poland Says It Is Making A Hard Fight

16 Killed, 35 Injured in Warsaw as Air Bombs Raze Workmen's Flats

## Secret Parliament Vows Not to Yield

Parties Swear to Fight to 'Last Drop' of Blood; Troops Battle in Silesia

In June 1940 France fell—and at once the Nazi threat to America's safety loomed larger. Within a few weeks both political parties held their conventions and put forward their candidates. The identity of the Democratic one was not exactly a surprise. Roosevelt had been coming to feel that no other man could align the United States against Hitler as he could, and had decided to defy precedent and run for a third term; so the convention proved a rubber-stamp affair, with Henry Wallace as the chief's choice for Vice President. But the Republican choice was astonishing. Prepared to nominate Taft or Dewey or some other politician, the party was swept off its feet by a burst of enthusiasm for a business man—Wendell Willkie of the Commonwealth and Southern utility group. He proved a refreshingly attractive and dynamic candidate, if usually hoarse; we show him above, riding in an ancient victoria at a frontier celebration at Cheyenne during the campaign. And at the left, we remind you of the variety of Willkie and Roosevelt buttons of 1940.

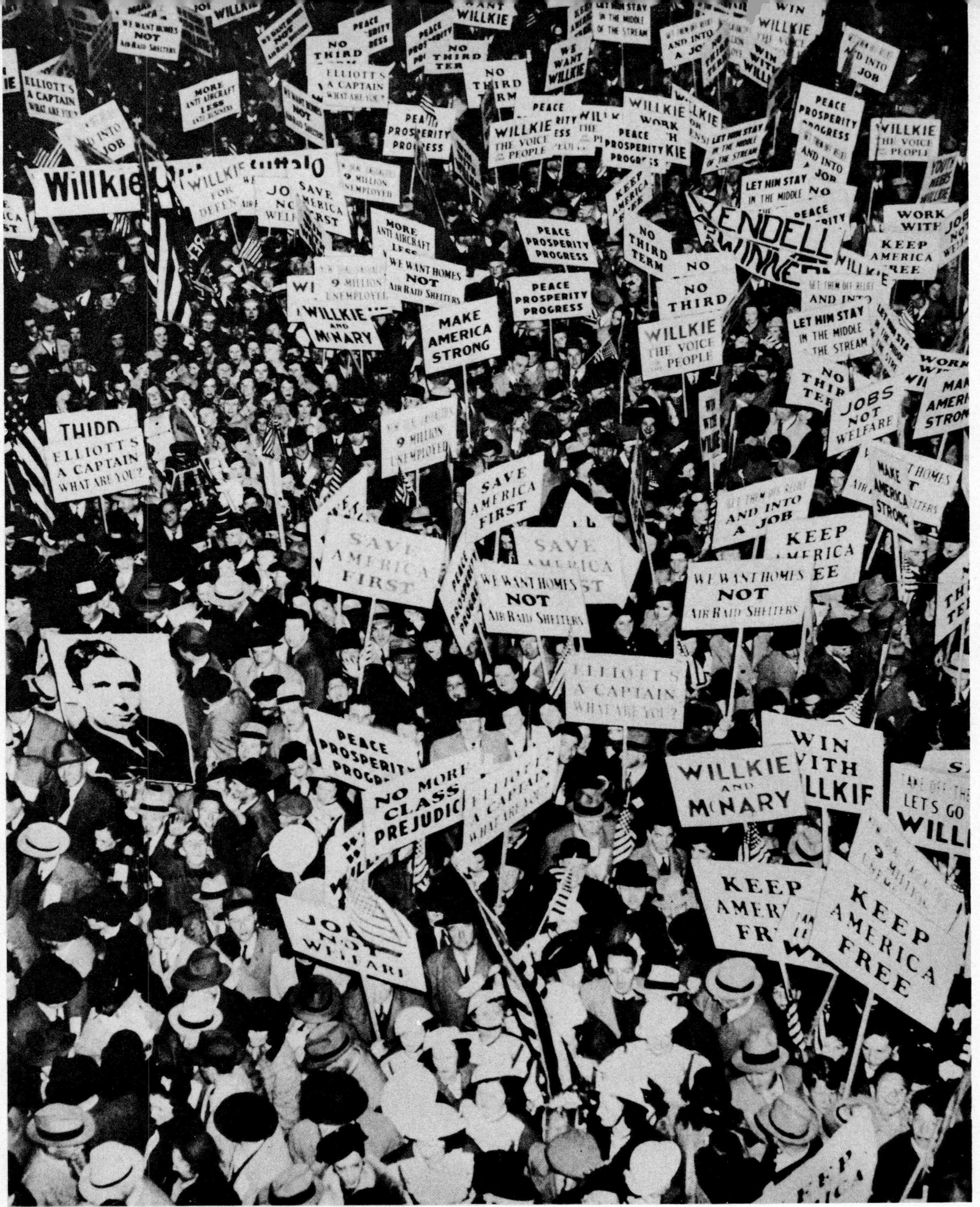


To taste the flavor of the 1940 campaign, read the signs carried by this crowd of more than 10,000 people who were unable to get into the Buffalo Memorial Auditorium for the Willkie rally there on the night of October 15, 1940. But this enthusiasm was of little avail against the great vote-getter. On Election Day, Roosevelt received 27 million votes to Willkie's 22 million; 449 electoral votes to Willkie's 82. And the third term began.

From 1939 until Pearl Harbor there
a new and deepening political divisior
the United States—and very confusin,
was to people who had been used to th
ing of one another as New Dealers
Roosevelt-haters, Republicans or De
crats. For a sort of Paul Jones took pl.
and the new line-up cut clear across
other groupings. It was isolationists vs.
terventionists. At the outset the isolati
ists had a big majority; but the tide
against them. One reason for this was t
the more substantial isolationists had sc
strange bedfellows, such as Father Cha
E. Coughlin (left) and Gerald L. K. Sm
In the view below, taken in 1936, Sn
is at the left, with old Dr. Francis E. To
send (of the Townsend Plan) flank
Father Coughlin on the other side.

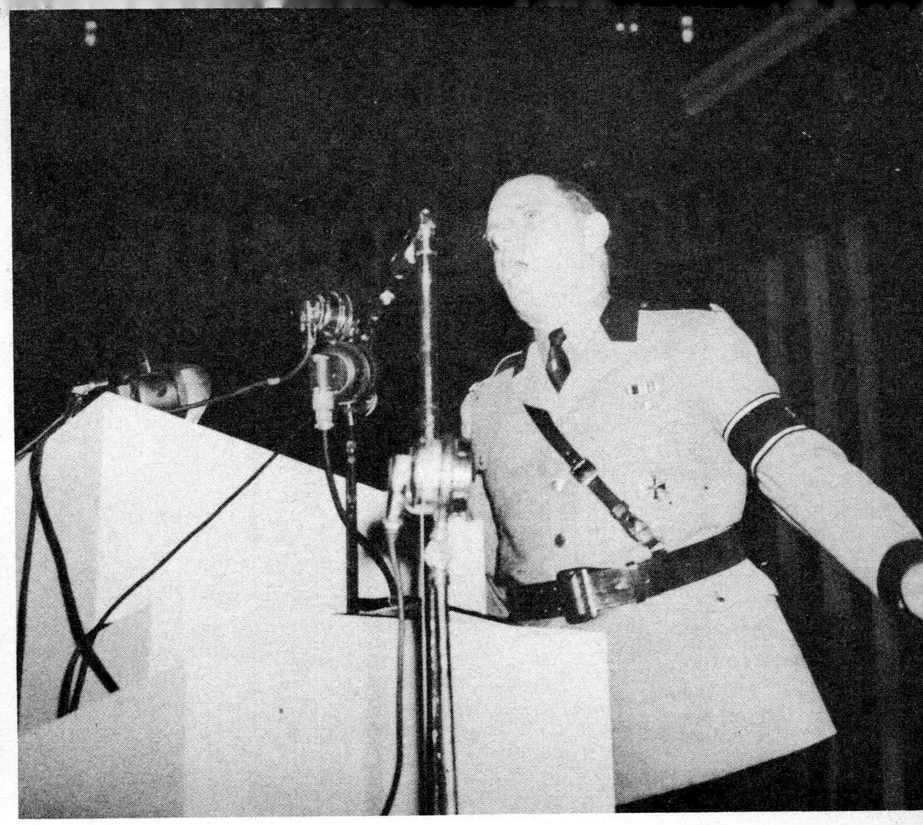

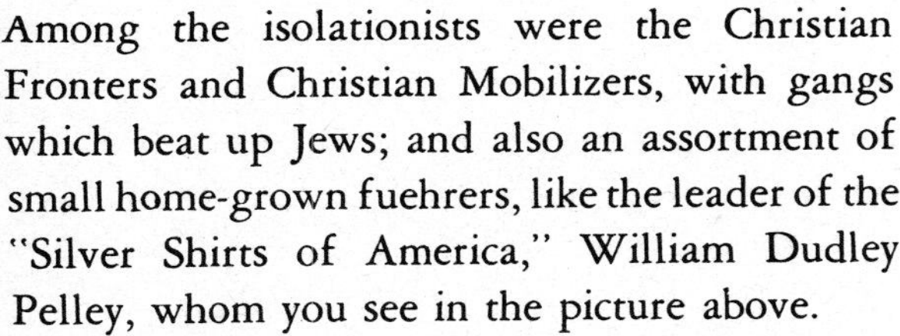

Among the isolationists were the Christian Fronters and Christian Mobilizers, with gangs which beat up Jews; and also an assortment of small home-grown fuehrers, like the leader of the "Silver Shirts of America," William Dudley Pelley, whom you see in the picture above.

More embarrassing still, there was Fritz Kuhn with his subversive German American Bund, an avowedly "100 per cent American and Christian" outfit. You see Kuhn above, speaking at a pro-Nazi rally at Madison Square Garden, New York, in 1939—and looking the part. Below are members of another and more pathetic anti-war group: the sect of Jehovah's Witnesses, convening in 1940.

As for the Communists—whose two chief leaders, William Z. Foster (left) and Earl Browder, appear above, whispering together on the platform at a Lenin memorial meeting in 1940—they were on-again-off-again, faithful to Soviet policy. Until August 23, 1939, they were ardently anti-Nazi. Then Russia signed up with Hitler and they became isolationist, saying that the Allies were engaged in an "imperialist" war. When on June 21, 1941, Hitler attacked Russia, they made a right-about turn and joined the interventionists. The Communists were few but active, had many fellow-travelers, and thus affected defense production—first impeding it, then speeding it.

Few of the interventionists wanted America to go to war. Most were for "aid short of war"; the mouth-filling name of their chief organization was The Committee to Defend America by Aiding the Allies. Later the more militant of them organized Fight for Freedom. Here is a platform group at a Fight for Freedom rally in New York in October 1941: Wendell L. Willkie (standing), Herbert Agar (left), William S. Knudsen, Mayor F. H. LaGuardia of New York, and the attractive actress Carole Landis.

At the right are the emblems of France Forever, British War Relief, and Fight for Freedom—familiar sights to many in 1940 and 1941. Below is a huge rally held by America First, the chief isolationist organization, in May 1941, at Madison Square Garden, with Charles A. Lindbergh speaking.

WEDNESDAY, MAY 29, 1940

C No. 34,163 — Copyright, 1940, New York Tribune Inc.

# 00,000 Allied Troops Try to Escape by Dunker
# As 300,000 Belgians Yield; Cabinet Disowns Leop
# U.S. Names Defense Board of Seven, Maps New T

Section One

SUNDAY, JUNE 23, 1940

C No. 34,188 — Copyright, 1940, New York Tribune Inc.

# rmistice Signed by France and Germany
# Nazis Reported Taking Fleet, Holding Coa

Events (see upper headlines) and Roosevelt (see lower ones) were both on the side of more and more intervention. In September 1940 Congress passed the Selective Service Act and the draft began. At the right is Secretary of War Stimson, blindfolded, drawing the first Order Number late in 1940—a matter of intense interest to millions of registrants, each of whom knew his own Serial Number by heart.

Vol. C No. 34,261 — Copyright, 1940, New York Tribune Inc.

WEDNESDAY, SEPTEMBER 4, 1940

# .S. Trades Britain 50 Destroyers for Air-Sea Ba
# oosevelt Concludes Deal, Then Informs Congr

Vol. C No. 34,378 — Copyright, 1940, New York Tribune Inc.

MONDAY, DECEMBER 30, 1940

# Roosevelt Calls for Full War-Basis Aid to Britai
# Says Axis Will Lose; U.S. the 'Arsenal of Democra

SUNDAY, APRIL 6, 1941

Section One

...rmans March on Yugoslavia and Gree...
...tacks in Thrace and Macedonia Resiste...
...scow and Belgrade Sign Friendship Pac...

...I No. 34,527

Copyright, 1941, New York Tribune Inc.

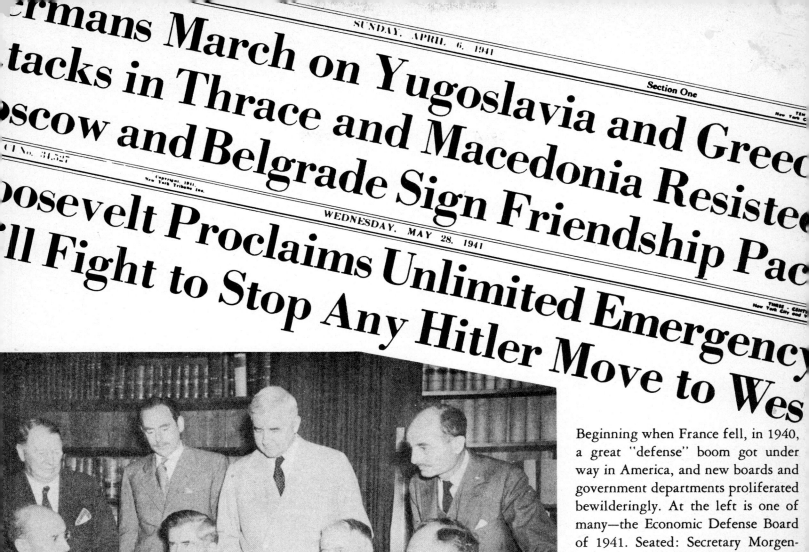

WEDNESDAY, MAY 28, 1941

THREE CENTS New York City and ...

...oosevelt Proclaims Unlimited Emergency
...ll Fight to Stop Any Hitler Move to Wes...

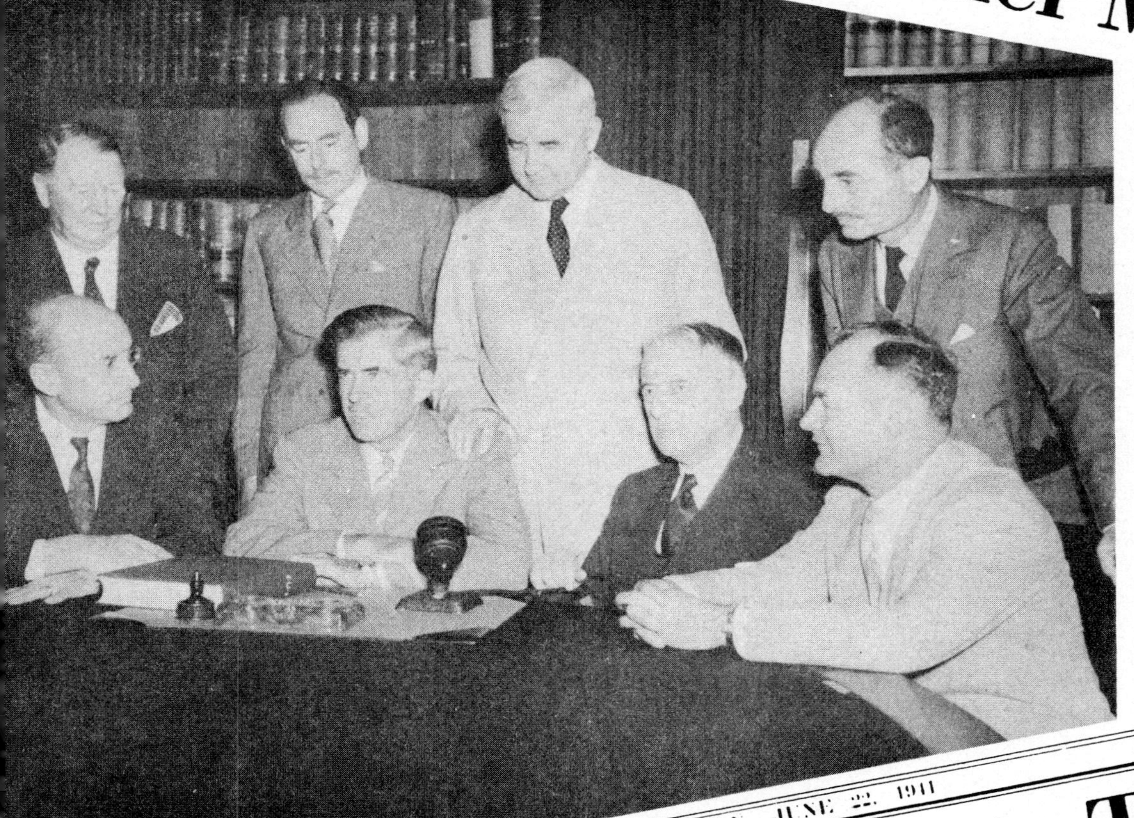

Beginning when France fell, in 1940, a great "defense" boom got under way in America, and new boards and government departments proliferated bewilderingly. At the left is one of many—the Economic Defense Board of 1941. Seated: Secretary Morgenthau, Vice President Wallace, Secretaries Stimson and Wickard. Standing: Secretary Knox, Assistant Secretary of State Acheson, Secretary Jones, and Attorney General Biddle.

TEN CENTS New York City and ...

Section One

SUNDAY, JUNE 22, 1941

...on Page 10, Sec. III

Copyright, 1941, New York Tribune Inc.

...o. 34,552

...tler Begins War on Russia, Troops Marc...
...ays Reds, U.S., Britain Try to 'Throttle' Hi...
...Drives From East Prussia, Finland, Ruma...

THREE CENTS New York City and ...

FRIDAY, AUGUST 15, 1941

Copyright, 1941, New York Tribune Inc.

...No. 34,606

...oosevelt and Churchill Reveal Their War Aims
...Sea Meeting Heralds Swift Blows at Ax...

We offer on these two pages one exhibit of the herculean job of building for arms production that was done in 1940 and 1941 while domestic goods were still being produced in unconverted factories. The picture at the left shows the ground being broken for the Chrysler Tank Arsenal. Note the date: *November 8, 1940.* The picture below shows engineers and draftsmen planning details; date, January 30, 1941. Now look at the opposite page for the sequel.

On April 22, 1941, they are installing heavy machinery in the already erected building. (You can see assembly lines in the distance.) And in the picture below, General Grant tanks, completed, are being loaded on railroad cars for shipment. And the date of this last picture? *September 25, 1941* — less than eleven months after the first one on the opposite page! In many such plants, the miracle of war production was already under way some time before Pearl Harbor.

What happened next upset all calculations. As the predicament of the Allies became more and more grave, American opinion, with Roosevelt leading it, had swung toward more and more intensive aid to Britain, and then Russia, and toward a stiffer and stiffer attitude toward Germany. By the fall of 1941 we were virtually conducting an undeclared war against Germany in the Atlantic Ocean. We also refused flatly to countenance Japan's imperial aggressions; and when in November 1941 the Japanese sent a special envoy, Saburu Kurusu, to Washington, there were scant hopes of a reconciliation. But nevertheless almost all eyes were turned toward the Atlantic, not the Pacific; toward Germany, not Japan. Above are Kurusu (left) and the Japanese Ambassador, Admiral Kichisaburo Nomura, waiting to talk with our Secretary of State, Cordell Hull, at the State Department on November 17, 1941.

Through the lengthening shadows of afternoon—and of a passing era of our history—the two Japanese envoys walked on either side of Secretary Hull to the White House to talk with President Roosevelt. The negotiations continued, fruitlessly, Kurusu remaining in Washington. Already word had gone out from Tokyo setting in motion the machinery for the attack on Pearl Harbor, but we had no knowledge of that, and our attention was still turned chiefly in the other direction—toward Germany. And then, on Sunday, December 7, came the blinding event. . . .

The Japanese bombs struck Pearl Harbor on the morning of December 7, 1941. Above, you see the U.S.S. *Arizona* keeling over under the impact of the blows. On the opposite page is shown the wreckage-strewn Naval Air Station, with an explosion in the background sending flames and smoke high into the sky.

Before the United States could get round to declaring war, the Japanese followed their bombs with an almost simultaneous declaration that a state of war existed between Japan and the United States "as of dawn" of that day.

Congress replied on the next day, December 8, by voting to declare war against Japan. The vote was 82 to 0 in the Senate; 388 to 1 in the House. Before the United States even had to face the question whether this would mean war with Germany and Italy, Hitler and Mussolini both declared war on us on December 11; we replied with counter-declarations, this time unanimous (except for one member of the House who answered the roll-call but refrained from voting).

Under such circumstances all argument between interventionists and isolationists ceased. The United States went to war unitedly—if reluctantly. The choice was inescapable.

When the bombs fell on Pearl Harbor, the twenty-three years and twenty-six days of the interwar period came to an end. During that time we, as a people, had often been guilty of myopia, irresponsibility, intolerance, and inanity. Struck by an economic storm, we had managed to ride it out, but no more; we had not conquered chronic unemployment—that negator of open opportunity—until deficit spending for armaments came to our rescue. Yet on the other hand our fits of intolerance had been fleeting. In the economic storm we had not yielded ourselves up to any tyrant; and on the whole we had been patient, humane, and loyal to the democratic decencies. When the test of war came, we were to show that despite our self-indulgences and our follies we still had the skill and the will to produce astonishingly and to fight victoriously. All in all, perhaps we had not done so badly.

Would we be able—looking back, later, over the record of our interwar achievements and idiocies—not simply to apply successfully the old maxim of a great schoolmaster, "To err is human, to make the same mistake twice is foolish," but also to gain the broader and more essential perspective needed to do the harder thing: to avoid making different mistakes springing from the same sort of myopia, the same sort of evasions and obsessions?

# SOURCES AND ACKNOWLEDGMENTS

The sources of the pictures in this book are here listed alphabetically, and we are grateful for the kindly cooperation of each and all of them:

B. Altman & Co.: illustrations from catalogues on pages 7, 8, 9, 10 (young men's fashions), 56, 57 (hats), 58, 59, 162, 163, 164, 165 (hostess gown), 170 (boy at upper left, men's shirts)

American Airlines: photographs on pages 186, 187 (DC-4)

American Broadcasting Co.: photographs on pages 4 (Paul Whiteman and band), 227 (Davis, Swing)

Appleton-Century Co.: photograph of Edith Wharton and reproduction of book jacket of *Miss Lulu Bett* on page 31

Black, Starr & Gorham: advertisement on pages 108, 109

Brown Brothers: photographs on pages 4 (Model T Ford; Fairbanks, Pickford, Chaplin, and Griffith; Ruth), 20 (MacArthur and Prince of Wales), 21 (suffragettes), 25, 26, 27 (Boston Police Strike, Coolidge), 29, 35 (portrait of Harding), 39 (Boardwalk scene), 41 (girls in boat), 67, 69 (Ruth batting), 71 (Dempsey-Tunney fight), 102, 122, 133, 174 (strikers at Monroe), 190, 206 ("It Happened One Night"), 216 (Goodman at the Paramount)

CBS: photographs on pages 141 (Gibbons, Husing, sound effects), 210 (Major Bowes, Kate Smith), 229 (Robeson)

Central Studios and Atlantic City Press Bureau: photographs on pages 39 (Miss America), 40, 41 (Miss America)

Chrysler Corporation: advertisement and photograph of car on page 185, photographs on pages 242, 243

Cluett, Peabody & Co.: Arrow collar advertisement on page 10

Crosley Corporation: advertisement of radio on page 38

Cunard White Star: photograph of *Queen Mary* (by Fairchild Aerial Surveys, Inc.) on page 188

*Current History:* advertisement for May 1919 issue on page 24

John Day Company: reproduction of book jacket of *The Good Earth* on page 140

Doubleday & Company: photograph of Tarkington and reproductions of book jackets of *Three Soldiers* and *Alice Adams* on page 31, photograph of Margaret Kennedy and reproductions of book jackets of *The Green Hat* and *So Big* on page 98

Douglas Aircraft: photograph on page 187 (DC-3)

E. I. du Pont de Nemours & Co.: photographs on page 182 (sale of nylons and lenses)

E. P. Dutton & Co.: reproduction of book jacket of *The Story of San Michele* on page 140

Board of Governors of the Federal Reserve System: basic charts on pages 104, 105, 106

Federal Works Agency: photograph on page 154 (laying concrete)

Finchley, Inc.: advertisements for plus fours and striped flannels on page 60

Ford Motor News Bureau: photographs on page 11 (Model T), 62, 63 (Ford coupé), 64 (Model T, Model A)

General Electric Co.: photographs on pages 179, 180, 183 (old style kitchen, kitchen 15 years ago), 184

General Motors: photographs on pages 11 (Oldsmobile), 12 (Cadillac), 63 (Buick), 64 (Cadillac)

Gotham Hosiery Co.: advertisement for Onyx stockings on page 40

Harcourt, Brace & Co.: photograph of Lewis, catalogue description of *Main Street* on page 31

Otto F. Hess: photographs on pages 213 (Condon), 214, 215, 216 (Goodman portrait), 217

Jantzen Knitting Mills: advertisement of bathing suit on page 170

Alfred A. Knopf: photograph of Willa Cather on page 98

Library of Congress: photographs on pages 196 (Rothstein for Farm Security Administration), 197 (abandoned farm—Lange for FSA), 198 (Lange for FSA), 218 (Lange for FSA)

*Life:* drawings by John Held, Jr., on pages 51, 53

Liggett & Myers Tobacco Co.: Chesterfield advertisement on page 54

Little, Brown & Co.: photographs of Remarque and Hutchinson and reproductions of book jackets of *All Quiet on the Western Front* and *If Winter Comes* on page 98, photograph of Marquand and reproduction of book jacket of *The Late George Apley* on page 202

Russell Lynes: photographs on pages 234 (campaign buttons), 239 (emblems)

Macmillan Company: photograph of Margaret Mitchell and reproduction of book jacket of *Gone With the Wind* on page 201

Robert McBride & Co.: photograph of Cabell on page 31

The Museum of Modern Art Film Library: photographs on pages 15, 16, 17, 51, 86-89, 132 ("Little Caesar"), 135-137, 205, 206 (Shirley Temple, Barrymore, Robinson), 207, 208, 230

National Archives: photographs on pages 14 (arrival of NC-4), 18 (Marshall and Allen), 19, 23, 24, 27 (rent strike), 34, 35 (Harding and Fall), 96, 113

National Industrial Conference Board, Inc.: chart on page 28

NBC: photographs on pages 36 (Melody Belles), 37 (Conrad), 141 (Amos 'n' Andy), 209, 210 (Fred Allen), 211

The New Haven Railroad: photographs on page 189

New York *Herald Tribune:* headlines on pages 233, 240, 241

*New York Times:* Lindbergh story on page 112, stock quotations on page 121, portion of front page of Jan. 31, 1933, on page 146, montage of headlines on page 219

*The New Yorker:* drawings on page 45 (by Gardner Rea), 48 and 49 (by Wallace Morgan), 104 (by Carl Rose), 107 (by Perry Barlow), 130 (by Perry Barlow), 158 (by Richard Decker), 159 (by Wallace Morgan), 190 (by Whitney Darrow)

Official Automobile Blue Book (1921): text on page 13

Official U. S. Navy Photographs: pages 228, 246, 247

Robert Osborn: drawings on page 5, animations of charts on pages 104-106

Pictograph Corporation: see *The United States, A Graphic History*

*Plastics:* photographs on page 182 (zipper, razors, plastic boxes)

Port of New York Authority: photograph of highway on page 185

Press Association: photographs on pages 1, 4 (MacArthur), 18 (Truman in store, Truman as officer), 20 (Dewey), 70 (Dempsey-Carpentier fight), 71 (Dempsey and Tunney in uniform), 76 (Jones in uniform), 101, 115, 124 (crowd outside Bowman's), 127, 148 (Moley), 149 (Corcoran and Pecora, Byrnes and Ickes), 151, 160 (Huey Long speaking), 172 (Warde), 178, 191 (goldfish swallowing), 193 (Louis-Baer fight), 229 (Welles), 237 (Pelley), 241

Public Roads Administration: photographs on pages 13, 65

Rinehart & Co.: reproduction of book jacket of *Anthony Adverse* on page 140

Rockefeller Center, Inc.: photographs on pages 176, 177 (by Thomas Airviews), 192 (by Wendell MacRae)

Signal Corps: photograph on page 240

Soil Conservation Service: photographs on pages 154 (drop inlet—by Hufnagle), 155, 195 (by McClean), 200 (by Mitchell)

Stork Club: photographs on page 212 (Douglas Fairbanks and Lady Ashley, Douglas Fairbanks Jr., and Vera Zorina, Winchell and Billingsley)

Tennessee Valley Authority: photographs on pages 156, 157

*The United States, A Graphic History*, by Louis M. Hacker, Rudolph Modley, and George R. Taylor, Modern Age Books (1937) and Pictograph Corporation: pictographs on pages 62, 125, 154

U. S. Department of Agriculture: photograph on page 197 (boy outside shack —by Rothstein)

Vandamm Studio: photographs on pages 82, 84, 85 ("Private Lives"), 138, 139, 199 ("Tobacco Road"), 203, 204 ("You Can't Take It With You"), 224-226

Vanguard Press: photograph of Farrell and reproduction of book jacket of *Studs Lonigan* on page 201

*Vanity Fair* (Courtesy the Condé Nast Publications, Inc.): drawings by Ann Fish on pages 47, 50, 52, 54; 60 (drawing of men's fashions); 67, drawing by Fish on page 78

Vassar College Library: photographs on pages 78, 79

Viking Press: photograph of Steinback and reproduction of jacket of *The Grapes of Wrath* on page 199, photograph of Woollcott and reproduction of book jacket of *While Rome Burns* on page 201

*Vogue* (Courtesy the Condé Nast Publications, Inc.): drawings on pages 4, 6, 7, 55, 57 (dresses), 161, 165 (street dresses, right)

Westinghouse: photographs on pages 36 (women listening to radio), 37 (tent on roof, first KDKA studio), 181, 183 (modern kitchen)

White Studio: photographs on pages 80, 81, 204 (Follies girls)

Wide World: photographs on pages 2, 3, 14 (personnel of NC-4), 20 (Lewis and Gallagher), 21 (Marines parading), 30, 32, 33, 42-46, 61, 68, 69 (Ruth after workout, Ruth and Gehrig), 70 (Dempsey-Firpo fight), 72-75, 76 (Jones and Alexa Sterling, Jones playing), 77, 83, 85 (Texas Guinan), 90-95, 97, 100, 110, 111, 114, 116-120, 123, 124 (apple-sellers), 126, 128, 129, 131, 132 ("Legs" Diamond), 134, 142-147, 148 (Tugwell, Wallace), 149 (Hopkins), 150, 152, 153, 160 (Long with Coca Cola bottle), 166-169, 171, 172 (*Morro Castle*), 173, 174 (Republic Steel strike, Columbia students), 175, 188, 191 (Bingo), 193 (Baer-Carnera fight), 194, 212 (Brenda Frazier), 213 (Irving Berlins), 219-223, 224 (Dorothy Thompson), 231, 232, 234 (Willkie), 235, 236, 237 (Kuhn, Jehovah's Witnesses), 238, 239 (Fight for Freedom rally, America First rally), 244, 245

We thank especially, for valuable assistance in the preparation of the book, Mary F. Russell and Else Ström, who tracked down for us many pictures and much information; John A. Kouwenhoven and Russell Lynes, for their fruitful suggestions; Cass Canfield, for the idea of compiling such a book; and Rosejeanne Slifer and Faith E. Willcox of B. Altman & Co., R. Hawley Truax of *The New Yorker*, Joan Gladstone of Press Association, and Rita F. Livingston of *Vogue*, for taking special pains to help us collect much needed material.

# INDEX